# TALES FROM THE SPECIAL FORCES CLUB

HIDDEN FROM THE MODERN WORLD,
THE UNTOLD STORIES OF BRITAIN'S ELITE WARRIORS

# TALES FROM THE
# SPECIAL
# FORCES CLUB
## SEAN RAYMENT

Collins

First published in 2013 by Collins

An imprint of HarperCollins*Publishers*
77–85 Fulham Palace Road
Hammersmith, London W6 8JB

www.harpercollins.co.uk

1 3 5 7 9 10 8 6 4 2

A catalogue record for this book is
available from the British Library

HB ISBN: 978-0-00-745253-8
TPB ISBN: 978-0-00-749875-8

*In memory of all the members of the special
forces who sacrificed their lives during the
Second World War*

*For Luca and Rafe*

# Contents

# Introduction

When I joined the Parachute Regiment in 1986 as a young officer I entered a world where the exceptional was commonplace and every soldier, no matter what rank, was always expected to perform to the highest possible standard.

Back then, my battalion, 3 Para, was still basking in the success of the Falklands War and was rightly regarded as one of the best, certainly one of the toughest infantry battalions in the entire British Army. It was an elite organisation, full of men who, just four years earlier, had marched across the demanding terrain of East Falkland and fought the Battle of Mount Longdon with bullet and bayonet.

I was a fresh-faced, inexperienced, 24-year-old lieutenant expected to take command of 27 hardened paratroopers, half of whom had served in the Falklands, where they had taken life and seen life taken.

Life in 3 Para was an unforgiving and at times humourless existence, where only professional excellence mattered and those unfortunate souls who could not deliver the goods fell by the wayside – and many did.

As a young platoon commander I was cut a bit of slack, but not much. While it was accepted that I might make mistakes, I was also expected to learn from them – second chances were a rarity. But with the help and understanding of a good but tough sergeant and excellent soldiers I survived that initial apprenticeship. Anyone who wants to serve in the Parachute Regiment, irrespective of rank, class, colour or creed, must pass the gruelling pre-parachute selection course, and that creates a special bond of mutual respect between the officers and other ranks.

But while we in the Paras rightly regarded ourselves as an elite force, none of us would have referred to ourselves as 'special forces'. That title was reserved for a very select few, those within the Army who were prepared to take another step and test themselves further.

In the late 1980s the special forces consisted of the Special Air Service, the Special Boat Service, the Force Research Unit, which ran agents in Northern Ireland, and the 14th Intelligence Company, a cover name for specially trained covert operatives who would spy on and monitor some of the most dangerous members of the IRA.

Those who undertook the various selection courses to join one of these special units were either successful and were rarely seen again or would return, having failed to make the grade for some reason or another, perhaps feeling sheepish, but admired by most for having the guts to give it a go.

Although I was obviously aware of the existence of the special forces, it wasn't until I served in Northern Ireland that I met members of those units in the flesh. In 1989, 3 Para was posted to Palace Barracks in Belfast on a 24-month residential tour. After a brief period training recruits at the Parachute Regiment depot I was posted to Belfast, where I became the second-in-command of B Company, 3 Para. Some weeks later I was offered the job of Close Observation Platoon (COP) commander, a position which was widely regarded as the best job for any young officer in Northern Ireland. COPs were usually composed of soldiers from the reconnaissance platoons of infantry battalions and can perhaps be described as being at the lower end of the covert intelligence-gathering operation in Northern Ireland. The Belfast COP was effectively an autonomous unit which, although housed within Palace Barracks just outside Belfast, was under the control of the Belfast Tasking and Coordination Group, known as TCG, a part of the Royal Ulster Constabulary's Special Branch.

The Belfast TCG consisted of two experienced warrant officers from the SAS and 14 Int, together with a senior Special Branch detective.

That 12-month period also instilled within me a lifelong interest in the special forces and those men and women who have served in their ranks. But after five years' Army service, during which time I had reached the rank of captain, I decided to resign my commission. Although I enjoyed the Army, I was never a 'lifer' and wanted to explore pastures new. In 1991 I embarked on a new career in journalism. By the mid-1990s I was reporting on the Balkans conflict, and I soon began to specialise in war reporting – a role which took me back to Northern Ireland and on to Iraq, Afghanistan, the Gulf, Africa, the Middle East and Guantanamo Bay in Cuba.

Western governments had hoped that the end of the Cold War would deliver an era of global stability, but instead a much more pernicious threat began to emerge with the rise of militant Islam across much of the Middle East, a phenomenon which would ultimately lead to the 9/11 attacks and the concept of 'asymmetric warfare'.

Those units in the British Army best equipped to deal with this new threat were the special forces, namely the SAS, the SBS, the Special Reconnaissance Regiment and the Joint Communications Unit, the last two being formed from units which had previously existed as the 14th Intelligence Company and the Force Research Unit in Northern Ireland, as well as the covert civilian agencies such as MI5, MI6, Government Communications Headquarters (GCHQ) and the Metropolitan Police's anti-terrorist squad.

For reasons of security, virtually all SF operations are classified, just as they were during the Second World War. But every so often a diamond emerges from the dust and allows one to understand why the special forces are so, well, special.

One such diamond, known as Operation Marlborough, came across my path in 2005, while I was reporting on the war in Iraq. Back in those dark days Baghdad was the most dangerous place on earth. Suicide bombers were routinely murdering hundreds of innocent civilians every week. The country was in anarchy and the West's 'war' was being lost.

Operation Marlborough was a 'take-down' – a hit on an al-Qaeda suicide bombing operation involving teams of British SAS snipers embedded with 'Task Force Black' – the joint British/US special forces unit operating in Baghdad with the sole aim of defeating al-Qaeda.

The Task Force had received specific intelligence suggesting that al-Qaeda were about to launch a series of coordinated suicide bomb attacks across the city. Three bombers were being fitted with devices at an al-Qaeda bomb factory within the city and targets were already being reconnoitred – street markets and schools had been chosen by the bombers.

The intelligence was passed to the SAS, who immediately began planning the ambush. I understand that a 15-man SAS team covertly observed the target house for several days, watching everyone who entered and left. Listening devices were used to monitor the plans being hatched, while a Reaper Unmanned Air Vehicle tracked the suspected terrorists as they moved around the city.

After several days of covert surveillance, the order for the 'take-down' was given.

Early one morning, as the sun began to climb over the city, three SAS sniper teams watched and waited. When all three suspects emerged, the SAS opened fire. The three bombers, each wearing a suicide vest impregnated with ball bearings, were killed by a single head shot. A follow-up operation also led to the arrest of several key al-Qaeda bomb-makers.

It was a classic special forces operation which, estimates suggest, may have saved the lives of over 100 civilians.

★    ★    ★

The modern SAS soldier is a highly trained, intelligent, excellently equipped, well-paid fighter who would have notched up several years in the ranks before being allowed to undertake the special forces selection. At the outbreak of war 70 years ago, by contrast, the majority of those who served in the special forces had very limited combat experience. Those 'originals' had to learn their skills very quickly, and once in the field largely had to survive on their wits. I wanted to find out what motivated thousands of young men and women to risk all in the service of their country, when many could have probably served out the war in a safe, comfortable operations room, many miles from the front line.

My search began at the Special Forces Club in London in early 2011. I had attended various functions at the club over the last few years and one or two of my friends were members.

The club was created in the immediate aftermath of the Second World War in August 1945, just as the various 'private armies', or special forces, which had evolved during the previous five years of conflict were disbanded. Within a year the Long Range Desert Group, the Jedburgh Teams, the Special Operations Executive (SOE), the Chindits, Popski's Private Army, the Commandos and the original Special Air Service all ceased to exist. The move was partly driven by 'old school' generals and the heads of the Secret Intelligence Service (SIS), who were never entirely comfortable with seemingly autonomous military or quasi-military organisations operating outside the established sphere of command.

Those who had served in these clandestine units were either posted back to their original units or, as in the majority of cases, returned to 'Civvy Street', seeking fresh challenges in a changed world. They were warned never to speak of covert operations, and some, especially those who had worked with foreign agents, were made to sign the Official Secrets Act. They were aware that to divulge any of their wartime activities could, in theory, result in imprisonment.

It was against this backdrop that the Special Forces Club was established in 1945 by Major-General Sir Colin Gubbins, KCMG, DSO, MC, the last chief of the Special Operations Executive. The general wanted to create a club where former members of the SOE could meet over lunch or dinner and chat about their wartime experiences, keeping alive the 'spirit of resistance', a phrase that became the club's motto. He wanted to preserve and develop the bonds of comradeship and mutual trust which had been forged between a special group of men and women in the war years.

Together with a small group of former SOE agents, he leased from the Grosvenor Estate a large townhouse in Knightsbridge, central London. Then, as today, the building gave little away, for the club never liked to advertise its existence. Like its members, the club has always preferred anonymity, a desire to remain in the shadows, out of prying eyes. It is quite possible even today that many people living and working in the Knightsbridge area know nothing of the club's existence. There has never been a name plaque to distinguish it from any other house in the same smart, leafy crescent.

The club was an immediate success and, unlike many other London clubs at the time, its doors were open to women, as many female soldiers and civilians had fought and died while serving in the SOE. Members were also welcomed from the wartime SAS, the Long Range Desert Group, the Jedburgh Teams and a host of organisations who had served behind enemy lines.

Only one covert unit was initially excluded from the club, the Secret Intelligence Service (MI6), which throughout the war years had been regarded as both a rival and an enemy of the SOE. I should add that the prohibition which prevented MI6 membership has since been lifted, and the club is used today by members of Britain's modern secret establishment – MI5, MI6, the SAS, SBS, the Special Reconnaissance Regiment and the various covert police organisations which have been created to fight organised crime and Islamist terror groups – as a secure meeting place.

Over the decades since the end of the Second World War the club was one of the few places, if not the only place, where former members of the SOE – indeed agents from all the Allied countries – could meet and reminisce about their lives some 70 years ago when they fought a secret war against Nazi Germany in occupied

Europe. Within the club's secure walls, former saboteurs, assassins, radio operators and those who trained agents in the secret arts of espionage and guerrilla warfare could meet and recount tales of derring-do among friends, over a glass of whisky, knowing that their secrets would be safe.

It was during many of these meetings, sometimes at the bar, late in the evening, or over lunch sharing a good bottle of claret, that the stories of what the special forces did during the Second World War began to emerge. Often those stories were never fully documented, which means that no historical record exists, and with the passing of time many of them have been lost for ever. That is why it seemed to be a good idea to interview a selection of those 'originals' and collect their stories in a book. Thanks to the club, it was possible to get in touch with some of them.

The Special Forces Club is one of the most friendly and least fussy of all London clubs – I don't think its members would have it any other way. It isn't large or grand and consists of a library, a bar, some rooms for meetings and a few bedrooms where members can spend the night at a pretty reasonable rate. The walls of the staircase which leads up to the bar are adorned with portrait photographs of members of the SOE who perished on operations, while most of the rooms have original paintings depicting clandestine meetings of agents in Nazi-occupied Europe.

It was during one of the various events I was attending at the club that I first heard the name of Noreen Riols, who had helped in the training of agents during the war. I eventually made contact with Noreen, one of the few surviving members of the SOE, and some time later we agreed to meet at the club so that I could learn about her secret wartime activities.

And so began a fascinating journey, during which I learnt of the heroics of men like Jimmy Patch, who was called up in 1940 before being sent to fight in the desert as a gunner in the Royal Artillery. To escape the drudgery and routine of the regular Army, he volunteered for special duties and was eventually accepted into the fabled Long Range Desert Group, taking part in some of the most celebrated covert operations of the North African campaign. Later, during an ill-fated operation in the Greek Islands, Jimmy was captured by the Germans but escaped to fight on in Yugoslavia.

Also serving in the North African campaign was Mike Sadler, who left England in the late 1930s with the intention of becoming a farmer in what was then Rhodesia but ended up becoming the 'best navigator' in the SAS. Mike served with soldiers whose names are now part of the historical fabric of the special forces, such as Lieutenant-Colonel Paddy Mayne and Lieutenant-Colonel David Stirling, the founder of the SAS. Mike took part in many of the early SAS missions, in which the elite fighting force built its reputation attacking German airfields deep behind enemy lines in North Africa. 'My resounding memory is that it was such tremendous fun,' Mike explains in the book.

The adventures of Captain John Campbell, who was erroneously branded a coward at El Alamein but later went on to win the Military Cross and bar, while in Italy serving with Popski's Private Army, make another remarkable story. He was later described by Popski, a charismatic British officer of East European heritage, as the 'most daring of us all'. John is the only surviving officer who served with that elite force.

Among the most dangerous ventures of the war were the night missions to occupied France flown by the RAF's Moonlight Squadrons, of which Leonard Ratcliff is a rare survivor; Corran Purdon recalls his part in the daring St Nazaire Raid, which led to imprisonment and the MC; and Bill Towill, a pacifist until Dunkirk, describes the horrors of jungle warfare behind enemy lines with the legendary Chindits.

Men who served in the Jedburgh Teams, a secret SOE unit, recall their experiences in France and the Far East. All were young volunteers who wanted to see some real action before the war ended. The soldiers were trained in covert communication, silent killing and sabotage, before being parachuted into occupied France just before D-Day to assist in organising the Resistance movement. Some of those who survived volunteered to serve in Burma, including men like John Sharp, who won the Military Medal, Fred Bailey, who fought alongside both the Maquis and Burmese guerrillas, and Harry Verlander, who escaped death by a hair's breadth when he was attacked by a Japanese officer wielding a samurai sword.

*Tales from the Special Forces Club* presents their unique stories of courage, conviction and fighting spirit. I hope you enjoy reading it as much as I have enjoyed writing it.

# CHAPTER 1

# The Secret Life of Noreen Riols

## *Training SOE Agents*

*'The disruption of enemy rail communications, the harassing of German road moves and the continual and increasing strain placed on German security services throughout occupied Europe by the organised forces of Resistance, played a very considerable part in our complete and final victory.'*
GENERAL EISENHOWER, May 1945

It was on a Monday morning in August 2011, when a black London taxi cab dropped me at the corner of a leafy crescent in Knightsbridge, that I made my first visit to the Special Forces Club as a guest of one of its original members.

The club is as anonymous today as it was when it opened after the Second World War, its address only known to a select few. I press a small bell fixed to the building's outer wall adjacent to a heavy, tan-coloured oak door, and a few seconds later the door clicks open.

'Yes, sir, can I help you?' a young receptionist enquires helpfully.

'My name is Sean Rayment and I'm here to see Noreen Riols,' I respond. A few elderly club members milling around in the lobby immediately turn and look at me, with a mixture of suspicion and interest.

'She is waiting for you through there,' responds the receptionist, pointing at a half-open door through which the morning sun is starting to shine. As I walk past another office two middle-aged men look up from behind their computer and stare unsmiling as I pass. I feel as though I have just been frisked.

Looking into the room, I see that Noreen Riols is reclining in a slightly worn, red velvet armchair which has the effect of diminishing her delicate frame. She is sipping a cup of breakfast tea while reading a copy of *The Times* and appears perfectly at home in the cosy, peach-coloured drawing room.

'Noreen?' I ask hesitantly as I enter the room.

'Yes?' she replies, looking slightly confused before a smile fills her face. 'You must be Sean. I'm sorry, I was expecting someone older. Please, come in and sit down. Now, would you like a cup of tea?'

After months of research, searching and seemingly endless emails and telephone calls, I have come face to face with Noreen Riols, one of the very few members of the SOE still alive.

As a journalist and former officer in the Parachute Regiment, I have met members of covert intelligence agencies, such as MI5, MI6, the SAS and more obscure organisations such as 14 Intelligence Company, which operated exclusively in Northern Ireland from the 1980s and whose existence was never officially acknowledged by the British government, on numerous occasions. I have always been struck by the physical ordinariness of those who inhabit the covert world. They might be super-fit and have brilliant analytical minds, but from the outside they tend not to stand out from the crowd; they are mostly neither too tall nor too short, fat or thin, handsome or ugly – just ordinary. For those who live their lives in the covert world of espionage and counter-espionage, blending in, being almost invisible within the crowd can be a life-saving quality. And Noreen is no exception. Sipping tea in the Special Forces Club she looked like everyone's favourite granny, with a kind, smiling, gentle face. It was curious, therefore, to think that some 70 years earlier Noreen was one of a select band of SOE personnel who were training agents to conduct assassinations and sabotage across Europe as Britain and its allies fought for their very existence.

Noreen and I shake hands before she adds: 'There aren't very many of us left, you know.' By that she means members of the SOE, the wartime clandestine force created in July 1940 on the orders of Winston Churchill, the Prime Minister, and Hugh Dalton, the Minister for Economic Warfare, with the aim of conducting sabotage, espionage, assassinations and forming resistance movements against the Axis powers in occupied countries.

Noreen was one of the many women employed by the secret organisation during the war. Today, aged 86, she is one of the few surviving members of F Section – the department which dispatched more than 400 agents, including 39 female spies, into France between 1941 and 1945. The methods of infiltration included parachuting, landing by aircraft and using fishing boats and submarines.

The section was one of SOE's most successful and was responsible for creating dozens of underground networks across France. Many of the agents were Britons who were fluent in French and were recruited from a wide range of backgrounds and occupations. Some were already serving in the armed forces, while others were recruited because of their knowledge of France, all united by their loathing of the Nazi ideology and the desire to strike back at a regime which had already enslaved millions of civilians.

But it was a dangerous and demanding occupation, and newly trained agents were warned that they had a 50 per cent chance of surviving the war. Those who were captured faced torture at the hands of the Gestapo followed by almost certain execution.

SOE's primary role was to help organise the French Resistance into a fighting force capable of mounting sabotage, with the primary targets being the rail and telephone networks.

'Isn't it funny that now that there are so few of us left we are in more demand than ever?' Noreen adds before returning to her seat. 'Now tell me, what do you want to know? There are no secrets any more.'

⋆　　⋆　　⋆

*Noreen Riols*

Noreen Riols was born into a naval family on the Mediterranean island of Malta. From an early age she had decided that she too wanted to lead an adventurous life which would begin with taking a degree at Oxford. War broke out before she was ready to go to university, but she was already becoming a capable linguist at the Lycée, the French school in South Kensington.

'The plan was this: before the war I had wanted to go to Oxford, take a degree in literature, then I was going to study medicine, then I was going to astound the world with my incredible medical knowledge and then I was going to marry a tall, dark handsome man, who would whisk me off to a thatched cottage in the country, which was suitably staffed and had a pony paddock, and then I was going to have six children, all boys with red hair. I had arranged the whole thing; the only thing I hadn't arranged was the bridegroom, but that was a detail which could be sorted out later – then the war came.

'The Lycée was evacuated early in the war, but a few girls remained in one class and I was one of those – but I can't remember doing any work at all and I seemed to spend the whole of my life tearing around South Kensington on the back of a Free French airman's motorbike.

'Life in London at that time was pretty dreadful because it was being bombed all the time and people were being killed, as you would expect, but I don't think we, girls of my age, ever realised how much danger we were in.

'I remember being in the Lycée when it was bombed in 1941. The school had been occupied by the Free French Air Force, and one day I heard a plane coming over and I'd just looked out of the window very excitedly when suddenly a French airman leapt on top of me and both of us were flat on the floor. Seconds later the bomb exploded and the window came crashing in. If he hadn't knocked me to the floor I would have been seriously injured or worse. That's why I say I don't think we really had any appreciation of the danger we faced daily. I don't ever remember being frightened – I don't think you do get frightened when you are young.'

'I got my call-up papers when I was 18. The papers said that either you joined the armed forces or you go and work in a munitions factory, but the idea of working in a munitions factory did not appeal to me in the slightest.

'All of my friends knew that we were going to be called up when we reached 18, and I thought I'll follow in my father's footsteps and I'll become a member of the Women's Royal Naval Service, WRNS. I thought the hat was very stylish and I could see myself in the uniform. But when I went to join up I was told that the only vacancies for women in the Royal Navy were for cooks and stewards, and the idea of making stew or suet pudding for the rest of the war was not the Mati Hari image I wanted to give to the waiting world, so I declined.

'My instructions were to report to a Labour Office somewhere in west London and when I was told by the female clerk behind the counter what my options were I said, "I'm not doing that or that," and frankly this woman wasn't having any of it, she got a bit ratty and said, "Make up your mind – it's this or that, and if you can't make up your mind I'll put you down for a factory."

'Well, you can imagine how I felt, and I started to cause a bit of a fuss and said, "I will not work in a factory," and stamped my feet and so on. At which point a door opened and a slightly irritated man looked out and said: "OK, I'll take over this one." He then proceeded to ask me a lot of questions which had nothing to do with the warship I intended to take charge of.

'He then picked up on my schooling and said, "I see you went to the Lycée. You speak French?" I said yes, and then he started speaking to me in several different languages. He was leaping about from one to another like a demented kangaroo and he seemed quite surprised that I could keep up with him in French, German and Spanish. After the interview he sent me to the Foreign Office, where I was ushered into a windowless room, where again I was questioned by a high-ranking officer. Of course I had no idea what I was being interviewed for at that stage, but looking back I think there was obviously some kind of liaison between the Lycée, the SOE and the Labour Office. At that stage there was a requirement for people who could speak languages to carry out secret work – but it's not the sort of thing you can advertise for.

'After that interview I ended up at 64 Baker Street, the head-quarters of SOE, but I had no idea where I was or what the building was for or the work they were doing. It was at Baker Street that I met Colonel Maurice Buckmaster, who was a major then and was in charge of SOE's French section.'

The SOE recruited people from all walks of life, with the primary requirement being a thorough knowledge of the country in which the agent was to operate. Fluency in the native language was vital, especially French for those entering France; thus exiled or escaped members of the armed forces of various occupied countries proved to be a fertile recruiting ground. Agents needed to be both ruthless and diplomatic, callous enough to slit a man's throat or execute an informer, while also able to master the politics of, say, the French Resistance movement and motivate members of it accordingly. Training was tough and, as we shall see later in the chapter, trainees could be failed at any stage.

While Baker Street was the main headquarters, the organisation's various branches and departments were strewn across London and much of England. Wireless production and research departments were based in Watford, Wembley and Birmingham. The camouflage, make-up and photography sections, Stations XVa, XVb and XVc, were largely based in the Kensington area of west London. Station XVb, a camouflage training base and briefing centre, was located in the Natural History Museum. In addition to the various stations there were over 60 separate training centres across Britain, where agents would be taught a wide variety of field skills, including demolition, sabotage and assassination techniques.

Station XV – The Thatched Barn – was one of the most important establishments within the SOE. It was a two-storey mock-Tudor hotel built in the 1930s in Borehamwood, Hertfordshire, and had been acquired by Billy Butlin, the holiday camp entrepreneur, before being requisitioned by SOE.

The Thatched Barn was the place where agents would be kitted out with clothing and equipment which was appropriate for the country in which they were about to infiltrate. Every item of clothing had to be an exact fit with what was expected for that particular country, or even region. So if the French in Brittany, say, stitched hems in a particular way, then that method needed to be used when fitting clothes for an agent about to be sent to that region. Nothing could be left to chance.

'At the time the headquarters was called the Inter-Allied Research Bureau – well, that meant absolutely nothing to me, as you can imagine. I was hopping from one office to the other. Buck sent me to another office and said this captain is expecting you – and he may have been, but by the time I'd got there he'd forgotten that he was meant to be interviewing me. He looked at me as though I had walked in from outer space and then said, "Nobody, but nobody must know what you do here. That includes brothers, sisters, aunts, uncles." Then an immensely tall man called Eddie

McGuire, an Irish Guards officer, shot into the room making very funny, squeaky sounds. It really was quite a bizarre scene. Then the two of them suddenly stopped talking and ran out of the room and down the corridor. I wondered where I was – I was only just 18 at the time and it felt like I was in a lunatic asylum being run by the Crazy Gang.

'I looked down the corridor and I could see that all the doors were open and people were running around. I learnt later that these two men had just returned from the field and were a bit on edge, and Eddie had been shot in the throat while escaping, which is why he spoke like a ventriloquist's doll.

'There was a FANY* inside the room who seemed to be completely unperturbed by everything that was going on, so I said to her, "Is it always like this here?" and she said, "Oh no, it's usually much worse, but don't worry, you'll get used to it," and I did.

'After that interview, I was in, although I didn't really know *what* I was in. I only knew that I was involved in something secret, because I kept being told not to reveal anything about what went on and not to ask questions. The view then, and it holds true today, is that the less you know, the less you can reveal, and if the worst happens, and the worst was of course a German invasion, then the less you could reveal under interrogation. I didn't know it at the time but everyone who worked for SOE was on the Gestapo's hit list.'

The interview was concluded and Noreen was asked if she could begin work immediately – by which she thought they meant the following morning, but inside the SOE immediately meant immediately. Within the hour she was ensconced inside an office in Montague Mansions, another building taken over by SOE as it grew almost daily, a few streets away from the Baker Street headquarters.

'I was a bit of a runaround at first, until I got to know how things worked. One of my first jobs was to ensure that special coded messages which were broadcast every evening by the BBC

---

* First Aid Nursing Yeomanry.

at Bush House were in the right place at the right time. That meant taking them down to the "Basement", as it was known somewhat sinisterly, which was run by a sergeant who was a veteran of the First World War. He wasn't a particularly happy person and he seemed to have a cigarette permanently glued to his top lip, but we seemed to get on after a while.

'Probably my most important job at that time was to get all the messages from all the various sections to him by 5pm, so that they could be sent over to the BBC – it was crucial that the messages went out so that the Resistance units could get their instructions.'

Noreen was working alongside living legends of the secret world such as Leo Marks, a cryptographer in charge of agent codes, and Forest Yeo-Thomas, codename the White Rabbit, one of the organisation's most celebrated agents. The two men were great friends, according to Noreen.

'Leo Marks's office was on the ground floor and mine was on the first floor but I saw a lot of him. He was a very nice chap, but his popularity was further increased because his mother was always sending him cakes, biscuits and freshly made sandwiches, which, because he was so nice, he always shared with other people so there was always a bit of a party taking place in his room.

'After a few months I was given better and more interesting jobs, and one of the most interesting was to attend agent debriefing sessions. There was a fairly straightforward routine when an agent came in. First of all they were given a huge cooked breakfast at the airport, after which they were taken to a place called Orchard Court, in Portman Square, close to the SOE headquarters. It could sometimes take months to get an agent back from the field for a debriefing session because of the complexities of living in occupied France. It was about at that stage that I really began to understand the sort of pressures the agents were under.

'It was always fascinating to see them just hours after they had left France. Some would be shaking and chain smoking, and others who had witnessed or suffered much worse experiences were as cool as cucumbers. I think it was awfully easy for a lot of people in England to say at the time, "I'd never talk if I was captured." But when you are actually over there none of us could tell what our reactions would be, and I suppose a time would come when the human spirit can no longer take any more punishment.

'The debriefing sessions were very relaxed, the agents were never rushed or pushed too hard, but the interviews were very detailed and could last several hours because the agents had so much information.

'A wireless operator for example was under enormous pressure, because he would have only about 15 minutes to send his message, which had to contain a lot of information about sabotage or enemy movements, but other information couldn't be included because it wasn't as crucial as operations.

'The idea of the debriefing sessions was to get into the real detail, such as the need to have a permit to put a bike on a train, or indeed the need for more bikes. The information was often the sort of detail a radio operator wouldn't be able to send because the need wasn't urgent. Every little bit of information helped in the preparation and briefing of agents who were just about to deploy on an operation. All of the agents had to be 100 per cent convincing all of the time, and it might be very small, almost insignificant details such as only being able to have coffee twice a week – that little bit of detail could be really important for a new agent going into an occupied country. Just imagine a new agent being lifted by the police and being asked a simple question like "How many cups of coffee do you drink a week?" The wrong answer could be a death sentence.'

By the middle of 1943 Noreen was a fully-fledged member of the SOE. She would begin work every morning, dressed in civilian clothes, at around 8am and work through until 6pm or later, depending on whether there was some sort of emergency. It became second nature never to talk about her work, and even her own mother was convinced Noreen was a secretary in the Ministry of Agriculture, Fisheries and Food. With her almost perfect French, Noreen worked exclusively in F Section, the department which looked after agents in France. SOE now occupied several buildings in central London, all close to the headquarters in Baker Street.

Working in the headquarters were citizens of every country occupied by the Axis powers – but there was, according to Noreen, an unwritten rule, which was that there could be absolutely no contact between people from the different sections for security reasons.

'We were all very aware that the agents' security, their lives in fact, depended on secrecy. One word, one slip of the tongue could result in a disaster. I loved the job, the people were fascinating and there was a real sense of purpose to the work.'

Then, in February 1944, Noreen was asked to go and work at what was known as the secret agents' finishing school at Beaulieu, the country seat of the Barons Montagu of Beaulieu.

By the time Noreen joined the SOE, the secret organisation has grown into a vast network of more than 60 training schools located across Britain, where at any one time hundreds of students were under training. There were also schools in Canada, for the training of US and Canadian agents, as well as in Palestine, at the Ramat David air base in Haifa, and in Singapore.

The training programme began at the 'Preliminary Schools', such as the Special Training School 5 (STS5) at Warnborough Manor, near Guildford in Surrey. The courses generally lasted two to three weeks, and it was here that they assessed the recruit's character and suitability for clandestine operations, without actually revealing what SOE did. (Interestingly, this same technique was adopted by 14 Intelligence Company during the initial selection when recruiting operatives for 'special duties' in Northern Ireland.)

Those potential SOE agents who passed were sent to one of several paramilitary schools, based at, amongst other establishments, the ten shooting lodges of Arisaig House (STS21), a forbidding granite country residence in Inverness-shire, which was requisitioned by the Army in 1941 and where Odette Churchill, one of the heroines of the SOE, was trained.

The locations were chosen for their remoteness and the gruelling terrain. Physical training was one of the key elements of the training, including many marches over the rugged Scottish countryside. For reasons of security, nationalities were kept separate, but virtually all students followed the same courses. Days were long and sleep was often in short supply, as the instructors piled on the pressure and assessed the recruits' ability to make decisions and think clearly under extreme duress.

The courses lasted for five weeks and included lessons in physical training, silent killing, weapons handling, demolition, field craft, navigation and signals. Weapons training was based on close-quarters combat, with two ex-Shanghai officers, William Fairbairn and Eric Anthony Sykes, teaching unarmed combat and silent killing. The two men gave their name to the FS fighting knife – a small knife used mainly by the Commandos – and the Fairbairn Fighting System, which was also taught to members of the CIA and FBI. The students learnt to master the Colt .45 and .38 and the Sten gun, a weapon regarded by many as being of dubious reliability. The recruits were taught the 'double tap' system of killing, firing two shots at a target, ideally the head, to ensure certain death.

Instructors also made use of the local train network, and trainees were given missions to 'sabotage' the West Highland Line using dummy explosives. Later in their training, the student agents also had to undertake a number of parachute jumps, six for men and five for women, at Ringway airport near Manchester.

Once these stages of training had been successfully mastered, agents moved to Beaulieu in Hampshire, the location of the Group B training school – 'the final stop before they drop', as some wag once observed.

Beaulieu was the perfect training school. It was located within the seclusion of the New Forest and the estate had numerous houses and outbuildings where students could perfect and hone their skills in relative secrecy. The training staff were housed in a central headquarters while the trainees were accommodated in a variety of different houses depending on their country sections.

Those destined for France were expected to know about all things French and adopt various customs, quirks and national idiosyncrasies, likewise for those being dispatched to Denmark, Belgium, Holland or other occupied countries. Each house had its own 'house commandant' whose job was to monitor and occasionally mentor the agents and keep them on the straight and narrow.

The one golden rule was that the trainee agents only ever associated with members of their own house for reasons of security, which meant that the training staff would come to each of the houses to give lectures.

During the course of the war more than 3,000 agents went through Beaulieu, whose vast rambling estate was built around the ruins of Beaulieu Abbey, and whose centrepiece is Palace House, the imposing Gothic grey stone mansion which was still used by members of the Montagu family.

'The gardener's cottage where I lived was really two cottages back to back. When we lived there we were three plus the housekeeper. Whoever was sleeping in the other (smaller) cottage had to go out and in through the front door to go to bed at night. And the winters were cold! "The House in the Woods", where the 25 officers lived – which had been a secret weekend rendezvous for Edward VIII and Mrs S. before he abdicated – was about ten minutes' walk away from the cottage, across the forest.

'In the middle of the estate was our HQ, a rather ugly stockbroker Tudor house called "The Rings", which has since been demolished and replaced with an equally ugly modern bungalow. The students were billeted in various houses away from us. We couldn't see their houses and they couldn't see us. The women were housed in "The House on the Shore", while the French students were mostly housed at "Boarman's" or "The Orchard" or "The Vineyard". The different nationalities were kept strictly apart, for security reasons. As were men and women – no unisex houses.'

The Beaulieu training houses were subdivided into five departments covering areas such as agent technique, clandestine life, personnel security, covert communication, cover story techniques and counter-surveillance. Agents were also taught how to change their appearance by using disguises. One of the instructors at the school, Peter Folis, who had trained as an actor, would often tell his students not to think 'false beards' but instead make small changes to the face such as wearing glasses, and part the hair differently.

'I was a little disappointed to be leaving London, because it was the heart of everything, but Buck said to me, "I want you to go to

Beaulieu," so I just got on with it. I went home, packed my bags, got on a train and that was it. I was at Beaulieu. My new home was a gardener's cottage on the estate and was shared by three of us: a South African FANY and a woman of about 35 who was very distinguished, and we had a splendid housekeeper who looked after us like a mother hen. It was a very gender segregated set-up, but that didn't stop all sorts of secret romances taking place.

'There was another house where 25 instructors were based, and they were mainly ex-agents. At first I didn't really know why I had been sent to Beaulieu, but after a very short time it became clear that I was going to help to instruct the students or agents, and that was a very exciting prospect. The men and women attending the courses were known as "students" while training, "bods" when they were sent on a mission and reached the rank of human being – if they made it back. It was all sort of light-hearted, designed, I suppose, to remove some of the fear.

'Kim Philby* had served as an instructor at Beaulieu for a short time and was very well liked. When I arrived he had already returned to London, but everyone spoke of him as being very charming, pleasant and efficient.

'But Kim was recalled to London; maybe his superiors were already a little suspicious. Another of the trainers was Paul Dehn, who became an art and theatre critic, and there was another one called Jock who was always very nice to me. Socially the set-up was very public school. For example, the instructors changed into service dress or black tie for dinner, so it was a little bit stiff. But Jock was different. He was always dressed in battledress and hobnail boots. The days were long and all of the staff worked seven days a week, but we finished at 1pm on a Sunday. Jock would come to our cottage after lunch and would bang on the door and say, in a very thick Glaswegian accent, "Does anyone want to come for a walk?" There was always a twinkle in his eye. I would often go for a walk with him and he might try and get a bit romantic. One only had to say "Shift it, Jock" – he never insisted. But what I didn't know at

---

* British double agent who spied for the KGB.

the time was that Jock was a specialist in silent killing. If I had known that at the time I'm not sure I would have had the courage to resist his advances.'

Noreen's main duty at Beaulieu was to help in the training of agents in a role known as a 'decoy'. All agents had to be able to follow targets and conduct close surveillance without being noticed. It was a specialist skill which took time to perfect. During the various exercises the student agents were ordered to follow Noreen and report on her movements, supposedly without being seen. The majority of the exercises took place in either Bournemouth or Southampton, the two large towns closest to Beaulieu.

'On a particular training day, we were given a scenario and told to head to a particular landmark in either Southampton or Bournemouth. I always worked in Bournemouth, and the agents were told, "You will see a girl in a headscarf and a dirty macintosh and a shopping basket, and she'll probably be wandering along in front of the pier at about 3pm: follow her and find out what she is up to." The idea was for them to try and follow me, find out who I met, where I went shopping and whether I had any sort of routine – exactly the sort of thing they might have to do in France. But the trick for them was not to be seen by me, and that was a very difficult skill to master. It was obviously easier for me to spot them than for them to spot me. It was wartime and there were a lot of women about, and most of them had baskets, because as soon as a woman in wartime saw a queue she would join it, because a queue would usually mean fresh food. But there was a shortage of men of a certain age. Most men between the ages of 19 and 40 were serving in the forces, so people looked very strangely at a man who was dressed in civilian clothes who was in his twenties or thirties, and quite often the agents would get abuse hurled at them. People, especially women who might have sons or husbands serving overseas, would walk right up to them and say things like, "It's disgusting, there's a war on and there you are wandering around Bournemouth in the middle of the afternoon – you should be ashamed of yourself."

'At the beginning of their training the agents were a bit ham-fisted. They would often stand very close to me, or if I was looking in a shop window then they would come and look in the window one shop along, but I wouldn't go, and in the end they would have to move on. And if they stopped to tie a shoelace – which usually wasn't undone – then I would know that I had got my man.

'There was a big department store called Plummers which I would often head straight for. I'd make for the ladies' lingerie department, and of course none of the men would like walking around that particular department. The students would come in following me and it would suddenly dawn on them that they were getting some very odd looks from other women and from the girls at the counters. I used to hold up a few unmentionables just to make them look a little more embarrassed. After that I would saunter up a few steps towards the lift and press the lift button. The target would then do one of two things: either he would get in the lift with me, or he would race up to the floor of the button I had pressed so he could continue following me. If he did that, I would quickly rush out of the lift and run down the stairwell by the side of the lift, and this is where my basket would come in useful, because I would whip off my headscarf and my mackintosh and put them in the basket, so all of a sudden I looked like someone different, and by the time he realised what had happened I had disappeared.

'Once I had gone through the door and was outside, that was it, he had lost me. Even if he realised what had happened, by the time he got outside I was gone. It was tremendous fun and, although in many respects it was a bit of a game, it was also deadly serious. You couldn't have an agent who stuck out like a sore thumb, either because he was just being clumsy or because he was being too suspicious, so the trick was to act as normally as possible and to try and blend in. There were some who were very good. In some cases you would report back and say, "He didn't turn up," and the instructors would say, "Ah, but she did."

'One of the other key skills an agent had to be adept at was using "live" and "dead" letterboxes – the passing of messages. A message might read: "Somebody will be sitting on a bench in the pier gardens about 11pm or 3pm and he's got a message for you," and you'd have to hope that somebody else, not a person taking part in the exercise, hadn't got on the bench too, because that could be a bit confusing.

'You'd be told that the contact would be reading a newspaper, so you would go and sit down and take out a cigarette – I've never been smoker but I didn't mind puffing away – and he would fold up the paper and put it down and I would pick it up, and that was quite normal because there were very few papers published and it was first come, first served, and everyone wanted to read a paper, so if you saw a paper lying around you always picked it up.

'We would also pass messages in cinemas and tea rooms, which was quite difficult because you had to make sure you found the right person, especially if you were a woman. If you started passing messages to a strange man you could be had up for soliciting, so you had to make sure you were giving the messages to the right person.'

Noreen also had to become proficient at the so-called 'honey trap', a tactic in which female agents use their feminine allure to 'convince' enemy agents to confess or at least admit their activities. It was a demanding task, not least because if Noreen was successful it might mean the end of an agent's career even before it had begun. Curiously, some male agents did give some indication that they were involved in covert activities, often within just an hour or so of meeting Noreen.

'During this stage of the training we would work very closely with the students' conducting officer. He wasn't part of the Beaulieu staff, instead his job was to act as a sort of mother hen to the students, giving them a bit of inspiration when needed but also listening to their troubles and soothing their fears, reassuring them, when needed, that they were up to the task and also explaining the risks of the job. I think that certainly some of the students, as time went on and news came in of field agents who had been captured and killed, would think about their own mortality – that was only natural. There was nothing wrong with agents worrying about being killed; at the very least it demonstrated that they had grasped the reality of what they were about to do.

'Of most concern, however, were agents who might talk or give away what they were up to, either by boasting or through fear or torture, and who might display characteristics which would ultimately compromise their role. The conducting officer would sit in on various exercises and watch the students, and he would pick out anybody he thought might be likely to talk. This wasn't a test which all of them had to pass. He would approach one who he thought might be a bit suspect and say, "Let's go out for a drink, or dinner or something – you've been working hard and deserve a bit of a break." He would often do this to students, so there was nothing that unusual in it.

'Together, the conducting officer and I would act out a couple of different scenarios which we had worked out beforehand, planning down to quite a lot of detail. One was known as the Royal Bath Dinner, named after the hotel where we often worked. I also worked at the Lincoln Hotel, but I preferred the Royal Bath because it had a terrace off the dining room and if there was a full moon shining on to the sea it was very romantic and much easier for me to work.

'The two men would go off and have dinner and I would wander into the dining room out of the blue and the conducting officer would say, "Oh, Noreen, what are you doing in Bournemouth? How lovely to see you." He would explain that I was some old friend of the family or something believable and would then ask me to stay for dinner. And the three of us would chat for a while and then someone would come along and say to the conducting officer, "Sir, there is a phone call for you" or something like that, and he would return and say, "I'm frightfully sorry, I've been called away, but you two stay here and have some fun and if I can I'll come along and join you later." And that's how it began.

'We had another scenario where he would say to one of the agents, "I met a girl today, I used to be at school with her brother, and I've invited her to join us for a drink." And the students never minded. Well, the Brits minded a bit, because they were looking forward to a good old boozy evening and along came this blasted woman who was going to spoil everything. But agents with other nationalities were very accommodating, they quite liked it because they didn't get the chance to meet many English women, so they were quite pleased.

'I found that the Brits didn't talk much. My job was to try and get them to talk. The Brits were very stuffy and came out with a series of stories without actually saying anything. One told me that he was a representative for a toothpaste company, which was a bit daft because we didn't have any toothpaste, we used to clean our teeth with soot or salt. They pretended they were all sorts of things, but the most obvious excuse they gave was that they were on a very boring course with the War Office. The clever ones would always try and steer the subject of conversation back to me, so that I had to talk about myself or what I did, so I had to be careful too.

'But the foreign agents were different, especially the younger ones. I think they were lonely, they were often far from their families and their culture – it was isolating for them. It must have been very flattering for them to have a young English girl chatting away to them, hanging on their every word. I remember one, a Dane, a beautiful blond Adonis. I managed to get him out on to the terrace – he didn't need a lot of persuading actually, I think he was rather taken with me. I weighed about 18 kilos less then, and didn't have white hair, and I didn't need glasses in those days.

'As we chatted on the terrace, he asked me if we could spend Sunday together. I took a little persuading, just so that he didn't get suspicious, but I knew of course that we couldn't. I became a very accomplished liar, I lied to everyone – my family, my friends – I just lived a lie. But once he said that, I felt a real surge of adrenaline because that was my lead, it was wonderful feeling that I might be on to something. I said, "Yes, I'd love to meet up on Sunday. But what is going to happen afterwards? Am I just the sort of thing you pick up on one day and then off you disappear, or are you going to be around?"

'He looked slightly crestfallen and told me he was going away, so I responded, "Oh, you're going away. Well, where are you going? Could we write? Could we meet again? I don't particularly want to get involved unless we could meet again." This went on for a while as we chatted over coffee and perhaps a whisky or two. After a while he told me that he would be going back to Denmark, which at the time was still occupied by the Nazis – and the only people who did that sort of work were agents. It was almost like a bit of a confession or perhaps he just wanted to unload some of his concerns. He said, "I won't be able to write, I won't be here, I'm being repatriated back into my country."'

The Danish agent had committed a cardinal sin. Although the trainee spy hadn't actually admitted that he was a member of the SOE, he had provided a clue, and in the world of espionage that is often all that is needed. Had his admission been made in the field he could have jeopardised himself, his team and an entire network, leading to the deaths of hundreds of men and women.

'I felt terrible when he said that, because I knew I was going to have to betray him. That was my job – it was the sort of job you hoped you would never succeed at. It was exciting up until the end, when you felt awful. But the reality was that I was helping to save the agent's life and possibly the lives of many others. It was a horrible job but it had to be done.'

Noreen kept up the pretence all evening, which ended with a gentle kiss on the Dane's cheek. The student spy returned to his quarters while Noreen headed straight to her house to write up her report. Once written, it was submitted that same evening to the debriefing officer, Colonel Woolrych, known to everyone as 'Woolly Bags', an intelligence specialist who had served in the First World War and later went on to become the commandant at Beaulieu.

'Like many people in that world, Woolrych didn't suffer fools gladly, but I found that he had a very compassionate side. All the reports from all the different spy schools were sent to Woolly Bags. He then made an assessment and sent the final report to the head of section. For French students it would have been Buck, and he would have the final say as to whether the student should be sent into the field. But if someone had spoken about their role, that was a very different matter.

'The following morning I was called into an office, and sitting there was the Dane. I stopped in front of him and we both looked at each other and I think it slowly began to dawn on him what had happened. At first there was a look of confusion and then, when Woolly Bags said, "Do you know this woman?" the look on his face turned to complete hatred. On previous occasions when I had done this, I had found that most of the students took it well, even if it meant that their careers in the SOE were compromised. But the Dane was different.

'He leapt to his feet with this infuriated look on his face and he said, "You bitch!" Well, no woman likes to be called a bitch. I was quite upset. I was then asked to leave the office and the two officers continued with the debriefing.

'Afterwards I was called back into Woolly Bags' office and in his very blunt way he said: "There's no point being upset about it. If he can't resist talking to a pretty face in Denmark he won't last an hour. He more or less told you that he was going to be an agent after dinner and a few drinks. Imagine what you could get out of him if you had a week, or if he was threatened with torture or execution. And remember it's not only his life he's putting in danger, he could bring down an entire network." I did realise that, of course, but Woolly Bags' words were of little comfort to me. The poor chap had gone through six months of very tough training, and Beaulieu was by no means a holiday camp.

'Beaulieu was known as the Finishing School for Spies – it was where everything they had learnt for the last six months was supposed to come together, so that the agents could deploy into the field and hopefully survive and carry out the tasks for which they had been trained. But it was also a very tough place, and if the students weren't up to the task then they could be failed at any moment. Some students were failed on the last day because the instructors could not be sure that they would survive as an agent.

'But Buck could be very generous – and even for those students who talked it didn't always mean the end. Buck used to say, "They've learnt their lesson, they won't do it again." Of course Buck had to be absolutely sure about this, because it was his reputation on the line also. His attitude was that lots of agents made mistakes in train-ing, and it was better to make the mistakes in training rather than on an actual live mission. But this attitude was always a risk and I'm not sure that the other section heads had such an enlightened approach as Buck.'

Noreen never saw the Danish student again and never discovered whether he actually became a spy.

★    ★    ★

The students at Beaulieu were also taught how to pick locks and enter buildings and factories without being heard or seen. The instructors were former spies, but some rehabilitated criminals, often ex-burglars, also served at Beaulieu and they were known as Method of Entry (MOE) men. One of the trainers was Johnny Childs, a lock-picker extraordinaire.

'Johnny was always easy to recognise because he was always driving around in a truck and on the back of this truck was a huge door covered in locks – every conceivable type of lock you could imagine. His job was to teach the students how to pick the locks, so there were locks from every country, French, German, Dutch, Danish. As an agent you might have to enter a building to which you didn't have a key – it might be in an emergency so this was a really vital art. Johnny had learnt his skills from a burglar. The story was that the burglar was serving a long stretch in Pentonville Prison.'

When the war broke out the SOE realised they needed help to enter buildings, and the experts of the trade were burglars. A senior SOE officer approached the authorities and asked for an expert burglar to be released into their care on the condition that he willingly passed on his skills – or so the story goes.

The lessons in 'breaking and entering' took place towards the end of the course when the students were preparing for the final exercise – a 96-hour test which all students had to pass. On one occasion Noreen was sent to accompany one of the students taking part in the exercise whose task was to travel to London and reconnoitre a certain address.

'The student who asked me to accompany him was very dashing, a member of the Parachute Regiment, and very handsome. And so I was delighted to go along. I also thought it would be fun and a chance to be in London for a few hours. We got the train up to London and went to the address, which was in central London close to Westminster Cathedral. I thought we were just going to look at the building so that he could say he had been there, but he wanted to go up to the fourth floor, which was fine, but when we got to the door he began to pick the lock and then went inside the flat.

'It was a Saturday afternoon, about 4pm, and I had never been so terrified in my life. He looked at me shaking and said, "Don't just stand there dithering, come in." I went in and I thought he was just going to have a quick look and then leave. Not a bit of it. He went into the bedroom and bounced on the bed, went into the bathroom and turned on taps, went through some drawers and cupboards. It was awful, every time we heard the lift I thought Wormwood Scrubs here we come. Then he started fiddling with the curtains, examining the photos on the piano – it probably lasted 10 minutes but it felt as if it was about four days. I was almost fainting by the end of it.

'As part of the compensation for this ordeal he took me to an underground pub in Piccadilly where he managed to revive me. We had a few drinks and then he took me to the theatre. What amazed me, when I thought about it afterwards, was how cool he was, completely unflappable. I was almost rigid with panic and my only thought was to get out, but he was completely comfortable.'

The experience was both fascinating and frightening for Noreen, who now fully realised how agents in the field had to work under conditions of almost unimaginable stress and still be able to think clearly.

There were occasions during the 96-hour exercise when events seemed to become almost tragically real. The agents were now so close to deploying into occupied countries that they no longer regarded themselves as students – the lines between exercise and reality became blurred. One such occasion involved a French SOE member who excelled in sabotage and silent killing in training.

'When he went on his 96, one of the decoys had been ordered by Buck to see if she could get him to talk about what he was doing. She met him in a bar, a classic scenario, and they spent the whole evening chatting, and the next day they had lunch together and went on a romantic walk together in a forest somewhere. She was chatting to him and becoming more and more romantic and they got into some sort of passionate embrace, at which point he grabbed her by the throat and began to squeeze until this poor girl almost fell into unconsciousness. At that point he released his grip and as the girl gasped for breath he said, "Now go back and tell Buckmaster to be more careful next time."'

Everyone was fully aware of the risks involved with being an agent, although, according to Noreen, the knowledge that death and torture would almost certainly follow capture was not something anyone dwelt upon.

'We weren't told about deaths or executions immediately after they happened – the news sort of filtered down. For example, if a radio op came up on schedule every day and then one day he didn't, Baker Street might suspect that he was wary that the Germans were on to him and he was trying to find a safe house. But if there was still silence after six or seven days you had to accept that he or she had been killed or captured. Everyone was obviously very sad when the news came through, but no one made a fuss. There was never any real outpouring of emotion. I think we mourned privately.

'I always thought the work was particularly dangerous for the radio operators. They were told that they had just a 50 per cent chance of surviving the mission – imagine what that must have been like. They received no extra pay for the work they were undertaking, it would have been the same rate as anyone of equal rank.

'The radio operators must have had nerves of steel – it was the most dangerous job, and they were highly valued and looked after very carefully. If a group lost their radio operator they lost all contact, because he was the only one who knew how to encode and decode messages.

'The golden rule for radio operators was never to transmit for more than 15 minutes, because it took the Germans 20 minutes to get a fix on a location.

'One radio operator told me that he had a horror of transmitting from inside a house, because he had this terrible feeling that the door would one day burst open and the Germans would catch him in the act, so to avoid this he always tried to transmit in the open. He would throw his aerial over a tree and always had two members of the Resistance with him who stood with guns at the ready and would warn him if there were any Germans approaching.'

Noreen also recalled the exploits of one agent called Benny Cowburn who was parachuted into occupied France four times between 1939 and 1941. He was awarded the MC and Bar, the France and Germany Star, the Defence Medal War medal, 1939–45, the Légion d'Honneur and the Croix de Guerre avec Palme.

Cowburn was extremely self-reliant and even used to make his own bombs. His base was a hut in the mountains.

'Benny played a very dangerous game, because he pretended to be friendly with the Germans. He must have had a tremendous confidence in his Resistance group, because they could have shot him for being a traitor. But he became quite friendly with the Germans, and one night, when he had been busy making his bombs, at about 3am, there was a terrible banging on the door. He opened the door and the German soldiers wanted to come in for a drink and a smoke, saying words to the effect of, "What are you doing up at this time of night?" and he said, "Oh, I'm making some bombs to blow up a bridge."

'But the Germans didn't take any notice because they thought he was joking, obviously, and said, "Have you got any beer?" He let them come in and gave them some beer. They asked him if he was going to have one and he said, "No, you have to keep a clear head when you are playing with dynamite," and they all thought he was terribly funny and screamed with laughter. After they had their beer they left. I think Benny was probably the coolest man I knew.'

Noreen harboured a secret ambition to become an agent herself, but two critical facts were against her – she was too young and the war was coming to an end. The youngest female agent was Anne-Marie Walters, who was aged just 21 when she arrived in France, but Noreen was only 20 at the end of the war in Europe.

Walters was recruited into the SOE from the Women's Auxiliary Air Force in July 1943, aged just 20. She was born in Geneva to a French mother and an English father. The family left Switzerland at the outbreak of war, and two years later Walters joined the WAAF. Her SOE codename was Colette and she parachuted into south-west France in January 1944, where she remained until the invasion of Normandy. She survived the war and was decorated by both the British and French governments for her work in occupied France.

'One of my last memories from life at Beaulieu involved a little Cockney corporal called Frank, whose job seemed to be getting us girls out of scrapes. Frank was engaged to a girl called Doris who worked in Woolworths. On VE Day we had a party and I was staggering over to The Rings, our HQ, a rather ugly stockbroker Tudor house in the middle of the estate. I was rather worse for wear because I had danced until dawn and had a few drinks. Suddenly out of a rhododendron bush appeared Frank and he said, "As it's VE Day, could I kiss you?" and I said, "Frank, what about Doris?" and he said, "I'll tell her that it's my last sacrifice for the war effort." Not really very flattering for me.'

As the Allied forces began pushing through France the need for agents to be sent into Europe decreased rapidly, but there was still a need for volunteers for service in the Far East, especially Burma, where Force 136, also part of SOE, were harrying the retreating Japanese.

'We all knew that the war in Europe was coming to an end. By the end of 1944, or even as early as D-Day, there was a certain inevitability about it. But when the end came at Beaulieu it was all a bit sudden. But there was still a war to be fought in Burma and I hoped to be sent there. In fact I was actually on embarkation leave when the atomic bomb was dropped in August 1945.

'By October 1945 Beaulieu had pretty well closed down, and by January 1946 SOE had ceased to exist. MI6 didn't like the organisation, I think they saw SOE as a threat to their existence, and after all both organisations were competing for the same meagre resources. We in SOE all knew that MI6 regarded us as a "load of amateur bandits" – well, we were all amateurs and we were bandits.

SOE was made up of lawyers, accountants, teachers, businessmen, bankers and future housewives. None of us were professional spies, but I think we were pretty good at what we did.'

Noreen had left the SOE in September 1945 and, like all agents and members of the organisation, she was sworn to secrecy. They were ordered to sign the Official Secrets Act and effectively told to keep their collective mouths shut.

After the war she put her language skills to good effect and joined the BBC's French Service, where she remained for five and a half years.

'Occasionally you would come across an agent from F Section, and we would acknowledge each other and perhaps have a quiet word over lunch or a cup of tea in the canteen, where we'd talk about our time in SOE and catch up on news of old friends such as Harry Ree,* Eddie McGuire, George Millar, Odette Churchill, Peter Churchill and Bob Maloubier.

'Then one day Buck turned up and it was a bit like being back on home ground. Some time later my future husband, Jacques, arrived at the BBC. Jacques had served as a captain in the French 1st Army and under Général de Lattre de Tassigny with the 19th battalion of the Chasseurs Alpins, and was awarded the Croix de Guerre with Bar. We got to know each other and we later married and I moved to France, where I have now lived for 56 years.'

Noreen remains an active member of the Special Forces Club, regularly attending reunions and meetings, where she often hears previously untold stories from her former colleagues of 70 years ago.

* Member of the SOE who started the war as a conscientious objector.

# CHAPTER 2

# The Two Wars of Jimmy Patch

## *The Long Range Desert Group*

*'Danger has some kind of satanic appeal to me. I am drawn
towards it in an octopus-like grip of fear.'*
MAJOR-GENERAL DAVID LLOYD OWEN,
the commander of the Long Range Desert Group

In addition to the SOE, the Second World War saw the emergence
of private armies, those units which became the special forces. This
was partly because the rules of warfare had changed, and the vast
distances over which the conflict was being played demanded
something new. In the North African campaign, for example, the
theatre of operations was the size of Europe, with most of the fighting taking place along or in close proximity to the Mediterranean
coast. This meant that small, self-contained military units could
disappear into the vastness of the desert and monitor the activities
of the enemy unseen and unheard.

Every commander wanted to know what his enemy opposite
number was doing or planning, and any unit which could help achieve
this was worth its weight in gold. The Long Range Desert Group was
created during that campaign in July 1940, about the same time that
the SOE became operational, specifically to conduct long-range
reconnaissance and raids deep behind enemy lines. It was founded by
Major Ralph Bagnold and originally called Long Range Patrol.

When I began carrying out research for this book and inquired
amongst veterans of the Second World War who, if anyone, might

be able to help me paint a picture of what life was like operating deep behind enemy lines in one of the most hostile environments on earth, one name kept surfacing.

'Speak to Jimmy Patch,' I was told by members of the Special Forces Club. 'He was there, he did the business. Fought in the desert,' said one veteran who got to know Jimmy after the war, 'and was captured by the Germans but escaped.' 'He'll have a good tale to tell, if you can get him to talk,' said another. Clearly Jimmy Patch was something of a legend within the Long Range Desert Group.

So on a cold January morning in 2011 it was with a keen sense of anticipation that I visited Jimmy, now 92, at his wonderfully serene hillside home in rural Kent.

'I'm not sure there's very much I can tell you,' said Jimmy diffidently. 'But why don't we have a cup of tea and then we can chat.'

Fortified by a cup of tea and some of my wife's home-made cake, Jimmy began to talk.

★　　★　　★

Jimmy's life in the special forces began while he was stationed in a large, tented camp on the outskirts of Cairo in the summer of 1941. One day as he walked through the pristine, whitewashed headquarters of the Royal Artillery Depot at Al Maza with his friend Bill Morrison, he saw a note pinned to a noticeboard bearing the following typed message: 'Volunteers required for special duties with the Long Range Desert Group. Details from the orderly room clerk.'

The two wiry young Royal Artillery gunners, who had long been in search of wartime adventure, looked at each other and smiled.

Almost from the moment of their call-up, a year earlier in May 1940 in the wake of the British Expeditionary Force's calamity in France, Jimmy, who was born in east London, and Bill, a proud Cornishman of Scottish descent, had been seeking an escape from the drudgery which typified the life of the private soldier during the early war years.

On that early summer's day within the vast training camp on the outskirts of Cairo, both men thought their prayers had been answered as they joined a growing queue of volunteers who were being assessed for their suitability for 'special operations' by Lieutenant Paul Eitzen, a young, diminutive South African who spoke with the clipped, confident tones of a public school boy. Eitzen, a member of the Royal Artillery attached to the Long Range Desert Group, wanted suitable volunteers to boost numbers of a covert unit which had begun experimenting with a 25lb artillery field gun while on operations behind enemy lines.

'Eitzen was very pleasant to both of us,' recalled Jimmy, 70 years later. 'He asked us a few questions, made a quick assessment of our intelligence and our suitability to operate in small groups. He must have been satisfied with Bill and myself because we learnt within a day or so that we were in, or at least attached to, the LRDG. It was probably the easiest interview of my life. I think he sensed our suitability very quickly. We were two young, impressionable men, happy to try anything and full of initiative, and that is what Eitzen was after.'

A few days later Jimmy, Bill and Lieutenant Eitzen left Al Maza in a 15cwt Ford truck, one of several in an LRDG replenishment convoy, and began the long, arduous journey across the scorching desert to the group's main base at the Siwa Oasis, which was about 350 miles south-west of Cairo and just 30 miles from the Libyan border.

Despite the demands and dangers of undertaking such a mission, Jimmy and Bill were gripped by a sense of excitement which they had not previously experienced as soldiers in an army at war. As the convoy entered the Sahara, Jimmy was immediately struck by the colossal expanse of the North African desert.

'I was 21 and had never left Britain. Now I was in the desert and the natural beauty was staggering. It was something you couldn't possibly hope to imagine. I had read about the Sahara in books but to see it with one's eyes was breathtaking.'

Back in 1941 the wider Army knew little about the LRDG, or any of the so-called 'private armies' emerging during the North

*Jimmy Patch*

African campaign. But gradually stories revealing their exploits began to seep out, often in the bars of Cairo, and for men with a sense of adventure the LRDG held a certain allure.

'We knew precious little about the LRDG and we didn't find out much more after the interview with Eitzen. But we knew it would be something different, and that would have to be better than our current situation. For the first time since being called up, I did feel a sense of excitement.'

\*   \*   \*

Jimmy Patch was born in 1920 and attended the Aldersbrook Elementary School in Wanstead before winning a scholarship to the Wanstead County High School where he was educated until the age of 16. Although he possessed the intellectual ability to attend university, his father, who had served in the First World War and won the Military Cross, had other ideas. After being demobbed in 1919, Jimmy's father was employed in the Ministry of Labour during the depression and, after seeing hundreds of men join the dole following the collapse of the economy, decided that his son would get a 'nice steady job'.

'I left school and joined the Post Office as a counter clerk. I worked there for three years, based in Loughton, Essex; then I passed a clerical exam and was transferred to London. It was a very comfortable existence; the hours were nine to four, and nine to twelve-thirty on Saturday.'

When war was declared in September 1939, Jimmy, like hundreds of thousands of young men of his generation, soon began to accept the inevitability of being called up to train, fight and possibly die in a war of national survival.

'I was 19 at the outbreak of war. I didn't volunteer to serve in the Army, I waited until I was called up, which happened in May 1940, at the time of Dunkirk. I was told that I would be going to the Royal Artillery and would be a signaller – there was no option. Basic training took place in Scarborough at the Royal Artillery Signals Training Regiment. Obviously the threat of invasion at the time was very real. With practically no training at all – we certainly hadn't fired a rifle – we were marched up to Scarborough Castle dyke every evening and spent the night guarding England. We each had a rifle and 50 rounds of ammunition in a cardboard box. We were the only thing that stood between Britain and being invaded by Hitler.'

For Jimmy, life in the Army was everything he had feared. He found the discipline and the endless inspections tiresome beyond belief, although he did enjoy the signals training, which taught him how to use a Number 11 radio* and how to send messages by radio or light-flashes using Morse code.

---

* The Number 11 radio set was the standard radio for an LRDG vehicle. Transmission range was 15 miles but could be extended to over 1,000 miles by using an external antenna and Morse code.

'I didn't regard being called up as an adventure, I just looked upon it as something that was inevitably happening to me. I had to submit to the discipline of the Army, of course, which I found very tiresome. In fact at one stage in 1941 I volunteered to be transferred to the RAF, because volunteers were called for, but nothing happened.'

The training continued until the late spring of 1941, when both Jimmy and Bill learnt that they were to be sent to fight in the North African campaign. Both men were given embarkation leave, but Jimmy's leave was extended by another week after his parents' house was damaged during a German bombing raid. 'It was pretty scary. The house was badly damaged, but no one was injured and I got an extra week's leave before being sent up to Liverpool to board a troopship bound for the Middle East.'

The Mediterranean Sea was a war zone in 1941, and the only relatively safe way for ships to reach Cairo was to travel in convoys via the Cape of Good Hope and up the east coast of Africa. For Jimmy and hundreds of others aboard, it was a journey into the unknown from which many would never return.

'We were packed cheek by jowl on the troopship. There were dozens of us in a huge dormitory, each with a hammock. It was impossible to sleep. The atmosphere was hot, fetid and noisy. Every night a group of us would collect our blankets and try and find a sheltered spot on the deck and sleep there, and we did it in all weathers.

'We all soon settled into a routine. There was a bit of training and PT to do, but we also played a lot of housey-housey – now called bingo. The voyage seemed to take an age but it ended up being quite enjoyable. We steamed almost to the other side of the Atlantic before heading back to the West African coast and pulling into Sierra Leone to refuel. Then we travelled down to Durban, where we transferred to another ship, the *New Mauritania*. In a convoy of three ships we moved up the east coast of Africa, into the Red Sea and on into the Suez Canal and Port Tufic.'

The LRDG was the creation of Major Ralph Bagnold of the Royal Signals, a man regarded by many within the new world of special forces as a genius. In the late 1920s and 30s, Bagnold, together with a collection of friends such as Bill Kennedy Shaw, Guy Prendergast and Rupert Harding-Newman, spent a great deal of time exploring the region of desert between the Mediterranean and Sudan. During those years Bagnold designed and perfected expeditionary equipment which would later be used by the LRDG. He created a simple sun compass to make navigation easier, perfected the condenser to conserve water in car radiators, thought up the idea of sand mats to help extricate vehicles stuck in soft sand, and developed properly balanced rations when travelling in such austere conditions.

Bagnold originally came up with the idea for the LRDG in November 1939, but it wasn't until Italy entered the war, in June 1940, that his proposals were taken seriously and approved by the Middle East commander-in-chief, General Sir Archibald Wavell. Following a meeting between the two men, Wavell asked Bagnold if he could create an operational unit within six weeks.

Bagnold's aim was to build a force capable of mechanised reconnaissance, intelligence gathering, navigation and mapping vast areas of the North African desert.

It was a massive undertaking but Bagnold set about achieving his mission with his customary zeal and over the next six weeks he recruited a force of New Zealanders who were regarded as both self-reliant and full of initiative and therefore perfect for working in enemy territory in small groups for weeks on end. While Bagnold began to select the men for his force, Harding-Newman, who had also been recruited into the unit, was given the responsibility of acquiring transportation.

The British Army in the Middle East in 1940 had no vehicles remotely suitable for desert warfare, and so Bagnold approached the Chevrolet company in Alexandria and acquired 14 vehicles, while Harding-Newman managed to obtain a further 19 from the Egyptian Army. The vehicles were quickly modified for the desert and long-range patrolling and repainted in camouflage colours.

The vehicles were fitted with a variety of weapons. These included the old Lewis machine-guns, which were initially fitted to 11 of the trucks and later replaced by the twin Vickers machine-gun, as well as four Boys anti-tank rifles and one 37mm Bofors anti-aircraft gun.

During those six weeks the men also had to be trained in desert navigation. This required detailed knowledge of how to calculate one's location with sun compasses and theodolites, which use the position of the sun and the stars respectively.

Once all the men and equipment had been gathered, Bagnold took his force on two exercises into the desert to test their newly acquired skills and tactics. It was a tough ask, and many mistakes were made during that hectic period. Days were long and sleep was always welcomed. For some the demands of desert life proved too much, and they either asked to be returned to their units or were told their services were no longer required. Bagnold wanted to test his unit on every eventuality they might find in the desert, but their future success would depend above all on their ability to navigate and survive in one of the most hostile terrains on earth. Despite the huge challenges, however, by August 1940 the LRDG was operational.

★　　★　　★

Despite being accepted by the LRDG, Jimmy was only 'attached' to the unit; he would become a permanent member within a few months only if he proved his worth. In those early days the LRDG was composed of two squadrons, A and B. A Squadron consisted of four New Zealand patrols, while B Squadron was composed of two Yeomanry and two Rhodesian patrols, and two patrols from the British Brigade of Guards.

The composition of the patrols varied slightly according to the commander, but essentially they consisted of a variety of 15cwt and 30cwt Chevrolet trucks and, later on in the campaign, US jeeps. All the trucks were unarmoured and stripped down to their bare essentials. Having no doors or windshields, the vehicles offered little protection to the crews if they were attacked, but they were fast and manoeuvrable. The strength of the patrols also varied but was somewhere between 15 and 20 men. The vehicles were repaired, modified and improved after each mission. Every patrol had to be self-sustaining and contained a medic, navigator, mechanic, signaller and cook.

The Siwa Oasis base was close to the Libyan–Egyptian border and a world away from the regular Army. It was a long journey through the dust and the heat of the North African desert, but Jimmy and Bill were not bothered by the discomfort, and a week after leaving Al Maza the convoy arrived at the base.

Siwa was unlike any military establishment either Jimmy or Bill had previously experienced. The oasis was composed of a small village with a number of dwellings and an Arab hotel, used by some of the French forces who were also camped at the oasis.

Most of the LRDG troops chose to make their camp beneath the shade of a collection of lush date palms growing close to the numerous ponds which provided the Arab population and the military units with vital supplies of clean, fresh water. The oasis was also the perfect location for a forward operating base. It was in Egypt, 150 miles south of the coast, which was the main fighting area, and therefore relatively safe. But its presence was not secret, and the Italian forces certainly knew of its existence. Italian reconnaissance flights would fly over the oasis every week, and there was the occasional bombing run, but despite the threat the soldiers felt quite safe.

Discipline was different from the regular Army. Members of the LRDG were expected to be professional at all times; those who weren't were sent back to their original units. It was, Jimmy thought at the time, like a breath of fresh air. There was hardly any saluting, no drill, no inspections. All patrol commanders were called 'Skipper', while all other ranks were on first-name terms.

The two new arrivals quickly settled into the relaxed atmosphere of desert life, and it hardly seemed that a violent war was raging across North Africa and much of Europe. In fact, life was so idyllic at Siwa that the troops called it 'Hollywood'. Within the privations of desert warfare, the LRDG at Siwa wanted for nothing – there was always a plentiful supply of fresh water, and rations were brought in by the unit's Heavy Section on regular administration runs.

'Life in Siwa was very comfortable and we were a tight-knit, self-contained unit,' Jimmy recalled. 'Everyone was very professional and got on with what they had to do. There was no shouting and no punishments – the only punishment was to be sent back to your unit, and no one wanted that. We even had a little pond where we could go for a swim and keep cool and wash.

'We wore whatever we liked and, more often than not, it was a mishmash of uniforms. We soon learnt what was practical for the conditions and what wasn't, and that's how we operated.

'We had army rations we cooked ourselves and we had a rum ration every night – some people didn't have it so there was a little bit more for others. We received the rum in bulk but it was rationed out. There was one character, an ex-tank soldier in his 40s, who was older than the rest of us and he used to take damn near a mug full every night and would go to bed stupid. The only real threat was from aircraft, which would come over most days either to take pictures or sometimes drop a bomb from a height well out of range. Life was also made a little bit more comfortable because the LRDG was issued 50 per cent more rations than other units because we worked in small patrol groups.

'The Sahara is a vast area; you can fit the entire sub-continent of India into it, and we had behind us all the experience Ralph Bagnold had gained from his various expeditions into the desert in the late 1920s and 30s.

'Bagnold developed the sun compass, which was a beautifully accurate instrument and it would give navigators a precise fix of the patrol's location providing they knew what they were doing. Behind enemy lines you could keep way away from the fighting line, which was around the coast, but the danger was always aircraft. There were occasions when the LRDG were attacked by friendly aircraft and men were killed because the aircraft couldn't distinguish between friendly forces and the enemy. You can't fire effectively at an aircraft if you are on the move in vehicles, but if you are stationary then you become an easy target, so it's one or the other and you would choose what to do depending on the terrain.'

Speed in the desert depended on terrain and the vehicles being used. In areas where the terrain was particularly difficult the speed could fall to just 10mph, usually in rocky and hilly areas. But there were other areas, such as the Kalansho Seria, which were almost perfectly smooth, allowing convoys to travel at speeds of 60mph.

'Normally the terrain would be hilly and strewn with rocks, and it was often impassable, making navigation difficult. Then there was the sand sea, comprised of vast sand dunes. We tried to avoid the dunes, but sometimes you couldn't. The dunes were shaped by the wind; on the windward side the slope would be quite gradual and you could sail up them very easily, and then suddenly they would end in what amounted to a precipice. The gradual slope would stop and you would be confronted by an almost vertical drop the other side, which you couldn't see if the sun was shining in your eyes. There were one or two nasty accidents.'

Jimmy's first mission took place a few weeks after arriving at Siwa. The target was an Italian occupied fort called El Gtafia, about 25 miles south of Agedabia in an area 200 miles behind enemy lines. But as Jimmy was soon to learn, being located behind enemy lines was often much safer than being in front of them. It was the autumn of 1941 and, after the spectacular earlier success of the German Afrika Korps and their inspirational commander Erwin Rommel, the tide of the desert war was turning in favour of the Allied forces.

General Claude Auchinleck had replaced General Wavell as Commander-in-Chief Middle East theatre, and reinforcements in the form of a new Corps had arrived, which allowed the creation of the soon-to-be 8th Army.

'We didn't do a great deal of training prior to the first operation, because we were perfectly confident and trained in what we had to do. It was also quite an easy function to take the gun, a 25-pounder, out into the blue* and fire it. The gun was always ready for action. We made ourselves familiar with all of the equipment. There was a Number 11 wireless set and field telephones, and we

---

* Soldier slang for the desert.

just made sure that we had all the equipment we needed to do whatever was asked of us.'

Prior to departing, the vehicles were loaded with water, rations, food, radios, spare parts and ammunition. To cope with the loads, the trucks were fitted with reinforced springs, spares of which were also carried.

The convoy took around three days to reach its target. Progress was slow because of the 10-ton Mack truck which was needed to carry the 25lb artillery piece. When the patrol arrived at the target location, Jimmy and Paul Eitzen moved up to the top of a hill to get a better view of the fort, while at the same time laying a telephone cable back to the gun, so that the two observers could relay information back to the gun team.

'The fort was like one of those from the film *Beau Geste* which the Italians were very fond of building. It was being used to cache supplies for enemy troops on the move. It was a sitting duck – there were no troops outside covering the vulnerable points. Paul Eitzen gave direction orders to the gun team and we banged away for a pre-arranged number of rounds and minutes and then ceased. The first round we fired was a dud; it hadn't exploded and we later found it in the middle of the fort.

'Once the firing had ceased, some of the Rhodesians from S Patrol who had accompanied us went forward and captured the fort, which wasn't that difficult because after the first round the four Italians occupying the fort ran away, so the place was empty, but they were quickly captured. The structure hadn't been badly damaged because the 25-pounder isn't really a big gun.

'Once the fort had been captured, we withdrew into the desert with the four prisoners while the Rhodesians headed towards the coast on another reconnaissance mission. We made camp and tried to relax and explain to the Italians, as best as we could given the language problem, that we were going to look after them and that they would come to no harm. They responded to our friendship but I have to say they were a pretty unimpressive bunch – I think they were probably quite happy to have been captured because it meant they were out of the war. In fact, later that night we got out the rum ration and had a bit of a party. They couldn't speak English and we couldn't speak Italian, but it was all very friendly.

'After the Rhodesians came back from their reconnaissance patrol we started making our way back to Siwa, but on the way this dreadful 10-ton Mack truck kept getting stuck in the soft sand. It was very difficult to get it out, because it was too heavy for the sand trays – a device used to free vehicles stuck in soft sand. The vehicle also had brake problems, and the thing became such a nuisance that eventually the Rhodesian officer in command of the patrol lost his patience and said, "Leave it." We took the gun off the back of the truck and towed it behind one of the patrol vehicles and abandoned the 10-tonner.'

The LRDG had a limited number of vehicles at that stage of the war, and the difficulties with transporting even a relatively small gun such as a 25-pounder across the desert were immense. When the patrol arrived back at Siwa the artillery unit was given an Italian lorry to transport the gun, but it proved fairly ineffective, and after Christmas the unit was disbanded. Most of the gunners who had been recruited for the specialist unit were sent back to their former regiments. Jimmy and Bill were desperate to remain with the LRDG, but unfortunately Bill was taken ill with pleurisy.

'Bill was very ill. I don't think any of us thought that he was going to make it, and at one point his grave was dug; that was how close he was to death. Bill spent all his time back in the MO's truck, and the only thing which saved him was one of the new sulphur drugs. When he was cured, he went back to the LRDG but joined one of the New Zealand patrols as a signalman and stayed with them until the end of the desert campaign.

'Captain David Lloyd Owen, the skipper of the Yeomanry, or Y Patrol, asked me if I would like to join his patrol and I jumped at it. I became a Lewis gunner initially, but some time later the patrol navigator was selected for a commission and I began training to take his place, first as assistant navigator and then doing the full role.

'The main role of the LRDG was doing reconnaissance and "road watch". This involved monitoring the movements of enemy forces along the main coast road in the Benghazi area. The patrol would position itself a couple of miles from the road, camouflage up, and each evening two men would walk up to the road to a hide, rather like a birdwatching hide. They would sit there for 24 hours, making a note of everything which went past. All of this intelligence would be passed back up the chain of command to the staff officers at General Headquarters to help formulate future offensives or withdrawals.

'Apart from the enemy, one of the other great challenges of desert warfare is coping with the heat. In the summer the temperature often reached 120°F, while dropping to below zero at night. In the winter the weather could be miserable.

'The stripped-down vehicles kept the soldiers cool on long patrols and the men quickly acclimatised to the heat. To cope with the heat we dressed accordingly and often wore sandals – which were given to us as a special issue – instead of boots. We found that the standard issue baggy shorts were much more comfortable than long trousers, too. We were issued with these Arab headdresses which we folded into a triangle and fixed with a ring of black material known as an *egal*. These were meant to protect our heads but I didn't often wear one. I personally wore a cap comforter, a woollen thing which folded up into a cap. In the winter we wore full-length sheepskin coats, woolly hats, gloves and a thick jumper to keep out the cold.

'We'd have a variety of devices to keep ourselves warm. We would take an Italian water bottle, which was quite a capacious thing made of aluminium, fill it with water and break up a bar of chocolate into it and hang it over the exhaust and within five miles we would have a hot drink. We each had a blanket roll, no beds or sleeping bags, and we would just unroll that by the wheel of the truck. We had a rum ration every evening and some lime powder. We would mix the rum and lime with water and when we woke up we would have a nice cold drink.'

The LRDG continued with their reconnaissance operations and before long Jimmy was established as Lloyd Owen's personal navigator. It was at this stage that rumours began to surface about a large raid involving many different units – a major departure from the type of operations usually conducted by the LRDG.

It was widely believed that Field Marshal Erwin Rommel, known as the Desert Fox, and the commander of the Axis forces in North Africa, was planning a major offensive eastwards along the coast.

One of those working on the British plan was Colonel John 'Shan' Hackett, who would later command the 4th Parachute Brigade at Arnhem. In essence the plan would involve members of the LRDG, the SAS, Army Commandos, Royal Marines, Popski's Private Army,* the RAF and the Royal Navy launching simultaneous attacks on the Libyan coastal city of Benghazi, where a large German garrison was based, Tobruk and Barce. Once these attacks had succeeded, the Sudanese Defence Force were to attack the Jalo Oasis. If everything went to plan, Rommel's bold aggressive thrust to move east and destroy the 8th Army would lie in tatters.

But the plan quickly became over-ambitious and too complex. In simple terms, the plan was as follows: at Tobruk, Lieutenant-Colonel John Haselden,† a highly decorated British officer, would lead a force composed of around 80 commandos, engineers and Royal Artillery gunners, who were to capture the harbour and facilitate the landing of reinforcements by sea. Those reinforcements would then destroy underground fuel stores, release British POWs being held in the area and attack two airfields close to the city.

Meanwhile the SAS, supported by two Rhodesian LRDG patrols, would attack the harbour at Benghazi, destroying shipping and fuel storage tanks.

---

* Officially known as No. 1 Demolition Squadron, Popski's Private Army was founded in 1942 by (then) Major Vladimir Peniakoff, DSO, MC.

† British officer, born in Egypt, who had previously taken part in Operation Flipper, the abortive 1941 attempt to assassinate Rommel. Awarded MC and Bar.

The raid on the Barce airfield was to be conducted by the LRDG, who would also be supported by the commander of Popski's Private Army, Lieutenant-Colonel Vladimir Peniakoff.

Four days later the Sudanese Defence Force were to secure Jalo, which would then be used by David Stirling for further desert operations. D-Day for the operation was 13 September 1942.

But with so many staff officers now involved in the operation, security became a major concern. Gossip and rumours were rife in both Alexandria and Cairo, with some senior officers chatting openly about the operation over a gin and tonic in many of the bars and clubs which played host to the Allies.

In David Lloyd Owen's excellent memoir *Providence Their Guide: The Long Range Desert Group, 1940–45*, the author recalls his fears for the success of the operation because of the loose talk in the bars and cafés of Cairo.

'Even before I had first been put in the know by John Haselden in Cairo I had heard rumours; and I had heard these through gossip at parties and in the bars of Cairo. I was very suspicious that security had been blown, and I told John Haselden of my fears when he arrived in Kufra the day before we were due to set off on the 800-mile journey to Tobruk.

'There was little that John, or indeed myself, could do at that stage except to tell all those involved with us what was planned, in order to scotch all the rumours that were current. This did not help, however, to allay our fears that we would be walking into a trap.'

Despite the bond of trust which existed amongst and between members of the LRDG, Lloyd Owen refused to brief his troops on the operation until just a few hours before D-Day. The soldiers knew that something was afoot, but they also understood that surprise, and therefore secrecy, was vital if any behind-the-lines raid was to succeed. On 24 August the five vehicles and 20 men of Y Patrol left the Fayoum, 80 miles south of Cairo, for the first stage of the operation.

'We set out from the LRDG base at Fayoum and drove down to Asyut. We spent one night in a house which belonged to John Haselden. It was very comfortable, with a swimming pool and nice gardens. At that time we didn't really have any idea what the target was. We had heard the rumours, of course, and we knew something big was going to come off.

'At Asyut we met up with Haselden's force of commandos. There were about 80 of them in seven 3-ton trucks, together with some sappers and gunners. We didn't know it at the time, but the ruse was that the commandos were supposed to be POWs and their German guards were actually German Jews from the Special Interrogation Group (SIG). A great deal of planning had gone into making this work. The guards had proper German uniforms, faked papers, faked letters from girlfriends, and of course they spoke perfect German. Although the 3-tonners were British, they were painted with Afrika Korps markings. It was common practice at the time for both sides to use captured vehicles, so their presence should not have aroused suspicion.

'After we picked up the commandos, we travelled across the desert to Kufra. It was a four-day trip, made slower by seven lumbering 3-tonners which kept getting stuck in soft sand. By now we had covered around 1,000 miles when the desert heat was at its most fierce.

'We didn't know any detail, we didn't know where we were going. We just knew that something was coming off. We were to escort the commandos to the scene of the action, and that was to be done via Kufra.'

On 31 August Y Patrol and the commandos arrived at Kufra, the staging post for the combined operation, and the next six days were spent preparing for the mission. It was a relaxed yet busy period, and the troops quickly made themselves at home amongst the date palms which dotted the oasis.

As days passed, more men from other units began to arrive at Kufra, and rumours again began to surface. Haselden flew into the base on 5 September, and Lloyd Owen convinced him that the time had come to brief everyone on the mission.

Jimmy continued: 'We were eventually briefed the night before we left Kufra, and it was a great relief. D-Day was 13 September and everyone was very relieved that it didn't fall on a Friday.

'John Haselden briefed us on the operation on the night before we were due to leave Kufra. He unfurled a map and explained in detail what we were going to do. Everyone was very enthusiastic, there were no morbid thoughts, and we were all utterly convinced that the mission would be a total success.

'Our job was to deliver the commandos to Tobruk, secure the perimeter, then, at a given signal, move into the town and attack a radar station and then finally free some British POWs who were being held there. The idea was that the commandos would run amok, destroying as much as possible before being evacuated by sea.

'The thing I was most concerned with was making sure that I had the right maps. I would be navigating, so that was obviously on my mind. It was another six-day trip but although it was routine for the LRDG it would have been pretty tough for the commandos, who weren't use to these long-range desert patrols.

'At one stage we had to find our way between the oasis of Jalo, which was occupied at the time, and the Sand Sea. So we had to steer a very accurate passage through a narrow corridor and we couldn't show any light and had to be careful about noise.'

One of the main risks was being spotted by enemy aircraft and so some of the movement was conducted at night. The pace was slow and comfortable and the convoy arrived at Hatiet Etla on 10 September, where the small force took cover amongst the scrub and sand dunes. Y Patrol was now just 90 miles from Tobruk, and D-Day loomed ever closer.

'You get to a stage where you just want to get on with things, and that was the case at Hatiet Etla. There was a lot of scrub in the area, which was ideal for camouflaging our vehicles, and we remained there for the next two days, completing our final preparations. The plan was rehearsed several times so that everyone knew what part to play and also what to do if things went wrong.

'Everyone was making sure that their personal equipment was in perfect working order and that the vehicles were sound. It was that sort of thing, resting as much as possible and passing the time.'

The convoy moved off again on the morning of 13 September to an area called Ed Duda, 20 miles from the Tobruk perimeter. It was at this location that Haselden and his commandos went their separate way on what was ultimately to become a fatal mission. As the four 3-ton lorries containing the commandos departed, the men of the LRDG waved silently, many of them wondering what fate awaited their comrades.

As Haselden's party moved off to the north, a small party of German troops were spotted and the two groups passed within two miles of each other. Rather than hide and risk being reported to German intelligence, Lloyd Owen decided to bluff it out and ordered Y Patrol to spread out and advance, hoping that the Germans would assume they were friendly forces given that they were 300 miles behind enemy lines.

'We got right in amongst them before we opened fire. I think right up until that point they must have thought we were friendlies. We never gave them a chance, we just kept firing until all but one was dead and we captured him. It was kill or be killed. If we had let them go they would have reported us and we would probably have been bombed. That was the first time I had seen a dead body. It was the sort of thing you expect. If you are going to be involved in a war there are going to be dead bodies, but it didn't affect me at all. I didn't feel any sympathy, I didn't feel any fear. I was detached. I had grown used to war.'

The captured prisoner then broke the news that everyone feared, revealing that he was one of many reinforcements who had been sent into Tobruk in recent days to prepare for a possible attack.

'After that attack, we destroyed the enemy vehicles and moved off again briefly. Then we stopped, had a meal and waited to hear from the commandos. The idea was that Haselden would get in touch and brief us on the enemy situation so that we would be able to deal with any Germans on our route in. I think after about an hour we began to realise that something must have gone wrong. The radio operator kept trying to make contact but there was nothing. So after several hours we moved off down to the escarpment at Sidi Rezegh. Movement down the escarpment was painfully slow because it was so steep and covered in boulders.

'We eventually reached the perimeter fence well after midnight and everyone knew the plan was already seriously behind schedule. By now we could hear the sounds of battle in the distance. The RAF had flown over some hours earlier dropping their massive pay-loads.

'Lloyd Owen came over to me and said, "Patch, where do you think we are?" I pointed to the map and said "Here." I was absolutely certain that we were within 100 yards of the perimeter. The message then came around that we were going to stay put until dawn and then go in and destroy our first target, which was the radar station. So the vehicles moved into cover and we waited.

'I didn't know it at the time, but the radio operator had spent most of the night trying to raise Haselden while we either rested or mounted sentries. By the morning the battle was still raging, but without any radio contact it was impossible to know what was going on.

'Just before dawn Lloyd Owen called us all together and explained that he had been unable to contact Haselden or any of his commandos and that consequently we had no idea what was going on. The only option was to race back to the escarpment, set up the radio antennae and try and make contact with HQ to try and get an update on the situation.

'Within 10 minutes we were on the move, racing past these huge German tented camps. Titch Cave, a belligerent character, who was the skipper's gunner, wanted to open fire. He was manning a .50 calibre Vickers and he wanted to shoot up the camps as we drove past, but the Skipper said we just had to push on. It was quite an extraordinary sight. We could see all these German soldiers queuing for breakfast and we were racing past them. We could see them looking at us but no one tried to stop us.'

Y Patrol moved up and over the escarpment and continued for another 20 miles before halting and trying to reach HQ again, but it would take another seven hours before they eventually made contact and were given the dreadful news that the Tobruk element of the plan had been an abject failure. The large coastal guns which the commandos had been tasked with destroying had been moved, and the Royal Navy had suffered heavy casualties, losing two destroyers and a cruiser, and had also failed to land reinforcements. Y Patrol was ordered not to return to Tobruk but to make instead for Hatiet Etla and await further orders.

'We moved off just as it was beginning to get dark. I had managed to get a few hours' sleep but we were all pretty tired. But the worst feeling was knowing that the mission had been a failure. We still didn't know what had happened, only that the raid had failed and casualties were heavy. It was a huge anti-climax and we all felt very dejected. When we arrived at Hatiet we had to wait a bit and then we were told to move to a place called Landing Ground 125, an emergency airstrip near Barce, about 80 miles from our location, near the Kalansho Sand Sea. The landing ground was to be used as a rallying point and we were told that there would be a lot of injured soldiers and men who had been separated from their units heading there.

'I plotted a route and off we went. We left in the afternoon and arrived at LG125 when it was dark. LG125 was south of Barce, which was the scene of another raid which was exclusively LRDG, executed by New Zealanders and guardsmen, and that was quite a success. The LRDG destroyed a lot of aircraft, but they again ran into some resistance and had taken some casualties, and the theory was that the injured might have made their way to LG125.

'We eventually found them later that night. There were about eight of them under a tarpaulin, being looked after by our medical officer, Richard Lawson, who had behaved admirably throughout the whole of the Barce raid. He had been dashing around treating men under fire and was awarded the Military Cross. Popski was also amongst the wounded – he had lost his little finger. We helped in whatever way we could, gave them cigarettes, water, food and some rum. A message was also sent back to our base requesting a transport aircraft to come and pick up the wounded. The next day an RAF Bombay arrived, flown by an officer called Flight Lieutenant John Coles, a professional airman, who later became an Air Marshal. It was a masterpiece of navigation on his part. He had flown across the desert, which was flat and featureless, but he managed to find this little strip with practically nothing on it except a few oil drums to mark it out as an airfield. We didn't know precisely when he was coming and we didn't have any pre-arranged signals. He had a couple of men with him, but by the time he landed this old Bombay had used up all of its petrol. But it was carrying petrol for its return journey in four-gallon jerrycans. So we all helped in the refuelling and the injured were loaded on board, and by the next morning they had all arrived safely in Cairo.'

After the RAF Bombay had departed, Y Patrol were ordered to remain at LG125 for the next 24 hours to await and assist those who had become separated from their respective units during the raid. By the time Y Patrol was ready to depart, on 20 September, they had been joined by another 60 stragglers.

'We arrived back at Kufra on 25 September. I think we were all relieved to be back but also very angry about what had happened, because there was a very strong view that the failure could have been avoided if people had kept their mouths shut. It really was a case that careless talk costs lives.

'By the time we got back to Kufra, other soldiers who had taken part in the other raids were already there and we soon began to swap stories. The general consensus was that we had all been let down by staff officers in Cairo, because of their loose talk and bad planning.'

A few days after arriving at Kufra, one of the most extraordinary events of Jimmy's war took place during a German bombing raid. The Germans knew that Kufra was a British base and would occasionally attack. On this occasion, eight Junker 88s attacked the airfield where the RAF Bombays were located.

'The bombing run took the Jerry aircraft right over the top of the date palms beneath which we [Y Patrol], the New Zealanders, G Patrol and the SAS were billeted. Our guns were still mounted on our vehicles and as they passed over us we all let rip. There were dozens of machine-guns firing up at them and we managed to shoot down six out of the eight aircraft. It so happened I was on some sort of errand on foot in another part of the oasis so I didn't take part, I just heard this huge racket. Jerry made the mistake of assuming that we would be in the great fort built by the Italians, whereas that was the last thing we would think of doing, because it was such an obvious target. The 88s were easy targets because they were so low, just a couple of hundred feet, and so were difficult to miss – especially if you have several machine-guns all firing at the same time.

'As they came over they were met by this barrage of machine-gun fire. I was desperate to get back and have a go, but things like that are over in a couple of minutes and I was too late. It was unheard of to shoot down six aircraft.

'During the raid Lloyd Owen was wounded by a 20mm cannon shell which caught his back and arm. It was a very serious wound and I know that a lot of us thought he might not survive. But he eventually got back to Cairo and made a pretty good recovery.'

Over the following weeks the full catastrophe of the earlier mission began to unfold. It soon emerged that John Haselden had been killed leading an assault to capture the coastal guns. The commandos did achieve some initial success during the early stages of the operation but were overwhelmed by the size of the enemy force. Because the guns were not captured, the Royal Navy were unable to land the reinforcements who were supposed to bolster Haselden's commandos, and the mission was doomed.

The SAS also faced fierce resistance at Benghazi and the Sudanese Defence Force did not fare well at Jalo either. Only the raid on the airfield at Barce could be described as a success, so overall, as an attempt to delay Rommel's build-up for the offensive at El Alamein, the operation was a failure.

For Y Patrol the war seemed to be trundling along as they settled into a routine of road watch and long-range reconnaissance. Then planning began for a raid on the oasis at Hon, which at the time was occupied by the Italians.

'We set off from Kufra and it was planned to be a two- or three-day trip. The journey was very routine and went without a hitch. The idea was to see what sort of garrison the Germans had there, beat it up, see how the enemy would respond and get as much intelligence as we could so we could plan future operations. It was like a fighting reconnaissance patrol. The skipper, who by that time was a chap called Captain Spicer, went forward in his jeep to check things out at the oasis, while we took cover amongst a rocky outcrop.

'They went in and had a good look around, but they must have been spotted because some time later an Italian Caproni 309 Ghibli, a bomber, came over. We all opened fire at the aircraft and it veered away and that was the last we saw of it. But it was replaced by a number of CR42 biplanes. By now the Chevrolets had scattered and moved into defensive positions beneath a hill, with the sun behind us, so anyone attacking us would have to dive into the sun.

'Then these damn planes started attacking us, but we opened up with these wonderful twin Vickers and that kept them away. When a plane is diving straight at you, it is pretty terrifying. I remember thinking, "I don't want to be killed because of the effect it would have on my parents." That was all I was thinking about; I wasn't thinking about myself as such, just the grief it would cause my parents. It was a 50–50 chance that I would be killed. The bullets were coming in very close, and there was a sort of wop, wop sound as they hit the ground around me. As far as I was concerned, the pilot was trying to nail me. The sound of a round hitting the ground close to you is pretty terrifying, I can tell you, but the planes were put off by our shooting and they were unable to keep a direct course straight down to us. It was happening over and over, waves of planes attacking us. It was a very frightening incident indeed and that was about the closest I came to being killed, it was a pretty narrow squeak. If they had managed to get a bead on us for any length of time it would have been curtains, but to hit us they had to fly straight, and the pilots knew they were vulnerable when flying straight. The idea was to force them to twist and turn, which we did, and eventually they gave up and we hot-footed it back to Kufra.'

★　　★　　★

By May 1943 the whole of the North African coast was under Allied control. The LRDG had developed into a force of great renown. The challenge was to decide how the organisation should be used in the future and in what theatre.

One evening in late May, as the members of Y Patrol relaxed, the news came through that the LRDG were to be retrained for missions in Albania, Greece, Yugoslavia and Northern Italy.

The top brass had decided that there was no better force in the British Army than the LRDG to help train, equip and organise the various partisan groups fighting the Germans and Italians. But it would be a totally different type of warfare from that which the organisation had experienced in the vastness of the Libyan desert, where there was always plenty of room to hide.

The LRDG's mountain base was to be the Cedars Hotel in Lebanon, the British Army's Mountain Warfare Training Centre. The plan, for these one-time desert warriors, was to learn how to ski, climb and navigate in the mountains. For Jimmy and his colleagues it was an opportunity to recover from the months of arduous desert living, and although the training was going to be tough, the change, in many respects, was as good as a rest.

'It was quite different to anything we had done before and a lot of fun although the training was extremely hard. The officers lived in the hotel and we were billeted in large Indian tents and it was all quite comfortable. The officer in charge of the training school was a character called Jimmy Riddle. He was said to have been an Olympic skier, and I can well believe it having seen him perform. The instructor of our little group was a Czech, a private soldier. He took us in hand, but not very effectively as far as I was concerned because I was never any good at skiing. I was also set to learn Greek, at which I tried my best. As well as skiing, there were long hikes through the mountains, and we learnt how to live off dried rations. We also had to learn how to navigate and fight in this new environment which was obviously very different from the desert.

'We remained at the Cedars until early September 1943, at which point we were told that we were going to be trained as parachutists.

Again, everyone thought this was great fun. But first of all we needed to have a colour-blindness test because when it came to jumping out of aeroplanes we needed to be able to see the difference between red and green lights. We were all lined up ready to do this test at the medical officer's office, but all he had to test us with was the coloured cover of a magazine.

'He pointed to different colours and you had to say what they were. I was colour blind so I obviously got it wrong, but it didn't seem to matter – the medical officer said something like "Oh my God, you'll have to follow the man in front." That was my colour-blindness test.'

The Parachute Training Course took place at the Ramit David Airfield, close to Tel Aviv in what was then Palestine, now Israel. The soldiers were put through their paces and were taught how to fall and roll, a skill which would come in handy later when Jimmy had to make a quick exit – from a moving train!

'The training had to be quite relentless, and so the powers that be decided that we should be allowed an afternoon off before our first jump, which was supposed to take place the following morning. Free time was quite rare, so a group of us went into Tel Aviv for a few drinks and a bit of sightseeing. By the time we got back to camp that night there was a panic going on and we were told to grab our kit and be ready to leave for an unspecified location.

'We got our kit together, just what we could get into a little pack on our backs – a change of underclothes, socks, that sort of thing – together with our rifles, or whatever your weapon was, and we were taken down to Haifa harbour and were put on a Greek sloop bound for the Dodecanese Islands. It was quite clear that something big was going on because it was absolutely chaotic and no one seemed to have the slightest idea what we were doing or where we were going. One minute we had been enjoying ourselves looking forward to our first jump, and the next we were caught up in the whirlwind of confusion.'

On the evening of 13 September 1943 B Squadron of the LRDG, now commanded by David Lloyd Owen, who had recovered from the injuries he had sustained at Kufra, arrived at the Greek island of Kastelorizo. The Italian Armistice had just been signed, and Army headquarters in Cairo decided to send small garrisons of British troops to various Greek islands to try and encourage those Italian troops still based in the region to thwart any attempt by the Germans to seize them.

'We were greeted with great enthusiasm by the Greek inhabitants, but I was completely overcome by the poverty on the island. The Italians had kept the locals very poor, and I remember this one poor lady with a baby and the child was just skeletal. It was quite shocking and I think we all had a very low opinion of the Italians after witnessing that. But we did what we could for the locals, who were very appreciative, and in those first few days we became aware of the beauty of our surroundings. The islands were idyllic and we had a chance of swimming in this beautiful clear water every morning and you could almost forget that there was a war on.'

Within a matter of days of arriving, the squadron was ordered to move with all possible speed to the island of Leros. The island was important to whoever was going to control the Aegean Sea because of its strategic position and its natural harbour.

'We had hardly arrived at Leros when we were again ordered to move to an equally small island called Kalymnos. That was when the air raids on Kos began. The Germans were after a squadron of Hurricane aircraft, manned mainly by South Africans. We would watch these air battles taking place, with the Germans flying in from their base on Rhodes, and one by one the Hurricanes were shot out of the sky. The air battle lasted about a month or so – it was a terrible sight, and by then we realised that this whole operation was a complete mess.

'Then we woke up one morning to find that the strip of water between Kalymnos and Kos was full of enemy shipping and the Germans were invading Kos. We anticipated that we were going to be next, so it was decided to move back to Leros to concentrate our forces. We stowed all our gear on to a schooner and sailed from Kalymnos to Leros, which was no more than a mile or two so didn't take too long, but while we were unloading our gear we were attacked by Stukas. I don't know if the Germans were just lucky or whether they had a reconnaissance unit on the island, but we were sitting ducks and an easy target.

'All we had to hit back at them was our rifles and a few Bren guns. It was terrifying. I was behind this sort of low wall firing at the Stukas with my rifle as they dive-bombed.

'One of our chaps, "Pusher" Wheeldon, was killed in the bombing. He was in his early 20s and came from Chesterfield – a very fit, active chap who would have a go at anything. As the bombing was going on, he jumped back on board our boat and grabbed a Bren gun and set it up on a tripod on the quay so he could shoot at the planes. But he was completely in the open. Bombs were exploding everywhere and he was caught by the shock wave of a blast, which severely damaged his lungs. His face and chest were covered in red frothy blood – he was lying on his back coughing up his lungs, a dreadful sight. He was clearly on his way out, his lungs had been destroyed. The medics came and took him away in a jeep and I think he died about an hour later.'

Once the Stukas departed, the troops began to count the cost of the attack. Many soldiers had been killed and injured, some with appalling wounds. But the casualties amongst the LRDG were remarkably light.

'There was a row of bodies along a wall near where I had been shooting during the attack. The bodies were all in a line and had been blown there by the force of the blast. I noticed a chap moving along the row and checking for pulses. I don't know if he was the medical officer or a medical orderly. I saw him pick up the hand of one poor soul and I said, "It's no good checking his pulse, he hasn't got a head." It was carnage, and I think largely brought about by the confusion of that operation.'

On 23 October 1943 the LRDG were ordered to carry out a raid on the nearby island of Levita, which was believed to be in the hands of escaped German POWs. The mission was to typify the lack of intelligence which ultimately condemned the entire operation.

'We went over to Levita on these Royal Navy motor launches. Y Patrol and some Rhodesians went to the south-west of the island

and a New Zealand patrol went to the north-west. We made for a meteorological complex, which we thought might be occupied, and prepared for a bit of a firefight. The building was empty so we moved into the area quite easily. We began digging slit trenches and preparing the defensive position, which was just as well because we soon learnt that rather than just a few POWs there was a strong force of German mountain troops just a few hundred yards away across the valley and they must have spotted us pretty quickly because we were soon under attack.

'Fortunately, by the time the enemy attacked most of us were in cover. I was in a slit trench firing across the valley when suddenly the Germans started using a mortar. The first round overshot and the next one landed in front of the trench. I thought, "Oh Lord, the next one's going to come in between." I could hear it coming in and it landed on the parapet of my trench but didn't go off – it was about a foot away from my head. Had it gone off I would have been cut in half.'

The battle raged for several hours and it was also clear to Jimmy and his patrol members that bitter fighting was taking place on the other side of the small island.

'Our force was commanded by John Olivey, a Rhodesian who had already won the MC and was regarded as a very competent officer. Later that morning he sent a party to see what could be done about having a go at the Germans but they returned soon after with a wounded man and had made little impact. Then it was my turn. John Olivey turned to me and three others and told us to go and have a look and try and get an assessment of the enemy positions and strengths. So off we set, knowing that it was going to be pretty dangerous, but also convinced it was the right course of action.

'In our team we had one Bren gun and the rest had rifles. I was a lance-bombardier at this stage – it was only acting rank, but it meant that I was in charge. So we moved off and I decided to detour off a little and try and reach the Germans' flank. We were moving across open ground when a German flying-boat armed with machine-guns appeared and it was quite obvious that the aircraft had spotted us. The aircraft was flying over the top of us, mainly so that we kept our heads down. I couldn't move forward any further, so I decided to go back to the meteorological station and had just got within sight of the buildings when I saw a lot of people moving around. I obviously thought they were our chaps, but in fact Jerry had captured the meteorological station. I didn't know that at the time.

'We were just casually walking over this stretch of open ground, making our way back, when a German machine-gun team suddenly appeared. It would have been damn silly to try and do anything – they would have cut us to ribbons – so we just had to give up.

'I was absolutely furious because I thought, "That's it. War over." We didn't put our hands up, we thought that would be undignified. This one Jerry who they sent out to round us up indicated that we should put our rifles on our shoulders. We didn't even do that. We just carried the rifles in our hands and just walked up to where the Germans were and threw our weapons on to a dump. That was that, we were POWs. The rest of the men at the meteorological station had all given up – they must have given up pretty easily, because by the time we arrived they were being marched down to where the Germans had set up their HQ. The whole lot of us had been captured. Meanwhile the New Zealanders on the other side of the island were having a tremendous battle, so much so that they eventually ran out of ammo and they had to give up too. My friend Ron Hill was with them and he was also captured.

'The overriding sensation after being captured was one of disappointment and anger, but it was quite difficult to analyse one's feelings. You are in a situation and you have to make the best of it. The full force of being a POW hadn't hit me by then.'

Jimmy, Ron Hill and the other members of Y Patrol were all marched to the harbour at Levita. There they learnt that they were to be flown by seaplane to Piraeus, then taken to a German prison camp.

After arriving in Athens, the POWs were taken to an old Italian barracks where they were held for several days and questioned by two English-speaking German officers who wanted to discover whether any of the captured British were willing to change sides and fight with the Germans.

'The officers were very polite, very decent. My attitude was: what the devil are you on about? You can't possibly win this war. The Russians were well on the go, the US were in the war, Germany was being bombed to hell and it was quite clear what the outcome was going to be eventually. I didn't say that to them directly, I just implied it, but they wouldn't have any of it and they wanted us to switch sides and join them. "Germans and British are far too close to be enemies," they said. Our races were so similar that it was ridiculous that we were fighting one another. That was their attitude. They wanted us to fight against the Russians. Their argument was based on the grounds that the Jews were running our side in the war and that everything could be blamed on the Jews. Our attitude was "Don't be so bloody silly."'

By the time the POWs arrived in Athens, Ron Hill and Jimmy were determined to make their escape. Other members of the LRDG had managed to slip past the German guards while being marched through Athens.

'I, for one, was absolutely up for escaping, especially after a few days in the compound, which I soon became pretty fed up with. Right from the start, Ron and I said we were going to escape. But not before we had some fun with the guards. They were funny little gnome-like men from the Black Forest and they were armed with the most ancient of rifles, great long things which were as tall as they were.

'We used to make fun of them unmercifully. We would start a bit of a rumpus at one side of the compound and these poor little blokes would start shouting to one another and rush round to one side of the compound where the noise was. Then we would start a similar thing on the other side so they would have to rush back. And we'd sing funny songs to them. At the time, the Americans had a song which had rude noises in it which went like this: "When the Führer says we are the master race we heil, (raspberry noise), heil, (raspberry), right in the Führer's face. Not to love the Führer is a great disgrace so we heil, (raspberry), heil , (raspberry), right in the Führer's face." And these blokes loved it, though they didn't really understand what was going on.'

After a few days in Athens, rumours began circulating that the POWs were to be transported to Germany, and Jimmy and Ron knew that the opportunities for escape would soon be limited.

'We were put into cattle trucks with one kilogram of sour black bread and two small tins of Italian bully beef for a four-day journey. There were about 30 of us in each truck, the toilet was a bucket and one poor soul had dysentery, so you can imagine what it was like. As the train went through the villages and towns we were able to plot the route on a silk escape map which was sewn into my beret as part of my escape kit – most people in the LRDG had one. I also had a hacksaw blade sewn into the flies of my trousers and a small button compass hidden in the collar of my battledress tunic. There was no excuse for not at least trying to escape. I had managed to avoid being searched and the Germans never found my escape kit.

'Inside the trucks there were little openings in the four corners of the carriage which were criss-crossed with barbed wire, so I began sawing away at the barbed wire and then Ron and I took it in turns. The train frequently stopped and we were allowed out to go to the toilet, but we had to do our business in front of all these civilians who were passengers on the train and the whole thing was quite humiliating.

'The night before we planned our escape two LRDG men on the other truck kicked out some panels and managed to escape but they were later recaptured. The Jerry commander was furious and lined us all up in the morning and was walking up and down, bellowing at us, making all sorts of threats.

'By now the train had entered Macedonia, and that night, on 6 November 1943, just after we left the town of Veles, 13 days after we were captured, I managed to saw through the barbed wire. Ron and I tossed a coin to see who would get out first and I won. We bent the wire back and I climbed out and was hanging on to the side of the train as we passed through a tunnel, at which point I saw

Ron's boots appearing through the opening and so I jumped. The train was moving at about 25mph but my parachute training helped break my fall and I landed safely.

'The rest of the train passed and when I saw the red light on the back of the train disappearing into the distance I must say I felt pretty lonely. I didn't regret getting out at all, I was delighted to be free, but there I was in the middle of occupied Europe all by myself at that stage – Ron still hadn't jumped out. His jump was delayed and he was quite a little way from me. I walked up the track and found him hiding behind a telegraph pole because he thought I was a guard from the tunnel. Every tunnel and bridge we passed was guarded – but this one wasn't, fortunately. I spotted Ron and said something like, "Hello Ron, are you OK?" But he'd hurt his leg when he landed. He'd twisted a muscle in his thigh and had taken a couple of chips out of his lower leg when he hit the track.

'Ron and I used to speak quite openly about escaping and the extraordinary thing was that everyone in that truck could have got out, everyone, but they just didn't. I think they were just resigned to the fact that they were POWs and that was how they were going to spend the rest of the war. I felt very disappointed that no one else attempted to escape.

'Ron also had a map in his beret and he gave it to a couple of Scottish commandos who were with us in Y Patrol, but I don't think they used it. I think it was the shock of capture, and a sort of inertia developed in some people, but not in me. I deeply resented that I was a prisoner and I wasn't going to put up with it.

'It was raining, dark and cold. All we had to eat was a few items from a Red Cross parcel we had been given and in front of us was a very long journey through the Macedonian mountains. I asked Ron if he could walk. He said yes, so off we went – into the mountains on a compass bearing – and that was how our escape began.

'We figured that if we walked on a bearing slightly south of west we would eventually get to the Adriatic Sea, but that meant walk-ing through the whole of Albania. The plan was to get to the

Adriatic, steal a boat, row across the Adriatic and get to Italy, which was where the action was. What we wanted was to get back into the war.

'We didn't know what Albania was like but we soon found out that the country was really quite mountainous and swarming with enemy soldiers. We didn't know what to expect so we started off walking at night so that we wouldn't be spotted by the Germans, but poor old Ron's leg was getting worse all the time.

'The going was very rough, steep wooded hills and valleys made all the worse at night. One night we were on an open hillside, very rocky and blowing a gale. There was freezing rain, more like sleet, and we took it in turns with the compass to go on the right bearing. It was my turn to lead and I turned round to see how far behind Ron was and he wasn't there. I went back to see where he was and he was sitting on a rock. "Sorry, old son," he said, "I can't go any further." I believed him because he was a tough little bloke – quite small was Ron, about five foot six, but very tough. He'd seen active service in the tank regiment before the LRDG and had been injured when his tank was destroyed, so he knew what it was all about.

'I looked round for somewhere to spend the rest of the night, to see if I could find a dry spot. I found an area where there was an overhanging rock with a dry place underneath it, but with just room for one, so I installed Ron and I went to look for somewhere for myself, which I found but it wasn't as comfortable. By then I was very, very tired and went to sleep in spite of the conditions. I woke up at first light, freezing cold, and I couldn't move – I suppose I was close to hypothermia. I started moving my fingers and eventually got movement back in my body and went to find Ron and he was OK, he'd managed to recover a bit, and then off we went again.

'On about the fifth day it was clear that Ron's leg wasn't getting any better – we had virtually no food and so there was nothing for it but to get some help. We decided to enter a village called Belica in western Macedonia. It was a risk, but we thought that the locals might help us. I have to say that by that stage we were at a pretty low ebb; we were cold, exhausted and malnourished, and we needed some food and shelter.

'When we arrived in the village there were lots of locals filling water buckets from the stream, so we went over and filled our water bottles. I think it was obvious to them that we were soldiers, and they looked astonished to see us. We waved and smiled and walked off and were heading in the direction of some houses when this character appeared, waving his arms at us and making it quite clear that we couldn't go any further and that it was dangerous.

'Ron looked up at this house and saw uniformed men walking about, and they must have been Bulgar soldiers. We took this individual at his word and left the road, pushed up into the hills as fast as we could and disappeared. Fortunately no one fired at us or followed us. We went on walking for the rest of the day and came to a river flowing roughly in the direction we wanted to go, so we continued to walk beside it along a towpath. We walked on until it started getting dark. Ron's leg was getting no better so we continued until we came across this very primitive hut, which appeared to be occupied.

'We approached the hut cautiously and using sign language we tried to make it clear to the people inside who we were and how we had jumped off the train. But it was also clear that they didn't want us there. After a few minutes they got up and beckoned us to come with them; they led us outside and pointed up to a hill and just kept pointing. They wanted us to push off up the hill, so off we went, feeling very dejected. But after a few hundred yards it became apparent that the path wasn't going anywhere, so we thought bugger this and went back to the hut, and when we banged on the door for a second time the two men seemed to have had a change of heart and invited us in.

'It was the most primitive human habitation you could imagine. It had an earth floor, with a fire burning in the middle. The smoke rose up through the thatch – it was medieval.

'There was a cooking pot hanging by a chain from one of the roof timbers, with some water boiling in it, and that seemed to be the sole means of cooking and heating. The dwelling itself was divided by a wall and on the other side were cattle. The only furniture was a couple of little three-legged stools, wonderful things cut out of the trunk of a fir tree at a place where there were three side branches, so that you could stand it up.

'There were no cupboards, tables or chairs. Just these two men, who I think must have been father and son. It was all very odd, but we were so tired and hungry that to us it seemed like the lap of luxury. I think they took pity on us, and they invited us to a meal which consisted of what we later discovered was called *katchemak* – at least that's what we called it. The stew consisted mainly of maize flour dumped into the pot by the handful until it had piled up into a pyramid shape. The mixture was stirred until it took on the consistency of a thick porridge, and at some stage meat – mutton or pork or anything available really – would be added, and we would pick at it with our fingers. It tasted fine that night because we were so hungry and relieved that we would be spending the night somewhere dry and warm. After the food was finished they invited us to lie down by the fire and sleep, which we did with consummate ease.

'At some stage during the night some sort of official arrived at the hut, with a rifle slung over his shoulder, shouting, "Documenti, documenti!" Word must have circulated that there were two strangers in the area.

'We showed him our pay books, which was all we had. He looked through them but clearly couldn't find what he was looking for. He produced a Bulgarian banknote, and along the bottom it said "Thomas de la Rue, Angleterre", which was clearly the printers' name, and Angleterre was the word he was looking for.

'It then clicked that he wanted us to produce something showing Angleterre, but we had nothing. He must have trusted our word, because in the end he made a series of gestures which showed us that he was satisfied.'

Just after dawn Jimmy and Ron left the hut with their new friends, walked along the river they had followed the previous day, up through a deserted village and into a large cave which was occupied by Chetniks.*

The commander of the group of 30 guerrilla fighters was a Serb regular Army colonel called Stoyan Markovic. Markovic had learnt English from a book and was able to make himself understood to the two British soldiers. He explained to Jimmy and Ron that they were welcome to stay, and said he hoped that they would be prepared to join his band of fighters.

'A day or two later we went into a house in a village and several other members of the group came in. One chap, called Nikola Patriota, came bounding over to us with a huge smile on his face and said "Hiya, fellers" in a sort of American style. We thought, "Thank goodness, someone who speaks English," but it turned out that "Hiya, fellers" was all he knew.'

Jimmy and Ron were in pretty bad shape. They were exhausted and malnourished and Ron's leg was festering. They were grateful to the Chetniks for looking after them, but soon saw that they were doing nothing about fighting the enemy.

The days turned into weeks and the weeks into months. Christmas came and went and the two escapees remained almost permanently cold and hungry. The soldiers' now monotonous existence in the mountains was occasionally punctuated with brief periods of excitement when they encountered Bulgar patrols.

'There was the occasional skirmish with the Bulgars. There was one occasion when a Bulgar soldier was carrying a large battery, taking it from one place to another, and he stumbled upon our camp. The Chetniks didn't know what to do with him, so they took him up into the woods and shot him. It was quite pathetic really. Executing this poor chap served no real purpose. I think both sides – the Bulgars and the Chetniks – were pretty useless.

'On one or two occasions when we met up with a Bulgar patrol there was an exchange of fire, and in one attack a man was killed, but it was pretty quiet mostly. We stayed with them for nine months, having a pretty bad time of it. The hardest part was the hunger and

---

* Serbian nationalists who fought against the Nazis.

cold, more than anything. We hardly ever got into a house to spend the night in the warm. We were living mostly in the woods, but fortunately we were with peasants who were used to living pretty close to the earth. They were very adept at making shelters, tiny wigwams made of branches which they would cover with brush wood and turf, and these proved to be pretty waterproof structures. A fire could be made to keep out the cold, and the only thing missing was food. For this we had to rely on friendly villagers who risked their lives to bring it to us.'

The two LRDG men soon learnt that the Chetniks were 'all talk and no action'. Plans would be hatched and schemes would be made as to how they would launch 'this' attack or conduct 'that' ambush – but the plans amounted to nothing. But as Jimmy had seen on previous occasions, the Chetniks could be brutal.

'There was one occasion in April 1944 when we got a report that a certain man in a village was collaborating with the Bulgars, and a group of Chetniks went down into the village dressed in Bulgar uniforms. They knew the house where the suspect was living, knocked on the door and this unfortunate individual obviously thought they were Bulgars, so he invited them in and gave them food and drink. After the Chetniks had their fill they sprung the trap and marched this man at gunpoint to a bridge, where they killed him and then proceeded to dismember his body. The various body parts were laid across the bridge and this was supposed to serve as a deterrent to others.

'I was talking to one of them afterwards and asked him how they got on, and he said, "Oh, we had a great time." And he took a piece of filthy rag out of his pocket and in this rag there were these two obscene pieces of jelly. He showed them to me and said, "These are his eyes." They seemed to take a certain delight in that sort of thing. Their behaviour was very primitive.

'One of the group was called Kristo, the group's executioner. It was his job to hang collaborators, and by the time I met him he had hanged 83 people. He seemed a perfectly reasonable man and the last person you might think would be an executioner. He had this little joke where if you annoyed him he would trace out 84 on the palm of his hand and point to you and then laugh.

'Shortly after I met him he very cordially invited me to his next hanging, but I turned him down. He was totally committed to what he was doing; he felt it was his patriotic duty.'

Life continued in the same vein until August 1944, when Ron and Jimmy made contact with two members of the Special Operations Executive, Captain Hugh Miller and his radio operator Tom Smith, who were running a mission known as Bethesda in the area. The two men had been parachuted into the area some months earlier, and were helping to organise the partisan resistance forces.

'We were very fortunate that our Chetniks decided to join the partisans instead of fighting them, as had happened in other parts of Yugoslavia.

'It so happened that the Bethesda mission had recently radioed their HQ in Bari, Italy, asking for two more men to be flown out to them because of the expansion of their operational area. Hugh Miller was very suspicious of us at first. He questioned both Ron and me very closely, but seemed to be satisfied with our background in the end.'

Captain Miller suggested to Jimmy and Ron that they should join his mission, and the two men jumped at the chance.

'We all got on very well and Hugh was especially easy to work with and was a super chap, quite aristocratic.

'Our main role with the British mission was to arrange air drops for the partisan brigade and to keep them supplied with equipment such as weapons, radios, ammunition and uniforms.

'Jerry was pretty much on the run by then and had started to withdraw from Macedonia. A senior German officer managed to get a message to Captain Miller suggesting that to prevent bloodshed they should be allowed to withdraw without fighting but, although a meeting took place, nothing came of the plan. Eventually after a few more skirmishes the entire German force had withdrawn from the area.

'Once Jerry had gone we had the life of Riley. We moved to Skopje, the capital of Macedonia, where we set about repairing the airfield. By now it was November 1944 and the snow had come, but although it was getting very cold we were quite comfortable.

The mission had a supply of gold sovereigns, so we could buy food and we even managed to recruit a Yugoslav chef who had trained in all the posh hotels in New York. Captain Miller would give him a sovereign every now and again and he would go into the market and stock up on supplies and produce these sumptuous meals. He would cook us baked apples for breakfast, steaks for lunch or dinner and we had a barrel of beer on tap.'

The Bethesda mission eventually got the airport functioning and very soon Jimmy and Ron became redundant and were flown back to Bari to rejoin the LRDG on operations in Italy. But a new rule had been introduced which stated that escaped POWs could not re-engage in the same theatre of war in which they had been captured. Thus there was no hope of operating again with the LRDG. Shortly after they arrived in Bari they were sent back to Britain by boat, and arrived home in February 1945. Both men were sent to a camp in the north of England to more or less sit out the rest of the war, with other escaped POWs like themselves who were also barred from fighting. It was an uninspiring end to Jimmy's war, and neither man served with the LRDG again.

Jimmy's and Ron's war was over, and they were eventually demobbed in 1946. Jimmy returned to the Post Office, where he remained until retirement, and Ron became a librarian. In 1950, during the Korean War, Jimmy and Ron wrote jointly to David Lloyd Owen, who was still a serving officer, stating that they were prepared to serve under his command again during the war if needed, but nothing came of it.

The LRDG was disbanded in 1945, but those still serving wished to preserve the comradeship of this splendid unit. They therefore formed an association, with David Lloyd Owen, later to be promoted to major-general, as its chairman. The role of secretary was filled by a succession of individuals as the years went by until 1976, when David Lloyd Owen asked Jimmy Patch to take up the post. He accepted and continued to do the job until the year 2000 when, at the age of 80, he was obliged to give up after his wife became very ill and needed his full-time care. In that year the association was wound up and all its members, in accordance with an agreement made several years before, became members of the SAS Regimental Association.

★　　★　　★

By the time Jimmy joined the LRDG, many young men had already begun to look to the special forces as an alternative to service in the British Army. One of those was a young officer called Corran Purdon, and his unit of choice was the Commandos.

# CHAPTER 3

# The Greatest Raid of All

## Corran Purdon with the Commandos at St Nazaire

*The Commandos – 'Specially trained troops of the hunter class,
who can develop a reign of terror down the enemy coast'.*
WINSTON CHURCHILL, 1940

In early 1942 Britain stood alone – isolated and vulnerable. German U-boats had sunk almost 9 million tons of merchant shipping and the country's transatlantic supply of food and arms was seriously threatened. The North African campaign was grinding to bloody stalemate, British troops were being forced out of Burma and Malaya, and the nation's morale was beginning to crumble.

But the country's already perilous state appeared to significantly worsen with the arrival of the German super-battleship *Tirpitz*, the pride of the Nazi fleet.

*Tirpitz*, the second of two Bismarck-class battleships built for Germany's war navy, was operational by early 1941. At 251 metres in length and equipped with a main battery of eight 15-inch guns in four twin turrets, she was, like her sister ship the *Bismarck*, bigger and more powerful than any vessel the Royal Navy could muster. And although *Tirpitz* was protected by armour more than a foot thick, she could still reach a speed of up to 30 knots.

Prime Minister Winston Churchill, along with many senior officers in naval intelligence, feared that if *Tirpitz* was brought from the Baltic into the North Atlantic, beyond the range of the RAF, she would set about destroying those vast convoys of merchant vessels which had managed to escape the U-boats' torpedoes. If such a sequence of events evolved, then Britain would begin to starve and the country's chances of repelling a Nazi invasion would almost certainly be lost.

*Tirpitz*'s huge size, at 52,600 tons, however, also represented one of her greatest weaknesses. If she were damaged during an engagement in the North Atlantic, which was a strong likelihood given the attrition rates in Second World War sea battles, it would be too risky for her to try to return to Germany, given that she would be within range of RAF bombers for much of the voyage. The only dry dock on the Atlantic coast deep enough for repairs to be carried out to her was at St Nazaire, six miles up the Loire estuary. The Normandie dock at St Nazaire was 350 metres long, 50 metres wide and 16 metres deep and had been specially constructed to house the 80,000-ton passenger liner SS *Normandie*, launched in 1931. The decision was taken that, in order to keep *Tirpitz* out of the North Atlantic, the dry dock at St Nazaire would have to be destroyed.

But destroying such a vast site was easier said than done. An RAF bombing raid was ruled out because of the problem of inaccuracy. In 1941 only 5 per cent of the RAF's bombers that set out managed to land bombs within five miles of their target. Mass civilian casualties caused by bombing were still regarded as unacceptable. An attack by a naval task force was also ruled out when aerial photographs and reports from agents revealed that the six-mile route up the estuary from the Atlantic to St Nazaire was fortified by heavy gun emplacements. Sabotage by the Special Operations Executive was also a non-starter, because there were too few agents working in that area of France to carry and plant the estimated four tons of explosives required to destroy the dock gates.

Instead, the Combined Operations Headquarters decided that the best chance of achieving success was via a Commando raid, and planning began in earnest in early 1942.

In the early years of the Second World War the Commandos were something of an enigma – an unconventional force who did things differently, and in doing so often invoked the ire of senior officers. Commando units were created to carry out raids in enemy-occupied territory, such as Norway or coastal France, in order to maintain an offensive footing against the enemy but also to restore some national pride after the humiliation of the British Expeditionary Force's defeat in 1940.

Commando units did not use heavy equipment, such as tanks and artillery, and were only supposed to be on enemy territory for a maximum of two hours at that time. It was a tactic known as 'butcher and bolt', where the aim was to cause as much chaos and destruction as possible, and it immediately won Churchill's support.

Rather than being composed of three rifle companies, a support weapons company and a battalion headquarters, Commando units were composed of a headquarters, consisting of the commanding officer, the second-in-command (a major), an administrative officer and a medical officer. The remainder of the force was split into six 75-man troops each commanded by a captain, with a small head-quarters. Each troop was split into two sections of around 35 men, each commanded by a subaltern.

All the Commando units were composed of volunteers from other trained units, initially from the infantry but later from almost every arm of the services, and the majority joined on the promise of experiencing 'hazardous duty'. The men were chosen not just for their intelligence and independence of mind, but also for their physical fitness.

Training was tough and unconventional. Drill, or square bashing, was ignored and instead the commandos practised river crossings, tackled assault courses and conducted speed marches. Different units would compete against each other to see who could cover the longest distances in the shortest time while carrying 60lb packs – one group managed to cover 63 miles in 19 hours. Other units would attempt to march 15 miles in three hours, at the end of which they would have to tackle an assault course and then be expected to hit targets at 300 yards on a rifle range – the training was so advanced that much of it is still used today. The unconventional methods were all designed to create a body of men with the physical and mental attributes to tackle anything the enemy could throw at them.

The rulebook on weapon training was thrown away, and the Commandos began to develop their own tactics. The men were trained to fire the Bren light machine-gun – traditionally fired from the prone position – from the hip or while on the move.

Unlike conventional infantry units, Commandos had no fixed home or barracks and were billeted in private homes, with soldiers sleeping by their weapons.

The Commando units first formed as independent companies of men, often composed of territorial officers, who had been doctors, lawyers or architects in civilian life; men capable of independent thought and not blindsided to new ideas. These independent companies were formed into larger forces and were renamed Commandos.

The promise of seeing action proved to be an attractive proposition for many young men, and by the autumn of 1940 more than 2,000 had volunteered to serve and were initially organised into 11 Commando units, from No. 1 Commando to No. 9, plus Nos. 11 and 12. At the same time four Commando units were created in the Middle East. Other units would also be created over the coming months, such as the No. 10 (Inter-Allied) Commando. All of the Commandos came under the control of the Combined Operations Headquarters, an organisation initially commanded by Admiral Sir Roger Keyes, a veteran of the First World War, and from 1941 to 1943 by Lord Louis Mountbatten, who was a specialist in conducting raids.

One of those who volunteered for 'hazardous duty' was a young second lieutenant called Corran Purdon, the son of an Irish Royal Army Medical Corps Major-General, who had won the DSO and the MC and had been mentioned in dispatches three times during the First World War.

Corran was born in County Cork in 1921, while his father was stationed in Ireland, and was educated at Campbell College in Belfast, where he enjoyed rugby and all sports.

I met with Corran at his wonderful home near Devizes. At the age of 91 he is fit and healthy and still does push-ups every morning. As we sat in the drawing room, overlooking the Wiltshire countryside, he explained he had only ever had one ambition.

'From the age of 10, possibly earlier, all I ever wanted to do was be in the Army and the infantry. As a boy I had a huge collection of lead soldiers, some of which I still have, although sadly some were destroyed during the Blitz, and I played with them all the time.

'Back in those days, if you wanted to become an officer you sat an exam; there was no Regular Commissions Board.* I can still remember the day that I received notification that I had gained a place at Sandhurst. I was with my mother and father on Lough Currane, in County Kerry. It was my last holiday before the war and must have been in the early summer of 1939. War was looming on the horizon, but I don't really have any recollection that it was bearing down on me. I think I was just focused on joining the Army. We were fishing, and someone arrived with a letter and gave it to my father, who opened it and said, "Well, Corran has passed the Army exam and there is only one regiment for him – the Royal Ulster Rifles."

'Later that summer I went to Sandhurst, which I loved. War was declared that September and there was great anticipation that we, us cadets, would all see some action. In December 1939 I was commissioned into the Royal Ulster Rifles and was posted to Armagh, in Ulster, where the regiment had a depot. I then moved up to Ballymena, in County Antrim, where our training centre was based.'

By the time Corran had been commissioned, the Royal Ulster Rifles second battalion was already in France as part of the British Expeditionary Force, and like many young subalterns eager for their first experience of combat Corran expected to be posted to France.

'Obviously I wanted to join the 2nd Battalion, but was told that I couldn't because I was too young, I was only 18, and I was really frustrated. The 1st Battalion was on its way home from India – so I wasn't going to be joining them. The days began to slip past, and at

* A series of selection courses which must be passed before entry into the Royal Military Academy Sandhurst.

*Corran Purdon*

that point in time I saw myself stuck in Ballymena for a lot of the war. One of my friends who had been with me at Sandhurst had managed to get to France and I was very envious.

'Then one day I was walking around the parade square and Captain Norman Wheeler, who was the adjutant, called out to me from his office window and shouted, "Corran, I've got something here you might like to look at." I went into his office and he handed me a piece of paper. It was an Army Council Instruction describing the formation of the Commandos, and he said, "I thought that might be just up your street."

'The notice said something like "Volunteers wanted for hazardous service" – and right at that moment I thought, "I'm going to do this." The ACI stated that a Commando unit was being formed in Northern Ireland and volunteers were needed. It was obvious to me that the Commandos were being formed for active service and I wanted to be part of that.'

That afternoon in the early spring of 1940, Corran went to his commanding officer in order to get permission to volunteer for the Commandos, but his request was met with a resounding 'no' – an answer Corran refused to accept.

'I went to our Motor Transport Office and got a vehicle and a driver, without anyone's permission, and got the driver to take me over to Derry, where No. 12 Commando were being formed by Lieutenant-Colonel "Peachy" Harrison, who had won two Military Crosses in the First World War with the Irish Guards.

'When I arrived at the Boston Bar, the pub where 12 Commando was formed, I immediately made my way to see the commanding officer. I knocked on his door, walked straight in, saluted and said: "Sir, I have come to volunteer for service with No. 12 Commando." I explained my situation, said that I was highly motivated and didn't want to sit the war out in Ulster. I then asked, "Will you have me?" and he said yes.

'I was delighted and drove straight back to see my commanding officer. I could tell by the look on his face that he wasn't impressed by my actions, and at the end of the interview he said that he wasn't going to release me. Once again my age and inexperience were used as a reason.

'But I wasn't about to let the opportunity of serving with the Commandos slip away, and I got back in touch with Peachy Harrison and told him that my commanding officer had refused permission for me to join his unit and wondered whether there was anything he could do. To my delight he said that the ACI categorically stated that volunteers would "not be withheld". Peachy Harrison did whatever had to be done, and I was called in front of my colonel, who gave me quite a dressing down, then gave me a big smile and said, "I would have done just the same as you," and that was it. That was how I became a member of No. 12 Commando.'

Corran quickly became immersed in a world of shooting, physical training, unarmed combat and minor tactics organised by officers and senior non-commissioned officers who constantly set exacting standards. Like the rest of the Army, the training of new Commando units was initially hampered by equipment shortages following the débâcle of Dunkirk, where much of the Army's kit was abandoned. But gradually more equipment became available and the Commandos soon began to be armed with the weapons they would need to conduct lightning raids. All Commando units were equipped with standard-issue weapons but with larger numbers of Bren guns and tommy-guns; riflemen were armed with the Lee Enfield rifle; officers were issued with the powerful .45 Colt semi-automatic pistol, and every member of the force was eventually supplied with the double-bladed Fairbairn-Sykes Fighting Knife.

Training continued in and around the village of Crumlin, close to Lough Neagh, until in the late spring of 1941 the unit moved across the Irish Sea to Warsash on the Hampshire coast, where No. 12 Commando began training in amphibious warfare, using the Royal Navy's Assault Landing Craft (ALCs).

'Later that summer I learnt that my troop was going to take part in a raid on the French coast and that we would be departing from Dover. We were highly trained and ready to go and everybody was very excited.

'The plan was to raid the coastal town of Berck-sur-Mer. The idea was to beat the place up, kill a few Germans and take some prisoners.

'We had actually got into the ALCs, sat on the benches and prepared to sail over to France. We'd been sitting in the boats for quite a while when a message came through telling us that the operation was cancelled. We all climbed out of the ALCs feeling very dejected; no one uttered a word but I think we all felt the same. We climbed on board a fleet of coaches and headed back to Warsash. It was a gorgeous summer evening and I had never felt so ashamed as driving back that evening, having done nothing. At that point I thought to myself, "If this is life in the Commandos then I'm bloody well leaving." I was worried that I would spend all of my time conducting very tough training which would never be put to any use. I saw my colonel about it and said, "Sir, this is awful," and he said, "Don't worry, it will be OK."'

After the abortive raid, Corran was sent on an officers' course at the Special Warfare Centre at Loch Ailort, in the Western Highlands. There, in the depths of winter and living in bell tents, he and other young officers were instructed in the finer techniques of Commando training.

'We trained with all sorts of weapons, including firing the 2-inch mortar from the hip, firing the Bren gun on the move, and firing the Boys anti-tank gun standing up. All the things people said you couldn't do because it would damage your shoulder – nonsense! We did it all. We'd learnt an awful lot by that stage and we were terribly fit.

'Towards the end of my course No. 12 Commando moved up to Ayr, where I rejoined them. We continued training in the hills and sea, practising our raiding skills. We also went rock climbing in the Lake District – by then we were all longing for a raid.'

In early 1942 Corran was promoted to lieutenant and was sent on to a demolition course along with Lieutenants Gerard Brett and Paul Bassett-Wilson, fellow officers from No. 12 Commando, and a group of experienced corporals.

Also on the course were teams from Nos. 1, 3, 4, 5, 6 and 9 Commando. During the six-week course the students learnt how to prepare and set explosives in the destruction of dockyard installations.

By this stage of the war the planning for the St Nazaire Raid, codenamed Operation Chariot, was well advanced – but it remained top secret even for those who were to be taking part.

'Right at the beginning of the demolition course we were all told that we were going to be trained in the destruction of British docks – something which would be a necessity in the event of a German invasion. That was the cover story for what they really had in store for us. We learnt all about explosives, detonators, fuses, pressure and pull switches, and all the various ways of initiating explosives and where they needed to be placed to achieve the maximum effect. We visited the large docks at Rosyth, Cardiff, Burntisland and the King George V dock in Southampton, which was almost an exact replica of the St Nazaire dock. We trained during both night and day, and sometimes while wearing black eye-covers so that we were used to operating in night-time. As we became more adept, our instructors would put us under time pressure or remove one or two members of the team to see how we coped.

'That was an excellent training period because we all got a feel for how large dry docks worked. Our objectives were the pumping house, the caisson gates and the winding stations, but all of the team had to know how to destroy all the objectives.

'The training lasted about six weeks, and during that time the Bruneval Raid* took place, and that really whetted our appetites. I remember reading all about the raid in the *Daily Mirror* while standing in the main street in Cardiff. I was very proud of what they had achieved but also envious, and someone in my team who was reading the same story over my shoulder said, "Our turn will come next."'

Within a matter of days Corran and his four-man demolition team, composed of Corporals Bob Hoyle, Cab Callaway, Ron Chung and Johnny Johnson, received orders to travel by train to Falmouth, where they were to remain until further notice, living onboard HMS *Princess Josephine Charlotte*, a former cross-Channel ferry adapted to carry landing craft.

The briefings began a few hours after they arrived in Falmouth. The Commandos were told by Lieutenant-Colonel Charles Newman, the commanding officer of No. 2 Commando, that they would be taking part in Operation Chariot – a Commando raid on the town of St Nazaire, where their mission was to destroy the Normandie dock and its installations. Colonel Newman, who would lead the raid, explained the plan.

For Britain to survive in the war, the dry dock at St Nazaire would have to be destroyed, he told the assembled force. This would be achieved, he said, by ramming a Royal Navy destroyer packed

---

* Also known as Operation Biting, the raid was carried out on 27 February 1942 on a German radar station in France by members of a Commando force who parachuted into the area and were withdrawn by landing craft after the raid.

with four tons of high explosives into the dock gates during a Commando raid which would take place in approximately 10 days' time. Commando demolition teams and an assault force would travel to St Nazaire on the destroyer, while the remainder of the assault force would travel in a fleet of 16 motor launches, a motor gun boat and a motor torpedo boat. After the destroyer had been rammed into the gates, the colonel continued, the Commandos would set about destroying a series of pre-designated targets – the winding houses, pumping stations and the rear dock gate, as well as gun emplacements and, if possible, the submarine pens located on the far side of the dock.

Two Royal Navy Hunt class destroyers, HMS *Atherstone* and HMS *Tynedale*, would escort the flotilla close to the mouth of the estuary, where they would remain until the operation had been completed. The two ships would then escort the rest of the flotilla back to Falmouth after the raid had taken place. Supporting the naval flotilla would be five squadrons of RAF bombers, who would begin bombing runs prior to the main assault – but aircrews were under strict orders only to bomb clearly identified targets.

On paper the plan appeared simple, but there were many flaws, obvious to just about everyone. At the top of the list of concerns were the motor launches, 65-ton wooden boats, whose main role was anti-submarine or escort duties. The boats offered no protection for the 15-man Commando teams who would be travelling inside. More worrying, however, was the fact that in order to complete the journey the boats had been fitted with two 500-gallon high-octane petrol tanks in exposed positions on the deck. The other obvious problem was that St Nazaire was located six miles up the Loire estuary, a route which was defended by heavy gun emplacements on both banks.

Carl von Clausewitz, the 18th-century Prussian soldier and military theorist, once observed, 'Everything in war is very simple. But the simplest thing is very difficult.' That observation could almost have been tailor made for Operation Chariot.

The ship chosen to ferry the explosives across to France was the obsolete HMS *Campbeltown*, a former US Navy destroyer (USS

*Buchanan*) which had been transferred to the Royal Navy as part of the Destroyers for Bases Agreement.

The best route along the Loire estuary was a dredged passage close to the left shore which was fortified with heavy gun emplacements and therefore completely unsuitable for *Campbeltown* and her flotilla. Instead, the destroyer would proceed down the centre of the channel, where many sandbanks were located and the depth, in places, was less than 10 feet. *Campbeltown* would only be able to achieve this if she was made to resemble a German warship and her weight was significantly reduced, which was achieved by stripping out her internal compartments and removing four of her 3-inch guns, as well as her depth charges and torpedoes. Her bridge was reinforced with extra armour, while two of her four funnels were removed and the remaining two cut at an angle to resemble those of German destroyers. She was also fitted with a light, quick-firing 12lb gun, while her bows contained 4.5 tons of delayed-action high explosives hidden in a steel and concrete case.

The operation was under the command of Commander Robert Ryder, while the captain of *Campbeltown* was Commander Stephen 'Sam' Beattie. Motor Gun Boat 314 (MGB 314) became Ryder's floating headquarters and would be the location of Lieutenant-Colonel Newman and his small staff, while Major Bill Copland, the second-in-command of No. 2 Commando, would take command of the soldiers on *Campbeltown*. Major Bill, as he was known, was, at 44, one of the oldest men involved in the operation and had previously served at Passchendaele in the First World War, where he was gassed.

The total force consisted of 622 Commandos – the odds for the mission being a success were not, at least openly, discussed.

Intelligence estimates suggested that around 5,000 German troops were garrisoned in and around the town, which included a naval artillery battalion equipped with around 28 guns, some of which were on railways lines positioned to protect the harbour's approaches, while others were encased in concrete bunkers. Extra defences were provided by anti-aircraft batteries, searchlights and at least three German Navy ships – a minesweeper, a destroyer and an armed trawler.

Despite being heavily outnumbered and outgunned, Corran was convinced the operation would be a success.

'The Royal Navy had acquired a huge amount of intelligence and the RAF had built a scale model of the dockyard. We spent hours poring over aerial photographs and talking through the plan during the build-up to the operation. We also visited the King George V Dock at Southampton to practise laying our explosives and spent quite a bit of time conducting speed marches and weapon skills.

'I learnt that my objective was the winding house at the far end of the dock, so we made sure of the exact layout and tried to visualise how it would look on the ground.

'We seemed to spend days packing and repacking our equipment, trying to reduce it down to exactly what we would need and nothing more.

'We had about 10 days to get ready for the operation once we arrived in Falmouth, and by that stage it began to dawn on us that this was a very risky operation, but I never doubted that it would be a success. We were all sworn to secrecy and we knew then that it was only a matter of time before we departed.

'During the final planning stages we received a visit by the then Commodore Lord Louis Mountbatten, who was the chief of combined operations. He came to give us a bit of a pep talk before the start of the raid. He asked us a lot of questions and talked to us as though we were old comrades. He sat on a raft and chatted to us, and asked us if there was anything we needed and then began to make some notes.

'Some time later, at one of the many briefings, Colonel Newman read out a note from Lord Mountbatten in which he said that anyone who feels that he doesn't want to go on the raid may withdraw now and no one will think the worse of him.

'I was standing in a large group of these very tough-looking Commandos when he said this, and I remember thinking that it would take a bloody brave man to step forward now and say that he didn't want to take part. No one of course did step forward. But Mick Burns, a captain from No. 2 Commando, gave the colonel a note saying, "Please may I withdraw?" Colonel Newman was taken aback, but it was all a joke and we all had a good laugh, and he said, "Shut up, Micky."

'It was pretty clear that we were going to take casualties – the risks were tremendous. I think we all knew that a lot of us would not be coming back and that some would be killed or wounded. But I always thought that I would survive because I have always been an optimist. I think the reason was that I was so in love with my wife and I wanted to get back to her. That for me was very important. But there were plenty amongst us who felt differently and some were convinced that they would be killed.

'One day, I was swimming in the River Fal with a very good friend called Harry Pennington, a super chap, who was a captain from No. 4 Commando and an Oxford Blue rugby player.

'We had just finished swimming and were lying on the grass trying to dry off in the spring sunshine. Almost out of the blue he appeared to have some sort of premonition about his death because he said to me, "I've decided that England is worth dying for," and tragically he was killed during the raid.'

All of those taking part in the raid knew that once the Commandos stormed the dock the balloon would go up and chaos could ensue. There was also a very real risk that different groups of Commandos could mistakenly open fire on each other, given that the raid would be taking place at night. Therefore Colonel Newman ruled that the Commandos' webbing should be scrubbed white to aid in the identification of friendly forces.

'I suppose there was a possibility that we might be more obvious to the enemy, but we all thought it was a risk worth taking.

'Our equipment was very simple. I had a bergen containing all of my explosive equipment and a Colt .45. My webbing contained spare ammunition, and a fighting knife was strapped to my leg. We each had our own individual medical kits, consisting of a First Field Dressing and morphine, and apart from my tin helmet that was it – and the same went for everyone else. The idea was that we were not meant to be on the ground for very long so we only took the essentials. But one of the best pieces of kit with which we were issued were the new Commando boots, which had this wonderful composite sole and were both quiet and very comfortable.'

By 25 March 1942 all the preparations were complete and HMS *Campbeltown* had been fitted with her four tons of explosives, encased in steel and concrete and hidden within her bows. Corran's party, along with five other demolition teams and two assault teams, were to sail over to France on *Campbeltown*, now a floating time bomb. The soldiers were allowed on deck but only if they wore duffel coats to cover up their army uniforms. The presumption was that Nazi spies would be monitoring all docks, and no one wanted to risk warning the enemy that a Commando raid was underway.

'In those days in the Commandos, to be honest, we drank quite a lot off duty and had many good parties. The plan was that after the raid we would all go up to London and celebrate our success. Despite the risks, I think we all felt that the raid would be successful.'

The naval force left Falmouth at 2pm on 26 March 1942, and the voyage took the flotilla across the English Channel, around the Brittany peninsular and into the Bay of Biscay. By 10pm on 27 March the force was in battle formation and was ready for the final run into the Loire.

'Lieutenant-Commander Stephen Beattie was incredibly nice to us. We were only subalterns and he inspired great confidence, and the crew were all super as well. There was a great sense of euphoria on board. We were finally going to take part in a raid, and that is what we had spent months preparing for – that is why we became Commandos. If there was one concern, then it was the wooden MLs, which were pretty useless. Each was being used to transport around 15 Commandos into battle, and they were also supposed to help ferry us back down the Loire after the raid.'

Thirty-three hours after leaving Falmouth the flotilla arrived in the mouth of the estuary and began the six-mile voyage up the Loire to St Nazaire. At this point Commander Beattie gave the order for the fuses to be set, and the *Campbeltown*, flying a Nazi naval ensign, set a course down the middle of the river. Behind *Campbeltown*, in two parallel rows, came the vulnerable motor launches, each filled with a complement of Commandos.

'The demolition teams' action stations were in the ship's wardroom, and my team and Gerard Brett's had to sit on the floor with our backs against the bulkhead, so we wouldn't be thrown all over the place when we rammed the dock gates.

'The convoy passed the first couple of gun emplacements without any problems, but then the RAF bombers overhead caused a problem. For reasons of secrecy the pilots were unaware that a raid was in the process of being launched. Because of cloud cover the bombers were having trouble identifying their targets, and instead of aborting the operation they remained in the area, flying round and round, and so put the German garrison in the town on high alert.

'A searchlight came on and went off again and some of the shore batteries began to open fire at the convoy. The firing stopped and we were challenged in German Morse code.'

Unknown to the Germans, British naval intelligence had managed to acquire German naval codebooks, and on board the motor gun boat Leading Signalman Pike replied: 'Urgent – we are a friendly force coming in for the night. Have two damaged ships following enemy engagement. Demand immediate entry ...' or words to that effect, and that stopped them for a bit, but the deception didn't last long and the shore batteries opened fire again. The searchlights were absolutely blinding and they revealed us in our entirety. Signalman Pike did his stuff again, and they stopped for a bit but then started again.

'The date was chosen because there was a high spring tide which would give *Campbeltown* extra room to get over the sandbanks – but even with the extra height we still scraped over the top of them. The shore batteries really started hammering the ship. I could hear the shells slamming into the side, and suddenly I saw a red-hot glowing shell puncture the wardroom wall and fly out the other side at about shoulder height – we were bloody lucky it didn't explode.'

The *Campbeltown* and her accompanying vessels managed to get to within 2,000 yards of the dock gates before the Germans realised that a British raid was underway.

Within seconds the convoy was caught in a murderous crossfire from both banks of the estuary. *Campbeltown*'s decks were filled with prone Commandos in their assault positions, ready to disembark once she had ploughed into the dock, and many were killed or suffered horrific wounds as heavy machine-gun fire began to rake her decks.

Anti-aircraft guns switched targets and also set their range on *Campbeltown*, which suffered a series of direct hits under a hail of enemy fire. But despite sustaining severe damage she managed to achieve 22 knots and aimed her bows at the dock gates.

'At this point there was an awful lot of stuff hitting *Campbeltown*, which was now fully illuminated by searchlights. Our poor little MLs were also caught in the crossfire and several exploded.'

At 1.34am on 28 March, just four minutes later than had been predicted, the *Campbeltown* rammed into the gates of the Normandie dock.

'We had all expected there to be a huge jerk when we rammed the dock – but it was a strange grinding sensation of being slowed down. At that point everyone in the wardroom began to get up and make their way out on deck. As we emerged into the night the whole of the sky seemed to be illuminated by tracer fire. The battle going on around us was tremendous. The noise was deafening. Some of the assault team were already fighting in the dock, and *Campbeltown* was still attracting a lot of fire. We pushed our way along the deck, crouching low as bullets seemed to be ricocheting everywhere. I passed a four-pounder gun which had been knocked out, with the crew lying around it either dead or wounded. There was blood all over the place but we hardly gave it a second thought.

'One chap, Johnny Proctor, whose leg had more or less been blown off, was cheering us on. I didn't think it was a shocking sight – we were just totally focused on getting to the winding house at the far end of the dock. Then we were met by dear old Bill Copland, who had his rifle over his shoulder and very calmly announced,

"Right, boys, off we go – Purdon, you go now, Brett, you're off next," and off we went – he was so cool it might have been an exercise. He was standing in a very exposed position and was attracting a lot of fire, but he remained very calm.

'There were naval officers holding ladders for us to get down from the ship – which was amazing seeing as they were so exposed to gunfire. The plan was that I would rendezvous with a protection party, but they had become embroiled in a battle of their own, so we just trotted down to the far end of the dock where I knew my objective was located and it was all perfectly simple – we knew exactly where it was going to be because of the model and the aerial photographs.

'When I got to the winding house the metal door was locked, which came as a big surprise. I thought to myself, "Come on, Purdon, do something!" I took out my Colt .45 pistol, pressed it up against the lock and pulled the trigger, and there was this loud wang as the bullet ricocheted off the metal door. Corporal Ron Chung was standing beside me as the bullet passed us both – and he turned to me in the heat of battle and said, "Excuse me, sir. When I agreed to come on this raid I was quite prepared to be killed by Adolf Hitler, but not by you, sir."

'Then Ron moved in and began smashing the lock with this huge mallet which he had brought with him. The door flew open and in we went. At that point we could all take a bit of a breather because we were safe inside the winding house as the battle raged on outside.'

While Corran and his team were setting their charges, the other demolition teams located their targets and began placing their explosives. Elsewhere on the dock, groups of Commandos were making their way towards the submarine pens, destroying every-thing in their sights, while others assault teams attacked enemy gun emplacements. But the German forces greatly outnumbered the British and the casualties began to mount.

Back in the Loire, the motor launches were being decimated by the unrelenting automatic gun and one after the other burst into flames with their Commandos either drowning or being burnt to death. Seeing that the escape plan was beginning to fall apart, Colonel Newman left his headquarters on the gunboat and joined his men.

'As we began to lay our explosives,' Corran went on, 'I noticed that the chaps were chatting and cracking a few jokes. They were very relaxed, given that a huge battle was going on outside.

'While all this was happening I couldn't blow my charges because dear old Gerard Brett was next door to me laying his explosives in the rear caisson dock gates, which was right next to the winding house I was about to blow up. If I blew my charges first there was a strong possibility that we would kill him.

'Gerard was having a very tough time because the Germans had roofed over the top of the dock gate with railway sleepers and sealed it with tar and gravel and it was proving very difficult to get inside.

'The Germans had also spotted what Gerard's team were up to and opened fire, severely wounding him and killing a couple of his team. It was a pretty desperate situation, but very quickly a Royal Engineers sergeant-major, Frank Carr, emerged and he took control. I sent Ron Chung over to let him know that I would not detonate my explosives until they had placed their explosives and passed through us.

'I got everything ready and we waited for Gerard's lot to place theirs. My team kneeled outside and tried to stay out of the way of the searchlights. Every time the searchlights passed, other Germans on top of the submarine pens would open fire at us – the bullets were coming in fairly near. Then eventually Gerard came through, supported by two of his corporals. He had been very badly wounded in the legs and could barely walk. As he passed me by I said, "Well done, old boy," and that was the last I saw of him. Once they had all gone through I pulled my ignition switches. We moved away to a safe distance and watched the winding house jump about five feet in the air and then collapse – the explosives absolutely shattered the bloody thing.

'The job of every officer in charge of a demolition party was to go back and inspect the damage once the explosives had been detonated. I got up to go and inspect it although it was pretty obvious it had been blown to pieces, and as I got up and took a step forward a searchlight swept over as and several pairs of hands pulled me back down and wouldn't let go until the beam had gone past.

'Once the winding house had been destroyed we made our way back to the dockside where I found Colonel Newman. I walked up to him and, without really thinking, I saluted him in the middle of a battle, which to any watching sniper would have immediately identified a senior officer.

'I said, "Sir, we have destroyed the northern winding house and we are ready to return to England." The colonel turned to me and said, "I'm afraid, old boy, the transport home has rather let us down. Have a look at the river."'

Almost all of the motor launches which had crossed the Channel just a few hours earlier were now on fire. Eyewitnesses later said that the very estuary itself had been turned into an inferno.

'The MLs didn't stand a chance, and as soon as the fuel tanks were hit they burst into flames and a lot of chaps burnt to death. I'm thankful that I didn't hear their screams, but a friend of mine did and he later told me that he never wanted to hear a noise like that ever again.

'Despite the gunfire and the fact that our escape plan was now in tatters, the colonel remained very calm, and said, "We are going to have to fight our way through the town and we'll make our way down to Spain" – which was around 350 miles away. I remember thinking, amid the mayhem and the chaos, OK, if that's the plan, we'd better get on with it.'

With no means of escape by sea, the Commandos began to fight their way through St Nazaire. The dead were left where they fell and those too badly wounded to walk were patched up, injected with morphine and were left in the hope that they would be properly treated by the Germans once the battle was over. Those Commandos who could walk, even though they had sustained some appalling injuries, joined the group who were hurriedly reshaping their escape plan.

Colonel Newman quickly gave a set of battle orders to those who had assembled around him, explaining that they would attempt to fight their way out of the town and make for Spain.

'Around 30 of us formed up to make our way out of the dock area into the town. The battle was still raging at this point, lots of shooting going on. There were dead and wounded from both sides lying everywhere – a real battlefield. I found myself with the colonel and Bill Copland, and all I had was my Colt .45 and I wished I had a bloody submachine-gun of some kind. Then we literally fought our way from one patch of shadow to the next – they became our tactical bounds. We had to use fire and movement all the way.

'Bill was an extraordinarily brave chap – he at one point charged a German pill box on his own and emptied the whole magazine through the gun slot – as was Charles Newman.

'I remember tripping on a bloody great wire and a bullet struck the ground in front of me and hit the cobbles – had I not tripped it would have hit me. We couldn't take the wounded; we just had to leave them. My good friend Gerard Brett was left, too. They were patched up as best we could and we just had to hope that the Germans would look after them. We couldn't carry them. Where would you carry them to? At that stage we fully expected to be walking to Spain. Remember we were trying to get out of the bloody place.

'Our progress was slow because firefights were breaking out all over the place and we were heavily outnumbered. No one wanted to get themselves killed, but neither did we want to be captured.

'At one point we were confronted by an armoured car which began firing at us but we quickly managed to avoid it without taking any casualties. But to get out of the dock we had to cross a bridge which was being heavily defended by German soldiers.

'There was no tactical way you could get over it, so the colonel said, "We'll charge it," and so we did. The whole lot of us ran at the bridge just like a pack of rugger forwards. I think the Germans must have had their sights set too high, because we all managed to cross it. We ran over three or four abreast and if the Germans had fired into the mass of us all they would certainly have killed some of us. I managed to get myself wounded when a potato masher* landed under my feet and exploded. The blast blew me right up in the air and I landed on top of Captain Stan Day, the adjutant of No. 2 Commando, who I think must have thought I was dead when I hit him.

'I picked myself up and my leg was a bit odd. It was bleeding quite badly and I couldn't move my foot, but I could stand and still walk. I had also taken a couple of clips from bullets and shrapnel on the shoulders.'

The Commandos fought through the streets of the town, killing Germans wherever their paths crossed. They managed to avoid larger groups of German soldiers by creeping through alleyways and back gardens. But it was now almost four hours since the assault began and daylight was approaching.

'As we moved along one street a German motorbike and sidecar combination came tearing round the corner and I fired at them and they crashed into the wall, both dead. And I thought, "Right, well, I've done that." Later on it emerged that everyone had opened fire – they must have been really riddled with bullets.

'Daylight was approaching and we were running out of ammunition; in fact, most of us had no ammunition. Our group stopped by a rather large building which appeared to be empty. Colonel Newman turned to us and said, "Right, we'll lie up here now for the hours of daylight and then we'll get underway again at night." But he chose a building right opposite the German headquarters – we had no idea, of course.

'We all went down into the cellar and laid down our badly wounded on some mattresses, gave them first field dressings, any morphine we had amongst us, and tended to them as best we could. I remember feeling quite secure at that moment, even though the town was now swarming with Germans looking for us.

'The *Campbeltown* hadn't yet exploded, and I think some of the men may have wondered if it ever would. The realisation that a lot

* British Army slang name for the Model 24 German hand grenade.

of our friends had been killed and wounded began to hit home. We had been inside this house for about 30 minutes when there was a lot of very raucous stereotypical German shouting outside and suddenly the door burst open. At the top of the stairs a group of very tense-looking Germans with Schmeisser submachine-guns and potato mashers were standing there looking at us.

'Now if I had been them I would have wiped us out, I really would. I would have chucked a couple of grenades down the stairs and shot us all. But the Germans didn't, for some reason. Perhaps they knew we were trapped. They just stood there, and my dear old colonel, who was a very kind-hearted man, took his pipe out, put it in his mouth and said, "Well, we've done what we came here to do. I'm not going to have any more of my men killed," and we walked up the stairs and the Germans just let us pass through and form up outside in the street.

'Our weapons were wrenched off us, and they didn't like our fighting knives which we each had in a sheath strapped to the outside of our calf. They hated those and brandished them at us and all that sort of nonsense. No one had his or her hands up; we walked outside and were herded into a café. My overriding feeling was, "Oh bugger, I've been taken bloody prisoner." It was such a feeling of absolute anti-climax. I knew my boys and I had done our job, but we were sweating on whether the *Campbeltown* would now explode. That was quite a worrying few minutes.

'We were sitting around chatting quietly when all of a sudden we heard this enormous rumbling noise. We all immediately knew that it was the *Campbeltown* exploding and everyone began cheering, much to the chagrin of the Germans. The relief from knowing that we had completed the job was huge.

'I had a great friend called Bill Watson, known as Tiger, a lieutenant from No. 2 Commando, who led one of the sections in the assault troop. He had been wounded in the raid and wasn't feeling too clever. When the ship blew up one of the Germans came over to Tiger and began shouting, "We are going to shoot you, we are going to shoot you," and Tiger responded in a very bored fashion: "Oh for God's sake, just get on with it. If you are going to shoot us then bloody well do it, but stop shouting, you silly little man." This German just looked completely surprised. He probably didn't understand a word Tiger was saying, but it cheered us up.'

The *Campbeltown* had become something of a tourist attraction before she exploded, and early that morning several German officers took their French girlfriends on board to give them a quick tour.

An estimated 60 people were on board when she exploded – all were blown to pieces. Bits of their bodies were later found nearly 400 yards away lying close to the submarine pens. It is estimated that around 300 people, possibly more, were killed and many more wounded when the *Campbeltown* exploded.

It was at that point that, almost collectively, the surviving Commandos realised they would spend the rest of the war as prisoners. Many of those who took part in the raid had thought that they might be killed or wounded; few, if any, had given much consideration to becoming a POW.

'Although we had achieved the objective, I was a POW, which was a very depressing experience, and almost from the moment I was captured I began thinking about escaping. Before the operation began I had imagined how it would feel, arriving home after a successful operation, having achieved everything, having a big party and then going on another raid. But I had been captured, and that was the most depressing thing in my life.

'We beat them, to be honest, and we did what we bloody well set out to do. But there were so many Germans, thousands of them, so the odds were too great, but I just wish to God that we could have had a go at getting out of St Nazaire.'

An hour or so later the Commandos were put on trucks and driven the short distance across town to the German Naval Hospital, which was located inside the five-star Hermitage Hotel at La Baule, where they were made to lie in rows on the mattresses on the floor guarded by sailors armed with submachine-guns while the Germans decided what to do with them.

'I had a friend in No. 5 Commando, and he was convinced that the Royal Navy would come and rescue us. While we were lying on the ground, he kept saying, "They're not here yet, but they will be coming." I had to say to him, "Look, the Navy are never going to come, old boy. We are expendable. The job's done and that's all that matters. You won't see any British soldiers until the war's over."

'The very badly wounded were treated by German surgeons, wearing long white rubber aprons which went from their necks down to their shins and were covered in blood. I had to go to the hospital because of my injuries, and a moronic orderly was told to give me an injection. But this bastard threw the needle at my backside like a dart and it hurt like hell, although I didn't let on. I thought, "I'd like to get this bugger on his own." But that was the only time I was poorly treated.

'I was there for about a week, and during that time I was asked to go and identify some of our dead Commandos. I was taken into a room and the chaps were already in their coffins, standing upright against the wall.

'I remember seeing Sergeant Tommy Durrant* from No. 1 Commando, who won a posthumous Victoria Cross. He was manning a machine-gun on a motor launch and refused to surrender. He had been shot 26 times but just wouldn't give in and was the only soldier to be given a Victoria Cross in a naval action.'

Sergeant Durrant's Victoria Cross was one of five awarded for Operation Chariot; the other recipients were Lieutenant-Commander Beattie, Lieutenant-Colonel Newman, Commander Ryder and Able Seaman William Savage, who was also awarded his posthumously. In addition to the five VCs, a further 79 decorations

---

* Sgt Tommy Durrant was in charge of a Lewis gun on Motor Launch 306. As his vessel proceeded up the Loire to St Nazaire, it came under heavy fire from the German destroyer *Jaguar*. During the battle Sgt Durrant was wounded in the head, arms, legs, chest and stomach. Despite being ordered to surrender by the German destroyer, Sgt Durrant continued operating his Lewis gun, directing his fire at the destroyer's bridge. He only stopped firing when he collapsed unconscious through blood loss, and later died of his wounds. A week after the raid the commander of the German destroyer met with Col. Newman in a POW camp and recounted Durrant's heroics, recommending him for a high posthumous award.

were also awarded, including four Distinguished Service Orders, four Conspicuous Gallantry Medals, five Distinguished Conduct Medals, 17 Distinguished Service Crosses, 11 Military Crosses, 24 Distinguished Service Medals and 15 Military Medals. Four men were awarded the Croix de Guerre and a further 51 were mentioned in dispatches. Never before had so many honours been won by so few men in such a short period of time during a military action. But the awards came at a severe cost. More than 600 men took part in the operation, of which 228 returned to England; 64 Commandos and 105 members of the Royal Navy were killed in action and 215 became POWs, while five men escaped overland and returned to England via Gibraltar.

'The Germans, by and large, treated us correctly. It didn't happen to me personally but some of the soldiers received pats on the back from the German soldiers, who said things like, "Well done, Tommy."'

★   ★   ★

Corran and the other Commando officers were separated from their men and were sent to Spangenberg Castle, a POW camp for officers from which it was notoriously difficult to escape. But that served as no deterrent to the young British officer.

'The camp was full of officers who had been captured at Dunkirk, and life for them was relatively comfortable. But almost from the moment I arrived I set about trying to escape. I teamed up with Lieutenant Dick Morgan, who was from No. 2 Commando and had also been captured at St Nazaire, and we became escape partners. We had been at Spangenberg for several months when Bill Copland gave the two of us the idea for a plan. There was a theatre show put on by some chaps in the camp, and Bill told Dick and me that the Germans refused to allow the clothing for the theatre to remain in the prisoners' section of the camp, just in case they were used for an escape, and so someone had to go and collect the uniforms from outside the main prison and then take them back afterwards. This meant we had an opportunity of leaving the main POW camp within the castle. You had to go over a drawbridge and then through two huge gates. A sentry was guarding you all the time, while another unlocked the gates – and then you walked up the steps into the guardroom where the clothes were kept in a great wicker hamper, which you then carried over to the prison. The process was reversed in the evening. Dick and I collected and returned the clothes for a couple of days, and we agreed that we had to have a go at escaping, because if we didn't people would think we were windy.

'We made our plan for the third night. I hid a compass in my clothes and we got some rations together. Then, on 26 March 1943, a year to the day after we set sail from Falmouth, Dick and I managed to escape. Once we were out of the main camp we got ahead of the guard and dashed through a doorway – it was actually very simple. The guard fired at us and we both expected to get shot, but we were lucky. The castle was on a sort of hill, and as we ran we both went head over heels over and over again, and we lost our rations and compass, but we were out.'

Dick and Corran managed to stay on the run for 10 days. They had no food and were forced to drink water from stagnant ditches. Sadly, their luck ran out at a railway station during an air raid. They had hoped to jump on a train while all the lights in the area went out – but the only trains passing through didn't stop. After two hours the air raid was over, and when the lights came on the two British Commandos found themselves surrounded by armed German railway police.

'This chap stuffed a pistol into my chest and we were marched off to the local jail. We were put into a cell where an old German policeman with a huge moustache brought us a mug of ersatz coffee and a huge lump of rye bread, which we were bloody happy with. We were each given a bed with a polished metal cylinder as a pillow but slept like babies that night. The following morning a group of five German soldiers came and picked us up, and funnily enough they congratulated us – they were saying "Gut, Tommy, gut" and patted us on the backs. When we got on the train we were given a wonderful bowl of barley soup, I remember it till this day. It was the first decent scoff we'd had in 10 days and it tasted delicious. And to show what a shit I was after all of their kindness, I said to Dick, "We'll escape from here if we can." I went to the loo and tried to climb out of the window, which was too narrow for me and I got stuck. One of our guards burst in and wrenched me back in, and after that we were clamped together. Later that day we arrived back at Spangenberg, and as we marched into the castle all of the other prisoners cheered us, which was very nice but I felt a bit ashamed because we had failed to make it back home, and I know Dick felt the same.

'Later the commandant, who wasn't a bad chap actually, said to me, "Oberleutnant Purdon, I know that you are going to go on trying to escape, and I know you hate Germans, so I am sending you to the bad boys' camp." I had no idea what the bad boys' camp was, but we soon discovered that it was Colditz.'

Colditz Castle was a high-security POW camp for Allied officers who were regarded as security risks. The castle was and still is situated on a rocky outcrop near Leipzig, in eastern Germany, and during the Second World War was regarded by the Germans as 'escape-proof'. In reality, more than 30 Allied officers escaped from the castle or its grounds during the war.

'There were about 20 of us who were sent to Colditz in June 1943, and as we marched through the gates we could hear this tremendous shouting. The German guards had put all these tables around the courtyard to process the new prisoners and the inmates decided they were going to cause a bit of a riot. They were shouting and singing and dropping water bombs on the German guards, who were getting pretty fed up. Eventually one of the POWs got really carried away and set fire to a straw-filled mattress and pushed it through the window on to the guards below. That brought in the riot squad, and they pointed their rifles up at the windows, which quietened things down for a bit. That was my entry into Colditz.

'The escape committee at Colditz was a very professional outfit, much more so than at Spangenberg, and almost straight away I was working on a tunnel, deep in the bowels of the castle. I don't think it was ever going to get anywhere, but it gave you something to do – gave you a bit of hope.

'We kept ourselves fit by exercising with medicine balls and play-ing a game called stool ball, which was like rugger but with a stool at either end of the pitch in the cobbled courtyard. The game started with the ball in the middle and the idea was to get the ball to the stool. It was just like rugger with tackles and everything. I use to box as well, but most of the time I wanted to be involved in escaping.'

The regime in Colditz was deliberately austere. Food was 'horri-ble', according to Corran, and consisted of a diet of mainly watery soup and black bread, spread with a tasteless German margarine. Only the infrequent supply of Red Cross parcels, which contained luxuries like a few boiled sweets and a small dark chocolate as well as other rations, prevented severe malnutrition.

The POWs were woken around 6am every morning and made to attend a morning parade in the inner cobbled courtyard, where they were counted by the Germans, after which they were allowed to get dressed and wash.

'Douglas Bader* was locked up with me and I thought he was great. He was a jolly nice chap, always very nice to us young offic-ers, and we admired him a great deal. To think of everything he achieved with those two metal legs. Also in Colditz at the same time was David Stirling,† the founder of the SAS. I didn't know him terribly well. He was a tall, gangly man with a sallow complexion. But the extraordinary thing was that he wanted me to take command of an SAS troop in the Far East once Colditz had been liberated. He planned to raise a new regiment and take it to China to fight the Japanese. But of course everything changed after the atomic bomb was dropped.'

---

* Group Captain Douglas Bader, CBE, DSO and Bar, DFC and Bar, an RAF fighter ace during the Second World War. He was commissioned into the RAF in 1930, and in 1931 lost both legs while attempting aerobatics. He was medically retired from the RAF, but rejoined at the outbreak of war. He was credited with 20 aerial victories, four shared victories, six probables, one shared probable and 11 damaged aircraft. He was shot down over France in 1941.

† Lt-Col. David Stirling, the founder of the SAS, who was captured by the Germans in January 1943.

The days slowly passed by for Corran and the other Colditz inmates, who were always on the lookout for any escape opportunity that might arise. All lived in hope that they would one day escape and make it back to the Allied lines, where they could rejoin the fight against the Nazis.

'One day a lorry drove into the camp and it had a number of captured black French colonial soldiers in it. Here's an opportunity, I thought, and Dickie and I had just enough time to run upstairs and put black boot polish over our hair and faces. The plan was that we were going to jump into the lorry and be driven out of the camp and pass ourselves of as French colonials – all a bit mad, I know. And we were caught by the guards – I quickly ran up the stairs and washed the polish off, but Dickie had a bit of trouble getting the polish off his face, because he had a moustache as well, but we got away with it. Otherwise it would have been a couple of weeks in solitary.

'My attitude was that our fellow soldiers were risking their lives in the desert, Italy and later in France, and all we could do was risk our lives and try and escape. I didn't think about the risks or the consequences – it was my duty.'

Corran's life as a POW ended on 16 April 1945 when Colditz was liberated by the US Army, but rather than sit around and wait to be repatriated back to Britain, he decided to join up with the US forces.

'We could hear the Allies getting nearer, and then one day someone said they thought they could see US tanks. The castle was eventually liberated by the 273rd Infantry Regiment, 69th (Fighting Irish) Division of the US Army. As there were no officers around, Dickie and I asked the chaps if we could join them and they said yes. They gave us a US carbine and ammunition and we fought with the US Army for about a week. The US rank and file was great. No one seemed to object to two British Army officers who had been locked up for the past few years fighting with them. We weren't made to feel extraordinary or anything. We just got on with it and were completely accepted. The Americans were great – very tough and professional, warm and friendly. We took part in a number of skirmishes and I fired my rifle in anger – which was fantastic because I finished the war feeling like a soldier.'

The curtain was finally coming down on the war in Europe, and Dick Morgan and Corran were eventually repatriated to Britain.

On arriving home, Corran learnt that his days as a Commando were over – he was to become adjutant of the 1st Battalion, The Royal Ulster Rifles, who were now part of 6th Airborne Division. It was a heavy blow for Corran, made worse when he discovered some months later that all of the Army Commando units were to be disbanded, a fate which befell many of the Second World War's special forces. But he was happy and proud to be with the 1st Battalion.

The raid on St Nazaire remained firmly in the back of Corran's memory as he got to grips with the staff work which came with being an adjutant. Then, one morning as he headed down to breakfast in the Ulster Rifles officers' mess, he bumped into his commanding officer, who quizzically asked if he had read the morning paper.

'I said, "No, sir, I haven't," and he said, "Well, you'd better read it. Congratulations." I had no idea what he was talking about. I looked at the paper and I learnt that I had been awarded the Military Cross.'

The citation read: 'Lieutenant Corran William Brooke Purdon of the Royal Ulster Rifles. On the 28th March 1942 during the Commando raid in France, Lt Purdon, of No. 12 Commando, was in command of a demolition party. His duties were to carry out the destruction of the main dry dock installations. Although wounded, he led his men to their task and under intense fire carried through the work of destruction, completely destroying an important part of the dry machinery. Later in the street fighting, although suffering from a severe loss of blood, his determination, coolness and dash were fine examples to his men and his actions led to the destruction of many enemy and their equipment.' The citation was published in the *London Gazette* on 5 July 1945.

'I remained in the Army because that is all I wanted to do – I loved it, every minute. But I loved the Commandos more than anything because it was so free of bullshit. The best thing I ever did as a regular officer was to be in the Commandos.'

Corran remained in the Army for the next 30 years, retiring in 1976 as the General Officer Commanding the Near East Land Forces based in Cyprus. Afterwards he worked for British Aerospace and then joined the Royal Hong Kong Police, where he served as Deputy Commissioner for three years.

'I always wanted to command a foreign army – that was my last ambition. I like foreigners and serving abroad, and I commanded the Sultan of Oman's armed forces from 1967 to 1970.'

Corran is the life president of the St Nazaire Society, an organisation created to keep alive the memory of the raid.

Back in 1942, the St Nazaire Raid had been one of the great success stories of the war. The damage to the Normandie dock was tremendous, and it remained out of action for the entire war and wasn't fully repaired until 1947. The *Tirpitz* never reached the North Atlantic, remaining in the Baltic and the North Sea for the next two years, and after several crippling attacks by RAF bombers was finally destroyed in Norwegian waters in November 1944.

The decisive and morale-boosting raid also served to prove that in war almost anything was possible, providing soldiers were daring and prepared to take risks. They also needed to be well trained, properly equipped and led by first-class commanders at all ranks, just as the men of the Special Air Service were during the North African campaign.

CHAPTER 4

# 'The Best Navigator in the Western Desert'

## Mike Sadler with the SAS

'The boy Stirling is quite mad, quite, quite mad. However, in a
war there is often a place for mad people.'
FIELD-MARSHAL MONTGOMERY, describing David
Stirling, the founder of the SAS

Captain Mike Sadler and Jimmy Patch both served in the LRDG
during the North African campaign, but it was not until after the
war that the two men learnt of each other's existence and became
friends. It was Jimmy, in fact, who suggested that I contact Mike
and put me in touch with him. 'Mike is a very nice chap and saw
a great deal of action in the desert. Try and talk to him, he'll have
a great story to tell you.'

Captain Mike Sadler, MC, MM, has been famous within the
world of special forces since 1942. Even when he was serving
alongside Lieutenant-Colonel David Stirling, the founder of the
SAS, and Lieutenant-Colonel Paddy Mayne, his successor, Mike's
navigating skills were already legendary. He was regarded as one of
the best navigators in the western desert, possessing an unerring
ability to navigate by both day and night and in all weathers – a
skill which undoubtedly saved dozens of lives and helped to ensure
the success of some of the SAS's most spectacular missions during
the North African campaign. Typically, he himself says he was just
competent and lucky. Mike has been a longtime member of the
Special Forces Club. The establishment's walls are adorned with

some of the operations in which Mike was personally involved. He has led a varied and fascinating life but, like many of those early members of the club, in the 1930s Mike was heading in a completely different direction until war intervened.

Today Mike lives in Cheltenham, Gloucestershire, and we arranged to meet and have lunch and then, hopefully, chat about his wartime activities.

The years have been kind to Mike, who is aged 92 at the time of our meeting. Despite his failing eyesight and 'slightly dodgy memory', as he put it, he remains fit and active and insists we walk the mile to the restaurant for lunch.

Mike is easy-going and chats comfortably about his wartime activities. He enquires about Jimmy Patch, praising the courage and fortitude he demonstrated during the war as if it were yesterday. 'We didn't know each other back then, I think we must have served at different times. By the time Jimmy joined I had moved on.' One story rolls out after another. He talks about David Stirling, the founder of the SAS, as if he were still alive, and he was clearly a great fan of Paddy Mayne.

When we return to Mike's flat I ask if he minds if I take notes as we talk. He looks slightly uncomfortable, and I notice his brow furrowing before he replies: 'I shouldn't really be speaking about any of this.'

My heart begins to sink. 'Mike, you're 92 and you fought in a war 70 years ago. Those experiences belong to you and nobody else,' I say in desperation. 'You won't be breaking the Official Secrets Act by telling me about what you did in North Africa.'

Mike laughs. 'I suppose you're right.'

\*       \*       \*

Mike's war story began over 75 years ago when, after passing his school certificate in 1937, he left Bedales, his public school, and took 'more or less the next boat' to Rhodesia to become a farmer.

'My imagination was sparked by a friend at a dreadful prep school I attended called Oakley Hall, near Cirencester. I met this

Mike Sadler

chap called Rooney and he told me all about this wonderful country Rhodesia. His stories were full of lions, elephants and adventure. I suppose it may have been a way of escaping the rigours of school life, but from a very early age I had decided that was going to be the life for me.

'My family had a series of connections with people in Rhodesia and one of those was the owner of a tobacco farm. I headed off and went to work at the farm as a sort of apprentice. Tobacco was the cash crop and there were also hundreds of hectares of maize and cattle. I quickly settled into what was a really lovely life. There was a racehorse on the farm, and in the winter when there were no crops to look after we would train the horse. It was a wonderful country; it was a primitive life and it was very nice.'

His idyllic but austere lifestyle in southern Africa came to an end two years later in September 1939, when Britain declared war against Germany. Mike, like millions of other young men across Britain's vast empire, volunteered for active service.

'I joined the Rhodesian Artillery. The men within the unit were all very keen but our equipment was very basic. We had 3.7-inch Howitzers, screw guns from Kipling's day, all very antiquated but useful and still functional.

'During that period I learnt how to fire guns using aiming marks and also learnt the appropriate size of charge. Pretty soon after that we drove up to Kenya, chased the Italians up through Somaliland and into Southern Abyssinia, then moved up to Suez, where we joined up with the 8th Army. The Rhodesian Regiment was affiliated to the 60th Rifles,* so the connections were already strong.'

During the early part of 1941 Mike's battery, which had converted to an anti-tank unit, were based in the desert west of Mersa Matruh, a small town on the Egyptian coast west of Alexandria, preparing for the great German advance eastwards across the desert. The days were long, cold and mostly uneventful. Engagements with the enemy were rare events. The monotony of digging endless tank traps and bunkers was only broken by long and equally uneventful patrols out as far west as the escarpment at Tobruk in Libya.

But those dull days suddenly changed during a period of leave in Cairo. Mike and a few pals from his unit were enjoying an early evening drink at the Rhodesian Club when they started chatting to members of a unit whose name – the Long Range Desert Group – was unknown to them.

Mike was attracted by the stories of their exploits and the freedom they enjoyed to operate behind enemy lines with little interference from senior officers.

'My recollection is that we all got on very well. Their unit needed an anti-tank gunner and they said, "Why don't you come and join us?" I was young, keen and fit; I was delighted to be asked.

---

* 60th Rifles is the nickname for the King's Royal Rifle Corps, a British infantry regiment.

The work they were doing sounded infinitely more exciting than digging tank traps, so I joined. It was probably a bit more complicated than that, and I'm sure there was a lot of staff work that needed to be done to have me transferred across, but that's how I remember it.

'I spent two weeks at Abbassia Barracks in Cairo, and then joined up with an LRDG re-supply column, consisting of mostly 3-tonners and a couple of Fords, and their job was to keep the LRDG patrols supplied with food, ammunition and anything they needed.'

It was during Mike's long journey down to the headquarters at Kufra that he began to take an interest in desert navigation.

As the convoy headed south, Mike was struck by the beauty and majesty of the desert and was amazed at how quickly the hostile environment could change. Vehicles could be speeding along flat, road-like desert surfaces at one moment, only for the terrain to change in a matter of seconds to a rock-strewn wasteland capable of tearing tyres to shreds.

It was during those long days of patrolling that Mike learnt the routine of life in the desert followed by all of those who operated deep behind enemy lines. Soldiers would awake in the morning, cold and puffy-eyed. Weapons would be cleaned and checked before the preparation of a quick but nourishing breakfast. As the weak dawn sun slowly began to break the horizon, patrols would then break camp and push deeper into the desert. As the temperature began to rise, clothes which had kept the men warm during the freezing nights were jettisoned. Some of the vehicles' crews would strip to shorts and vests, and boots would be replaced with sandals. While the vehicles were on the move, the crews were kept cool and the flies, which seemed to appear from nowhere and were an ever-present menace, were kept at bay. Then, as the sun slipped into the western desert, the reverse would happen and warmer clothes – jumpers, long trousers and even woolly hats – would be needed. Once a suitable location for a camp was found, sentries would be posted, while the mechanics would carry out essential maintenance work on the vehicles. Food would be prepared while other patrol members cleaned weapons and camouflaged the vehicles. While the majority of men would try and get an early night's sleep, navigators and commanders would check maps and plan the route for the following day.

'I was absolutely intrigued by desert navigation. What amazed me was that even with the vast, featureless expanses of the desert, a good navigator could pinpoint his exact location by using a theodolite, an air almanac and air navigational tables, and having a good knowledge of the stars. It also dawned on me fairly quickly that the LRDG would be doing lots of long patrols, which can be quite boring, and I liked the idea of playing a role in the planning of the patrols.

'I also learnt on that first trip that few people had any real interest in becoming a navigator because it was regarded as being a bit of a black art which needed a bit of know-how. Navigators also had to sit up at night waiting to catch a star or receive a radio time signal while everyone else was tucked up and sleeping, so as a job it wasn't that popular. But as soon as I arrived at the headquarters I was offered the chance to become a navigator and I set about learning the trade from other navigators in the LRDG.

'I found it endlessly fascinating and eventually became patrol navigator for the Rhodesian S Patrol, which was the only patrol I served in during my time with the LRDG. At that stage nobody knew about the SAS; they were still to do their first mission.'

★    ★    ★

The SAS was the brainchild of David Stirling, who in July 1941 was serving within Brigadier Robert Laycock's small unit known as Layforce. In the spring of 1941 the German Afrika Korps led by Rommel had scored a series of stunning victories which had left 25,000 British troops cut off and isolated in Tobruk and the rest of the British Army in North Africa reeling from its wounds. The role of Layforce was to move along the coast and destroy enemy airfields in a series of well-planned attacks. But the Royal Navy was stretched and under orders not to take any risks. The plan was eventually shelved and Layforce was disbanded.

Stirling, then a lieutenant, who was commissioned into the Scots Guards, was attached to No. 8 Commando before serving in Layforce. He was convinced that a small elite force could parachute behind enemy lines and destroy huge numbers of enemy aircraft. He was able to convince General Claude Auchinleck, Commander-in-Chief Middle East theatre, of his plan. The young officer was promoted to the rank of captain and was allowed to recruit six officers and 60 non-commissioned officers and other ranks. The new unit was to be known as L Detachment of the Special Air Service. The SAS at that stage was a fictitious unit, whose name had been invented to make the Germans believe that a force of British paratroopers had arrived in the Middle East.

L Detachment's first mission took place in November 1941, during the 8th Army operation codenamed Crusader. The plan was to attack Axis airfields at Timini and Gazala in Libya with small teams of troops whose mission was to destroy as many aircraft as possible. The soldiers were to be dropped by parachute at night and make an advance on foot to the target areas. But the mission ended in disaster after the parachutists jumped into one of the worst gales to hit the area for almost 30 years. Of the 62 men who took part only 22 returned; the others were either killed or captured.

Three weeks later Stirling decided to try the same operation again, but rather than parachute in he asked the LRDG if they would 'taxi' the SAS to their target areas. After the failure of the earlier operation Stirling attempted to draw some positives, one of which was the involvement of the LRDG who had waited at a desert RV for the SAS men after the disaster of the first operation. 'If the LRDG can be used to take us out,' Stirling argued, 'why can't they be used to take us in?'

By this stage of the desert war Mike was earning a reputation as one of the best navigators in the LRDG. He seemed to be born to the role and had an uncanny ability to navigate a safe route through some of the most barren terrain on the planet.

'My first operation involving the SAS was in December 1941. It was the SAS's first ground operation after the earlier failed mission, so a lot rested on it. My job was to navigate from the Jalo Oasis to the German airfield at Tamet. The operation was being led by Lieutenant Paddy Mayne.

'Paddy was a very intriguing figure even then. I could tell almost immediately that he was a great operator, a great tactician. He was someone you had complete faith in. I think that was probably his greatest quality. His judgement was never questioned because he was such a superb operator, and he had this fantastically strong bond with his men. If he liked you, you were fine; but if not, if you didn't impress him, that was it, you were out.

'Shortly before we set off, a brigadier turned up to speak to us or wish us luck or something. But when he set eyes upon us he was horrified because some members of the patrol hadn't shaved for two weeks, our hair was thick with dust and we were wearing all different types of uniform. He looked at us and said "Oh my God!" in a very pompous way but he was effectively ignored by all of us. We were fighting men, and as far as we were concerned he was a desk officer who probably had no idea of the type of mission we were undertaking.

'I was to navigate from the Jalo Oasis to the airfield. It took between two and three days, and the going was bad. We stopped a couple of miles south of the airfield. Paddy and his team set off at about 6.30pm and returned at around 3am. The operation was entirely successful and a lot of aircraft were destroyed.'

The raiders managed to sneak into the airfield undetected and place bombs on around 30 aircraft, destroying at least 24. Ammunition and petrol dumps were also destroyed, and just for good measure a building where an estimated 30 Italian pilots were being billeted was attacked. According to newspaper reports at the time, all the German and Italian pilots were killed – but Mayne's report makes it clear that the extent of the casualties was unknown.

Mike continued: 'After the operation the LRDG's job was to get the SAS back, trying to evade Italian bombers at the same time, and that was my first experience with the SAS. The SAS joked about the LRDG being a taxi service. I think at that stage there was an increasing conflict of interest between the LRDG and the SAS. The LRDG's true role was long-range reconnaissance, which was vitally important, and the whole idea was that we should never be seen or heard. Although we could protect ourselves, we didn't set out to get into a fight with the enemy. But the SAS operations were designed to attack the enemy and stir up a hornet's nest, the complete opposite to us.'

Mike's navigational ability soon caught the eye of David Stirling. The SAS commander was impressed that Mike appeared to be completely lacking in any self-doubt – he was exactly the sort of navigator the SAS needed. By that stage of the war Mike had been promoted to corporal and had been awarded the Military Medal for his desert exploits.

Although Stirling was content with his relationship with the LRDG, he believed that if L Detachment was to become a fully-fledged regiment, which was his ambition, the SAS would ultimately have to be a self-contained unit with its own vehicles and therefore its own navigators.

As Mike recalls, 'There was some sort of deal struck between the SAS and the LRDG in which I joined the SAS through a request made by Stirling. It was all news to me, of course. I just discovered one day that I was being handed over, and that was how I joined the SAS. Almost from the beginning I became Stirling's principal navigator, although I also navigated for other patrols as required.'

In July 1942 the Allies were losing the war in North Africa. Tobruk, the so-called impregnable fortress, had fallen to the Afrika Korps, the Germans had advanced 40 miles into Egypt, and the British Army was locked into a fighting withdrawal back to El Alamein. But while the 8th Army was in chaos, the conditions were perfect for the SAS. The further Rommel pressed eastwards, the longer and more vulnerable became his supply chain, and Stirling was determined to exploit this open flank. Stirling moved L Detachment, which now numbered over 100 men, to a temporary base deep behind enemy lines and about 40 miles due south of Mersa Matruh.

Stirling had also managed to acquire a consignment of US jeeps, a vehicle which became synonymous with their desert operations and was to greatly enhance the fighting ability of the SAS. Each jeep was stripped of all its non-essential parts, including the wind-screen, to increase the load-carrying capacity of the vehicle. This innovation meant that the large amounts of fuel, water, ammunition and rations needed for long-range patrols could be carried without the need for support vehicles. Jeeps were also fitted with a sun compass, radios, sand mats and a condensing unit to help prevent water loss from the radiator. Each vehicle was also equipped with twin Vickers K machine-guns, often supported by a Bren gun.

Over the next few weeks, L Detachment set about attacking German airfields and supply dumps at every turn. The patrols were long, dangerous and gruelling but were having a huge impact on Rommel's exposed forces.

One evening towards the middle of July, Stirling returned from another visit to Cairo with fresh rations, supplies, more jeeps and a new set of targets given to him by the Middle East Headquarters, who wanted Stirling to concentrate on tank workshops, fuel dumps and water supplies – anything, in fact, which would slow down the German advance and buy time for the beleaguered 8th Army. Stirling also came equipped with a new tactic for attacking airfields.

Stirling gathered his men, spread his maps out and began to explain his plan for their next mission – a mass jeep raid on the German airfield at Fuka, near Sidi Hanish. The airfield, a base for the Junker 52 transport plane, was a major staging point for the front line and was essential to Rommel's plans.

The SAS had become a victim of its own success and the enemy had changed the way in which they guarded their airfields. As well as having sentry positions based on the perimeter, the Germans had also taken to guarding every individual plane. The tactic of sneaking unseen into an airfield and placing a Lewes bomb on to the wing of an aircraft could no longer be regarded as a reliable tactic. Stirling revealed that on this occasion the SAS would attack using 18 jeeps with all guns blazing.

'The plan was brilliant. He drew a diagram in the sand explaining how the jeeps would assault the airfield line abreast, laying down a tremendous weight of fire. A Vickers K can fire at a rate of 1,000 rounds a minute. Then, at a given signal, the firing of a green

Very light, the jeeps would move in two columns firing outwards. At the head would be a diamond of four jeeps led by Stirling. If it all went to plan, he said, there should be no casualties from friendly fire and the attack should be devastating. He said, "I want to attack tomorrow night. It's a full moon and intelligence says the airfield is in full swing."

'We all realised we had a lot to do. The vehicles had to be properly equipped, weapons and radios checked and I had to plan the route and, perhaps most importantly, we had to rehearse. We all had to know our position so that everyone could carry out their role almost instinctively. Every man had to know the plan as well as the overall commander, so the mission could still take place if the commander was killed or injured. There were no passengers in the SAS; everyone was vital to the success of the plan. It was a very long day and we were rehearsing well into the night. It was gone midnight by the time we eventually got to sleep, and we were up at 5am and continued with the preparations.'

The convoy of jeeps set out about an hour before dusk and headed for their target around 40 miles away. Each jeep was commanded by an officer or NCO and Mike Sadler was navigating.

'It was an arduous journey right from the very beginning. The route was strewn with rocks; driving in a straight line for a period of time was almost impossible and the going was bad.

'We stopped on the way to the airfield in the evening, about 20 miles or so from the coast, so that I could get star shots and get our position exactly right. When you are navigating you must be exactly sure of your position before proceeding, otherwise you could jeopardise the whole mission. I was happy, I knew our exact location, and so we pushed on, but I think David thought we should have been a lot closer to the airfield than we actually were. The convoy had been slowed down by the hard-going terrain.

'At one point we stopped and David came over to me and said, "Where the hell is this bloody airfield?" and I said, "Well, actually, it should be about a mile away dead ahead of us," and, remarkably, at that point the Germans switched on the runway landing lights right across the front of us to allow one of their JU52s to land. It was incredible and I have to say I felt extremely pleased with myself. My positioning was spot on and it was a moment of great triumph for me.

'When the aircraft landed, the lights went off. Stirling gave the order to move into line abreast and the attack went in with all guns blazing. The weight of fire was incredible and must have been quite deadly. Then, as per the plan, the green Very light went up and the jeeps moved into their two columns and proceeded to shoot up the airfield. My role during the attack was to establish an RV on the SE corner of the airfield for anyone whose jeep was knocked out and I got the most wonderful view of tracer fire illuminating the whole sky.'

The vehicles drove in formation, as had been rehearsed the previous evening, and began to let rip into the parked aircraft. The desert airfield seemed to be packed with every aircraft the Luftwaffe had deployed to North Africa – Stukas, Messerschmidts and the all-important JU52s. The Vickers were firing a mixture of ball and tracer ammunition at the maximum rate and soon the aircraft began to burst into flames. Although the German guards were not the primary target, they too were cut down by the enormous weight of fire.

'Pretty soon the Germans started shooting back and the fire-power from both sides was illuminating the airfield and the night sky around. It was a very surreal moment because it was almost like a huge fireworks display.

'It wasn't a battle as such, just a quick raid which really didn't last more than about 10 minutes. Only one of our chaps was hit and killed on the field. Everyone else got away one way or another and we destroyed 20 or 30 aircraft.

'After the raid all the jeeps headed off into the desert to various different places. We knew that the Germans would be conducting a follow-up operation so we had to get away as quickly as possible. Some of the crews had more time than I did, because I stayed until just before dawn, just in case some people did need picking up, but nobody turned up, so when it was daylight I decided to go.

'Luckily a thick sea mist enveloped the area, which covered our withdrawal, and we drove up a track into the desert, whereupon we suddenly found ourselves driving past a German column, who were actually going out to look for us. We were on the same road, they were on the side and we drove past them. They had stopped and were resting, some were brewing up tea or coffee and it was obvious they weren't expecting us. There were quite a lot of them, about 10 vehicles and maybe 40 to 50 men. If they had been awake we would have faced a bit of a problem.

'We headed out into the desert as far as we could get and then we ran into "Gentleman" Jim Almonds,* who was crouched down by a small ridge and waving to us to get down because there was a German unit just over the other side of the ridge. We kept a low profile for the rest of the day. A patrol of three Stukas circled us several times but did not attack, presumably because they associated us with the German unit on the other side of the ridge – we were that close to them and that night we proceeded back to the RV. The journey back almost felt longer than the journey to the target because we were so tired. It was very hot, especially on that particular operation because it was the height of summer, but it's surprising how quickly you got used to the environment.

'We had a few privileges, which made life just that little bit more bearable. Every evening we would have a tin of meat and veg, with a little bit of rum and some lime to ward off scurvy. Having that little bit of rum every evening did wonders for the morale and we always had supplies of rum and lime, whereas the average British soldier in the desert did not.'

The entire party eventually made it back to the base more or less intact, but the journey back for some of the soldiers took almost three days. The mission had been a huge success and the SAS had only suffered two casualties: one killed at the airfield, and a Frenchman serving with the SAS who had been killed in a Stuka attack on the route back to the base.

---

* One of the 'originals' of the SAS, who first served in L Detachment in 1941.

The tactic of the 'mass jeep raid' was regarded as a total success by Stirling and the SAS. When the unit was back within the relative safety of the RV, Stirling told his men that their role was now to destroy the enemy's equipment and supplies behind the lines. Stirling ordered half his force to return to Cairo and the rest to harry the enemy in the area of the El Alamein line. It was a mission fraught with danger but Stirling reckoned his small force spread out in small units could create havoc.

★    ★    ★

Mike worked with many officers, all of differing characters and abilities, but one who remains firmly lodged in his memory is Lieutenant Thomas Charles David Russell, of the Scots Guards, known to friends and colleagues as David. Russell, who was fluent in German, had transferred into the SAS from the Special Interrogation Group* a few months earlier.

Mike, Russell and four other men were conducting a recce patrol in the desert when they ran into a few difficulties. Russell, a very self-confident officer of great courage, came up with a unique solution to their problem, as Mike recalled.

'Our patrol consisted of just three vehicles, and as far as I can remember our brief seemed to be "to go and cause some trouble" and David Russell seemed to be the ideal man for the job. We had been looking for a number of targets, fuel and ammo dumps, that sort of thing, but we hadn't found any.

'At the time we were operating from a base about 100 miles west from the El Alamein line on the German side. One evening one of the vehicles got a puncture. We repaired the tyre, but our pump wasn't working, at which point David just turned to us and said we'd get one from the Germans. There was dead silence. We all looked at each other, wondering whether he was joking or being serious, and he said very calmly, "Don't worry, I speak perfect German," and he did. He had studied at a German university before the war.

* A covert British unit of German-speaking Jews from Palestine.

'He quickly hatched this plan which was for two of the vehicles to remain at an RV and for David and myself to drive to the location of a German Flak 88 anti-tank battery, where he would bluff his way in and ask to borrow a pump. David was so self-assured, he was convinced it would work. I drove him to the location of the German battery and he told me to wait where I was and that he was going to get a pump. Well, I couldn't speak a word of German and I told him this, and he said not to worry and if anybody said anything I was just to say, "Ich weiss nicht", which is "I don't know" in German, and with that he was gone. I sat there wondering what I should do if anyone came up to me. I was dressed in a khaki jersey, battledress trousers and boots and looked nothing at all like a German soldier.'

Russell walked up to a German sentry position and told the guard in perfect German that he was part of a German undercover unit and needed to speak to the battery commander immediately.

'David charmed the officer immediately and the two got along very well. David concocted some story about operating behind the British lines, basically the complete opposite of what we were doing. I thought he was mad but he was supremely confident. The German officer was so impressed that he gave David a tour of the gun battery, but every time the officer's back was turned David took a Lewes bomb from his pack and placed it on one of the guns. He managed to get away with planting several bombs, mainly on lorry-fuel tanks, and also got the pump.

'When he returned to the jeep we drove off, and at that stage he didn't say anything about the bombs. We drove back to where the others were waiting, but when we tried to use the pump we found it didn't work or didn't fit. Then the bombs exploded and a rather satisfied smile spread across David's face. Just as I was wondering what we were going to do, he said, "Right, let's go back and get another pump!" But the rest of us were horrified and we all made it clear that it would be suicide to go back because the bombs had just gone off and the Germans would have known it was us. But he said, "No, no, I didn't hear anything. It will be fine, you're worrying too much. Those explosions must have been something else," or something like that. Amazingly we all accepted his word and David and I returned to the battery location. But as we came into the view of the German soldiers they began firing at us immediately. The bullets were whizzing past, so we did a quick about turn and sped off. Dawn was approaching and we had to get back to the RV, collect the others and then find a place to lie up for the day. If we had tried to move during the day the Germans would have been on to us immediately.

'We found a small hill, no more than 10 feet high, with some gullies, and camouflaged the jeeps. The jeeps were very good for camouflaging because they were so low. If you dug the wheels down a little they had practically no profile – a great benefit in the desert.

'The Germans came after us in their lorry-loads – they must have been furious. They were scanning the horizon and looking at every conceivable hiding place. They must have known that we couldn't move around during the day without exposing ourselves to great risk. While the jeeps were hidden by camouflage, the crews hid in bushes some way from the vehicles. Curiously, it was all rather comical. I would look round one side of the bush and David would look round the other and we couldn't stop laughing even though we were at a very great risk of being shot.

'We managed to survive that first day, but unfortunately the Germans found two of our jeeps. Luckily for us they withdrew when it got dark, which was the time for us to make good our escape. The problem was, there were six of us and one jeep, which was the one with the punctured tyre – and we had 100 miles of desert to cross. We all piled in and set off, very slowly. But as we crossed the desert the jeep started to fall apart.

'Somebody, and it wasn't me, filled the petrol tank with water by mistake and that very quickly brought us to a standstill. We got the jeep going again but it was in a pretty bad way; gradually the thing disintegrated, then the wheel fell apart and finally we were driving along on the brake drum and the jeep wouldn't go any further. There was no other option but to walk the last 15 miles back to the RV where we were hoping the rest of our patrol would be waiting.

We got back just in the nick of time, because we were so late that the patrol had assumed we had been killed or captured and were planning on pulling out that night. Then some German Stukas appeared, but they didn't attack so they couldn't have spotted us.

'We had a bit of a rest, some food and water, and then we were on our way again, heading back to Cairo. It was a monumentally long journey, through the Qattara Depression,* which had once been thought impassable, and back to Cairo. As we moved eastwards the group grew in size with other SAS units joining us. One night we were driving along the desert with headlights on and we were spotted by an RAF Wellington bomber, but because we were so far behind enemy lines he must have assumed we were the enemy and shot us up. It was a very alarming experience – suddenly out of the night sky came this burst of machine-gun fire. We quickly turned off the headlights, scattered and waited for the aircraft to disappear.'

Shortly after that mission Captain Russell joined the Special Operations Executive. Before leaving the SAS he asked Mike if he was willing to transfer, but he declined. The desert had become a second home to him and he enjoyed the regiment's esprit de corps. The following year, Russell, who by then had been awarded the MC, was dead. After joining the SOE he was ordered to go into Romania to help the growing resistance movement. He parachuted into Romania as part of Mission Ranji but was murdered on 4 September 1943 by an unknown assailant. Later suspicions began to emerge that Russell was killed by one of his 'trusted' guides, who then stole the golden sovereigns he was carrying to pay the resistance fighters.

Mike enjoyed the relaxed informality of the SAS and the close relationship between the officers and the men. He also admired both David Stirling and Paddy Mayne, two very different characters.

'David Stirling was a very quiet chap, almost quieter than Paddy Mayne. But he was very thoughtful and I always thought that he was thinking about the next operation rather than the one we were

---

* The second lowest point in Egypt, covering an area of 7,570 square miles.

actually on. He was always looking at the lessons learnt and what was needed to ensure that the next mission would be successful. He always had a long-term view, more so than Paddy, who was second-in-command at the time. Paddy was a hands-on man, very much an operator. It was a very good relationship between the officers and men; they would generally call us by our first names and we would address David as Colonel David. There was none of that sort of stuffiness which you found in the Army. David wanted it to be a lot more civilised. Uniform consisted of whatever we felt like wearing, which was mainly shorts, desert boots or sandals, and we often wore an Arab headdress. David tended to wear a woolly hat whereas Paddy wore a very crumpled Army officer's cap. I sometimes wore Arab headdress or more often I wouldn't wear anything. I wasn't really a fan of headdress – at one time I had some tinted goggles but David had some sunglasses. He was not a very practical fellow, and he would often lose things.

'I think there was a view amongst some in the Army that the SAS and the LRDG were a bunch of scruffs, because of the way we dressed on operations, but that wasn't the case. The SAS liked to be smart in the right environment and Paddy was quite determined to keep up appearances, especially in barracks and when not on operations, but this wasn't the case out in the field, when life was utterly different. The reason why we wore what we wanted was because the Army hadn't really developed any sort of uniform for the type of warfare in which we were involved, so we wore what was comfortable and practical.

'We were also more or less allowed to choose our own weapons, provided there was a balance within the patrol. I always had a Browning 9mm pistol and a tommy-gun. But we also had to be familiar with the Vickers K, the Lewis gun and the Bren gun. There was no formal training as such, we just learnt how to use them on the job, I suppose. Once you know how to fire one weapon, it's just a matter of applying the same principles.'

It was around this period that Mike was told that he was going to be awarded the Military Medal for his activities in the desert. 'You could have knocked me down with a feather when I learnt that I was getting the MM. It was just something that I had never really thought about, and then one day it happened.'

Mike was also nominated to go to the Officer Cadet Training Unit (OCTU) but turned it down. 'It just wasn't my cup of tea and I felt that it would be so different to life in the SAS. I knew people who had been at the training depot and it didn't really sound like my scene. There was a Rhodesian fellow, one of my sergeants on my gun crew, who was the brother of the Secretary of State for War in the UK. He was sent to OCTU and after a few days he marched in to see the commanding officer, snapped his shoes together and said, "I have buggered up a perfectly good pair of shoes with all this stamping and marching. Now I demand to be flown back to my regiment."

In September 1942, Operation Agreement – the raid on Tobruk – was launched. The aim of the attack was to attempt to significantly disrupt the Axis war effort in North Africa by attacking port facilities, fuel dumps, airfields, ships and vehicles. The Axis powers were planning a large push eastwards across the Libyan desert and beyond. Tobruk was a key staging post for any German advance. A large raid on the town by land, sea and air, if executed correctly, would buy British commanders valuable time by delaying the German advance.

While the main attack was to take place at Tobruk, the SAS and the LRDG were ordered to carry out a diversionary attack known as Operation Bigamy, on Benghazi. The plan was to destroy the harbour at Benghazi and to attack an airfield at Beninia. But, as we have seen in an earlier chapter, the operation was a failure.

Stirling was wholly against the use of his troops for the raid, primarily because it was fundamental to the ethos of the SAS that only members of the regiment should plan SAS operations. He was also deeply sceptical of this plan and doubted very much whether surprise could be achieved, given the loose talk about the planning at the Middle East Headquarters in Cairo.

For Mike Sadler, the Benghazi raid was to be the only occasion on which he personally took part in a pitched battle during the entire North African campaign.

'The Benghazi raid was very different from anything the SAS had done before. We would be working with soldiers who were not members of the SAS and we would be a pretty big formation of around 200 men. For the SAS, that was huge. We had been used to working in small patrols that could hit and run and scatter, and the Benghazi raid would be very different. Everyone knew that David was not keen. He didn't let on to us directly but we knew.'

Stirling wasn't the only special forces commander to have his doubts. Lieutenant-Colonel Vladamir Peniakoff of No. 1 Demolition Squadron, also known as Popski's Private Army, who for many months had been organising Arab resistance, was critical of the entire plan. Peniakoff would later write that the operation had been planned with 'boyish enthusiasm'.

The planning appeared to be based on the best-case scenario rather than the worst, where everything would succeed without a hitch and the enemy would not put up a fight. Stirling knew that such plans were completely unrealistic. Nevertheless, on 13 September 1942 he found himself leading his force on the approach into Benghazi.

'The basic plan for the Benghazi raid was for the RAF to bomb the town and carry out a series of runs from midnight onwards which would appear like further bombing raids, keeping the Germans' heads down and allowing us to zing in and hit the harbour – one of our targets.

'The route in took us up through the escarpment, at the top of which was a fort full of Italians who were clearly prepared for an attack. We had to deal with that before we could move on, which we did. But that meant we were very delayed and we weren't going to meet the timings which were essential for the smooth running of the plan. It was also pretty clear that the people in the fort would have sent a message back stating that they were under attack, so the surprise element of the plan had gone.

'As we pushed on, the going became increasingly difficult and we were further delayed. Then we heard the RAF going in. We could see the flashes of explosions in the distance – the RAF were on time but we weren't. David decided that the best course of action was to make the best possible speed with headlights full on. By the time we reached the foot of the escarpment it was 3am and there was only a couple of hours of night left. We eventually found a track and then a tarmac road, which took us up to the perimeter of Benghazi. After a while the whole convoy stopped. We had hit a roadblock – a barrier. On the other side was a load of barbed wire. David sent Bill Cumper, a Royal Engineer officer, forward to open the gate and we all piled through. As we passed by, Bill said, "Let battle commence." His words were very apposite. Sergeant Jim Arnold was told to go and recce forward. He got about a hundred yards when a pillbox opened fire and all hell broke loose. I returned fire with my Vickers K. I couldn't see anyone, I was just aiming at the flashes. I certainly emptied a few magazines during that, but I don't know whether I ever killed anyone.

'Jim's vehicle was wrecked and burst into flames. He managed to get into a ditch on the side of the road but he was eventually captured in the mêlée. They must have expected us, and at that point it was clear to David that there was no way we were going anywhere. Even if we had managed to break through the ambush, the resistance was going to be pretty strong and they were already hitting us with everything they had – mortars, heavy machine-guns, Bredas.*

'We were stuck by the barrier for a bit even after David had ordered us to withdraw because we simply couldn't move. The plan was to get back to the RV, which was at the top of the escarpment.

'Then the air attacks started. We had a lot of 3-tonners full of stores which had been kept back at the escarpment. Unfortunately they too had been found by the Italian Air Force and they were sitting ducks. Many vehicles were destroyed and had burst into flames. It was a very desolate scene. As we were heading back up the escarpment we were machine-gunned by an Italian CR42 but luckily it missed. The whole mission had been a disaster and I can remember looking around and seeing lots of smouldering vehicles;

* Italian heavy machine-gun.

something like 20 trucks and a dozen jeeps had been destroyed.'

Although only a couple of men had been lightly wounded during the ambush at the barrier, many more had been injured or killed during the air raids. Tons of water, food and supplies were also destroyed in the attack, making the 800-mile return journey even more perilous. The lack of vehicles meant that there was no room for the severely injured, so the decision was made for the medical orderlies to take them back into Benghazi, where it was hoped that they would be given medical treatment by the Germans, which was the case.

Mike continued: 'We regrouped and tried to make our way as best as we could to Kufra. I didn't feel disappointment, I think one was only glad to still be alive. I never thought that I wouldn't survive the war; I think everybody thinks that it is always going to be somebody else who gets killed – you do think you are almost beyond it. But the raid was a pretty close-run thing for most of us.'

The Benghazi raid was an unmitigated disaster which was doomed to failure almost from its inception. For Stirling, the loss was huge: a quarter of his force was killed, wounded or missing, and three-quarters of his prize vehicles had been destroyed. But the SAS escaped any real blame and, despite the disastrous mission, Stirling was promoted to lieutenant-colonel and the SAS became a fully-fledged regiment (1 SAS) rather than a detachment. Ironically it was also at around this time that the brass at Middle East Headquarters (MEHQ) began to realise the full impact a unit like the SAS could actually have on the enemy. During that period the SAS became a strategic asset whose job was to attack the enemy, in Stirling's own words, 'wherever and whenever possible'.

In January 1943 Stirling designed four audacious raids for the SAS. Two were due to fit in with the 8th Army's planned offensive in the middle of January, with the other two timetabled for the final phase of the campaign. One group would raid the Axis lines of communication along the coast in Tunisia; another would act as a diversion on the western side of Tripoli while the 8th Army was attacking from the east and the south; a third group was to monitor the Mareth Line;* while Stirling's element was to reconnoitre the area of northern Tunisia and eventually join up with the 1st Army, which had landed in Algeria in November 1942.

Mike began planning for the operation, starting with how much fuel he needed. Stirling told Mike, now one of his trusted aides, that he hoped to link up with his brother, Bill, who was in command of 2 SAS. Stirling believed that the status of the SAS would be greatly enhanced if his organisation was the first combat unit to establish contact between the 8th and 1st Armies. Stirling at this time harboured ambitions for the SAS to achieve brigade status, and any event which could bring credit to the force would help the cause.

It was during the middle of this planning that Mike was promoted to lieutenant – but in a most unorthodox way. 'We were in David's brother's flat in Cairo, where we planned a lot of our missions, and David said, "I need you as an officer. Go down to the market and get yourself a couple of pips." Or words to that effect. So that's how I was promoted.

'We left around 10 January 1943. The plan was to get into Tunisia, do a raid and set up shop. I chose a route on a straight course to Ghadames. The going was good to start with and then got bad.

'At this stage we knew that Rommel's supply lines were vulnerable; he was on the back foot, and there was a lot of pressure on the SAS to attack his lines of communication. The orders from headquarters were to attack as often and as quickly as possible. I think because of that extra urgency David decided there was no alternative but to drive through the Gabes Gap, a very small gap of land only five miles wide at its narrowest point. The going was terrible and slow and I remember driving through the night. We were all exhausted. I don't think we had slept for about 48 hours. We had a few close encounters, including driving over an airfield which we only realised was an airfield when we saw German planes parked

---

* System of fortifications built by the French between Medenine and Gabes in southern Tunisia prior to the Second World War.

on it, and the morning after that we drove through a German camp. The soldiers were just getting up, cleaning their teeth, making coffee, that sort of thing, and we sped right past them. After that we headed northwards and made for a series of narrow hills which looked as if they would offer us some cover.

'In our patrol at that stage were about 14 or 15 men, including a Frenchman, Sergeant Taxis, an Arabic speaker. We settled into a wadi, which we thought would provide perfect cover, and went into the routine of camouflaging our vehicles. A fellow soldier, called Johnny Cooper, and I drove right to the top of the wadi and settled there, and the rest were scattered all the way down. We were all shattered, absolutely shattered, and David was determined to carry out a raid that night so it was vital that we got some sleep. We posted sentries and went to sleep. I just went to sleep in my kit, with my boots on next to my jeep.

'It seemed like the next moment that I was awoken by a German Afrika Korps soldier. Johnny also woke up. I looked at Johnny and he went rather green. I realised we'd been jumped. The weapons and jeeps were under tarpaulins and camouflage nets so we couldn't get to them. The only thing was to make a run for it. I thought, I've got to escape or we're prisoners. It was instantaneous, it took a second's deliberation, there was nothing else to do. I kept thinking how did we manage to get caught out when we had sentries, and I think it was because we were all deadbeat.

'Sergeant Taxis was also with us, and as soon as the German moved away, Johnny, Taxis and I made a run for it. We managed to get out of the side of the wadi and ran all the way up to the top of this hill. We had to move very quickly, so we couldn't take anything with us apart from what we were wearing. We had no food, water or weapons. We ran and ran until we couldn't take another step. It was one of the worst experiences that I had ever had, because we could have been shot at any moment and we were running up a very steep hill.

'Further up the hill we found a tiny little gully, and we lay down in it and spent the afternoon there, hoping that they wouldn't find us.

'We could hear a certain amount of noise so we knew what was going on. We knew that they had captured at least some of the patrol. We had no idea if anyone else had escaped, but it was fairly obvious that it had been a disaster.

'The Germans sent out search parties to round up any stragglers. We heard them firing and setting off grenades, and that continued until dark. I had managed to escape with some confidential signals so I buried those just in case we were captured. There was one point when we thought our luck was up because the Germans were getting close. Suddenly an Arab goatherd appeared and the goats surrounded us, which provided us with a bit of cover and a bit of protection from the Germans. But in the late afternoon the Germans drove off with the prisoners.

'We then had to decide what to do. We had no compasses but I had a good idea of the lay of the land. It was a very depressing time, because we assumed that they had captured David and all the others – that meant the SAS had lost its commander and we thought the whole future of the SAS might be in jeopardy.

'Our destination, where we thought we might be able to contact friendly forces, was around 100 miles away. That first night we set off and walked until dawn, and during the day we rested in a cave, which was shown to us by local Arabs. Taxis was able to speak with some of them and they told him that there was water about five miles away. In the evening we started off again and found the well. The water was a bit murky but at least it was water.

'We walked all through the night until day and came across some other, less friendly Arabs, armed with a shotgun, who demanded our clothes. I gave them my battledress jacket and Taxis, who was conversing with them, said, "No, they want every-thing, they want us to give them everything because they are going to kill us." At which point I said, "No fear!" and then they started throwing stones at us and one hit Johnny in the head. The blood was gushing into his eyes and he was temporarily blinded. Taxis and I grabbed him and we made a dash for it across some stones – the Arabs gave chase but they were in bare feet and soon gave up.

'Johnny was a bit shaken up. He had a nasty gash but he was able to carry on. We walked for three days, mainly at night.

'It was later on the third day that we came across another Arab. We were obviously a little bit concerned, given our earlier experience. But he was very friendly and gave us his terribly smelly goatskin bag full of water and told us where we could find some more. He also said, "Be careful, there are some very bad Arab men around." The goatskin bag was leaky. We tied it up with boot laces but the water soon leaked out.

'Later on we found the well and were able to bathe Johnny's wound and have a bit of a wash and a good drink of water. We later came across another camp near the salt lake which we were using as a navigation mark – the place we were trying to get to was at the far edge of the lake, in Tunisia. Taxis was hallucinating and thought the Arabs would attack us. To evade the Arabs we crept out on to the salt and kept a wide birth. The lake was quite easy to walk on in some places, but in others you could easily go through the top layer of crust. We had taken our boots off to make as little noise as possible and it was at that moment that we discovered that Taxis had six toes on one foot, which was rather peculiar.

'Taxis was really struggling at this stage, and the following morning he said, "I can't go on any further, you will have to leave me." It was a sort of Captain Oates moment but obviously we weren't going to leave him. We were just all weak from lack of food. We walked for a few more miles and saw a town in the distance. Obviously, we were slightly cautious because we didn't know whether it was going to be occupied by the Germans. Nevertheless we decided to risk it. As we approached we were greeted by some French West African soldiers, who took us to a barracks where we were given food, water and wine – it was such a relief. The three of us were looked after very well, especially by a French colonel. We had walked for four nights and days and were exhausted. After we rested for an hour or so the colonel told us that we would have to be handed over to the Americans because we were in their zone. Later that day we were taken up to the US headquarters, and their approach was very different to the French.

'We had long hair and beards and were looking very bedraggled. Our feet were in tatters – I don't think we looked very much like soldiers. We were taken to a room and a Colonel Bowman appeared with a squad of soldiers and said, "Keep these men covered, sergeant," because he didn't believe that we were British soldiers; he thought we were Germans or something sinister. We tried to explain, but it was no good. Eventually he said that we would have to go up to Tebessa, in northern Tunisia, where someone would decide what to do with us.

'We were loaded into an ambulance and drove up to Tebessa followed by a jeep full of American soldiers and some newspaper correspondents, who thought they were on to a great story. We moved overnight, so we didn't get much time with the French. It was a pretty wearing time and then we got up to Gafsa where it was rapidly established that we were who we said we were. We were allowed to clean ourselves up, get some more medical attention and I was given an American lieutenant's uniform to wear. After that I was flown back to 8th Army Headquarters and then attached to General Freyberg's New Zealand Division for a short time to act as a guide.

'By that stage we were pretty certain that David had been captured. We were delighted to have escaped but saddened by what fate awaited David. There was always the possibility that he might be executed.'

Mike's part in the desert war had come to an end. He was sent to Palestine to learn how to parachute and would later take part in fighting in Normandy, where he won the Military Cross. Lieutenant-Colonel Stirling had indeed been taken prisoner and, despite escaping several times, he spent the rest of the war in captivity.

The North African campaign eventually came to an end when the German Army was cornered in a pincer movement composed of the British 8th and 1st Armies. The Axis forces surrendered on 13 May 1943, and 275,000 prisoners of war were taken. In the course of the campaign the SAS destroyed 250 aircraft, hundreds of vehicles, and many fuel and ammunition dumps.

Two months after the North African campaign ended, the invasion of Sicily began.

# CHAPTER 5

# Popski's Private Army

## John Campbell's Italian Jobs

*'Victory is never final. Defeat is never fatal.*
*It is courage that counts.'*
WINSTON CHURCHILL

The name, Captain John Campbell, CVO, CBE, MC and Bar, still manages to cause a slight stir amongst the ageing warriors who frequent the Special Forces Club. Although more than 70 years have passed since John first donned an Army uniform, the story of his wartime service within Popski's Private Army remains an inspiration. It is a tale of triumph over adversity, of how a man who was wrongly branded a coward became, according to his commanding officer, 'the most daring of us all'.

I learnt of John's existence through members of the Special Forces Club and tracked him down with the help of the Friends of Popski's Private Army, an association which seeks to ensure that the PPA will not be air-brushed out of history. As well as being the PPA's last surviving officer,* John is also the association's chairman, and we met at his wonderful home near Leominster in Herefordshire.

John greets me with a firm handshake and a warm smile. Despite his age he retains the bearing of an Army officer, and I immediately sense he is eager to talk. After lunch in his dining room, we retire

---

* The actor Christopher Lee was briefly attached as an RAF Intelligence Officer.

to a conservatory and John begins to explain his wartime story. He begins by saying: 'I will tell you something in a few minutes which I have only discussed with a few close friends. I couldn't even begin to talk about it for almost 50 years.'

⋆　　⋆　　⋆

Second Lieutenant Campbell arrived at the 8th Army's El Alamein perimeter – the Allied front line – in the autumn of 1942, in the weeks before Operation Lightfoot,* General Montgomery's two-pronged attack against the Axis forces.

His fresh complexion, innocence and sense of optimism seemed at odds with the drudgery of life on the front line in North Africa, where days seemed to merge seamlessly into one another.

John had spent many hours contemplating how he would cope in the heat of battle, amid the death and destruction, watching men die terrible deaths whilst being able to kill an enemy at close quarters, if necessary, with a knife, spade or even with his bare hands. Above all else, John hoped that courage would not desert him. Like many young men in the Second World War, he wholly believed that it was better to die in battle than live with the shame of being labelled a coward.

Courage was something every officer was expected to demonstrate in the heat of battle, especially those serving in the 7th Battalion, The Argyll and Sutherland Highlanders, the unit to which the young Lieutenant Campbell had been posted.

The battalion's commanding officer was Lieutenant-Colonel Lorne Campbell,† a man who had courage in abundance. He had already been mentioned in dispatches and won the Distinguished Service Order while fighting in France. He would go on to receive a bar to his DSO and win the Victoria Cross the following year.

When John arrived at the front, Colonel Campbell shook his hand as if he were an old friend and welcomed him to the battal-

---

* The second Battle of El Alamein, 23 October to 4 November 1942.

† Commanding Officer, 7th Argylls, awarded the Victoria Cross at the battle of Wadi Akarit.

*John Campbell*

ion, before adding, 'You've arrived just in time. We are going to attack in half an hour. Just pick up a rifle and join in. You'll soon learn what to do.'

But the attack was cancelled, and while many soldiers were relieved John was frustrated at missing out on the chance to make his name so early on in his military career.

★ ★ ★

Before the war John had lived by his own admission a comfortable, classically middle-class life. He was educated at St Anthony's preparatory school, Eastbourne, and Cheltenham College. His father's plan was that John would join ICI, the chemical production company, but following the German invasion of Poland John's only ambition was to join the Army.

At the outbreak of war in September 1939 John was reading for a physics, chemistry and mathematics degree at St Andrews University in Scotland. His scientific studies were cut short and John joined the East Kent Regiment the following year as a private soldier. Once he had passed his basic training John was selected for officer training and was commissioned into the Argyll and Sutherland Highlanders on 5 August 1941.

John was one of many young officers who had watched the desert campaign from afar with the excitement of a young boy about to attend his first football match.

After the fall of France, North Africa was 'the only show in town'. The campaign began with the Italian declaration of war in June 1940, a move which gave rise to a series of battles which would eventually see the Italian army in North Africa destroyed and the subsequent arrival of the Afrika Korps, under the command of Erwin Rommel. The months that ensued resulted in a series of battles for Libya and parts of Egypt, leading to victories and defeats for both sides. By October 1942 the Germans were on the back foot and Lieutenant-General Bernard Montgomery was in charge of British forces.

The campaign also saw the first use of what became known as the 'private armies' such as the Long Range Desert Group (1940), the Special Air Service (1941) and No. 1 Demolition Squadron (1942), otherwise known as Popski's Private Army – another smaller raiding unit, also operating and intelligence-collecting behind enemy lines in the desert.

John quickly settled into life as a desert infantry officer and learned how to cope with the daytime temperatures, freezing nights, swarms of flies, indescribable boredom and, worst of all, the monotony of Army rations.

Four days after arriving at the front, a private soldier arrived slightly out of breath at John's slit trench and said, 'Sir, the commanding officer sends his compliments and requests your presence at battalion HQ.'

Making his way to the briefing tent which formed part of the battalion headquarters, John wondered what unknown misde-

meanour he had made that had incurred the wrath of his commanding officer. The young second lieutenant was ushered into the tent,
where his CO was waiting for him.

'I'm sending you on a standing patrol, John,' Colonel Campbell
said calmly as he strode around the tent. 'You'll be moving out just
before last light. Take a section of men with you and move out to
that small rise you can see in the distance. You'll need to move
quickly but you'll be in dead ground, you'll be quite safe. I want
you to take a telephone with you, the signallers will explain the
detail, and report everything you can see. I want to know what
Jerry's up to, and you're going to be my eyes and ears. It's a straightforward job so there shouldn't be any problems.'

As John left the CO's briefing tent he was perspiring heavily but
excited at the prospect of leading his first patrol.

'I think my commanding officer was absolutely delighted that
there was another Campbell in the Mess,' he recalls, 'so he gave me
this job – which was really pretty straightforward – as a way of
proving myself.'

John outlined the plan to his less than enthusiastic section of six
men, most of whom were already weary of desert life, and explained
what was required of them. 'We're going to move out to a ridge
line as part of a standing patrol ordered by the commanding officer.
We will carry a field telephone out to a fixed position and lay a
cable as we move forward, so that we will have direct communications once we arrive in position. We will remain in position until
dawn, reporting on any enemy activity. We'll be moving through
dead ground so we should be able to get into position without any
trouble at all.'

The men prepared for the operation. Weapons were cleaned and
checked, ammunition pouches were loaded with extra magazines
and grenades, and water bottles were filled. John ordered them all
to have a final meal before departing, as there would be little
opportunity for hot food once the soldiers were in position.

At the allotted hour the section extinguished cigarettes and
moved off into the desert as the sun began its steady descent
beneath the horizon.

The soldiers moved gingerly in single file, trying not to step on the electric cable being played out by the signaller, when suddenly on the far left of the Argylls' position, where the Middlesex Regiment were based, a Vickers machine-gun opened up, sending a stream of tracer in an arc of fire over their heads towards the German trenches. Yellow Very lights lit up the darkening sky and the soldiers froze.

'Don't worry, lads,' John encouraged, 'it's only someone getting a bit windy.' But almost immediately the enemy returned fire towards the Middlesex Regiment. At first the bullets from the Spandau machine-gun passed harmlessly overhead. But after a few moments' firing some began to fall amongst John's section.

'The chap who was winding the telephone out was hit at an angle on his tin hat and was sort of knocked out. He was lying on the ground, dazed and confused, and almost instantaneously another soldier was struck in the calf and he went down, and you could hear the bullets zipping just overhead. The Germans hadn't seen us, they were just firing on a fixed line and we were caught in the middle.

'It was at that point a corporal shouted, "Come on, boys, let's get out of this. That bloody fool will get us all killed." I looked round, only to see my patrol running back to our lines.

'I shouted, "Stop, don't go," but they didn't stop. They all ran, taking the injured with them, and I was left alone, so eventually I had to follow them into our lines and face the awful prospect of having to explain myself.

'When I got back to our lines my company commander appeared and I could immediately sense that he thought that I had panicked and lost it. It was an utterly dreadful moment – and that was a view which prevailed amongst many in the battalion until long after the war.'

John had considered seeking out the offending corporal and challenging him on his actions as well as reporting his clear cowardice in the face of the enemy, but he assumed, probably wrongly, that any attempt to blame the corporal for the mission's failure would backfire on him.

'There was no question about it but my reputation within the battalion had gone. No one actually said anything to me, but I could tell by a variety of ways. There was a general silence when I was around, there were looks and mutterings. It was cool and unchummy. I felt that if I tried to explain things I would have only made matters worse, so no one ever knew the truth.'

That experience still pains John today, more than 70 years after the event. The incident recalled to my memory a lecture I attended during my Army career given by General Sir Peter de la Billière, a former 22 SAS commander who served as a young officer during the Korean War.

The lecture focused on the subject of leadership, and Sir Peter recalled an incident during the Korean War when one of his young riflemen refused to take part in a fighting patrol. 'I drew my revolver, went over to the tent where the young soldier was and told him that if he didn't join the patrol I would shoot him on the spot.' The soldier joined the patrol and subsequently survived the war.

Given the nature of John's dilemma on the battlefield, I asked him whether he thought about shooting the corporal who had inspired the panic.

'If we had been in the thick of battle, then I think that course of action might have been appropriate, but we weren't. We were caught in a crossfire so it was never an option. I was tempted to draw my pistol and shoot the corporal but I couldn't.'

John learned to live with the unfair reputation he had acquired and set about trying to prove himself at every opportunity.

A few weeks later during one of the many advances to contact conducted by the 8th Army during Operation Lightfoot, John thought all his problems had come to an end.

Operation Lightfoot was the second battle of El Alamein and a major turning point in the Western Desert Campaign. The operation was a success, and it ended the Axis hopes of occupying Egypt and beyond and ultimately taking control of the Persian oil fields, which Hitler needed to fuel his military ambitions.

'We were moving across no man's land during one battle and the Germans started shelling us, and just to one side of me there was a huge explosion and I was knocked to the ground. In that instant I thought to myself, "I'm dead and now I'm a war hero." And, briefly, I suddenly felt very content and not at all afraid. But obviously I wasn't dead – I was still alive, and just stunned by the effects of the blast, so I picked myself up and pushed on feeling somewhat disappointed.'

Despite John's efforts to clear his name through demonstrating his fearlessness in battle, he soon discovered that the old adage 'mud sticks' was very true when he found himself being heavily shelled while manning a forward observation post.

'The position was supposed to be camouflaged to enable us to spot for the artillery, but at some point we must have been spotted because we started taking very heavy fire. Shells were bursting around us, and so I informed the battalion headquarters that we were taking very heavy fire and that our position had obviously been compromised. As I was listening to the radio, waiting for a response, I heard someone say, "It's that yellow bastard Campbell."'

And so John's war in the desert continued, but there was one final humiliation he still had to suffer, and it came at the moment of victory in May 1943, when the Axis powers in North Africa were defeated. Even before the end of the campaign, rumours began to circulate amongst the troops that the 8th Army would be involved in the invasion of Sicily before the summer was over.

'At the end of the battle of El Alamein, when we were in Tunisia, Lorne Campbell asked to see me. He told me to sit, offered me a cup of tea and I had a sense that I wasn't about to be the recipient of good news. The CO by this stage was a living legend, having won the Victoria Cross. Instead of giving me good news he said: "Not everyone can be a great performer in war, and I think you have many qualities, and never feel that you cannot turn up to reunions of the 51st Highland Division or that sort of thing, just remember you have lots of qualities, but I am going to recommend that you are given a non-combatant post." He said it in a very nice way, which was even more humiliating for me.'

John pauses, lost in thought, perhaps remembering the exact moment of the conversation. I can see that simply talking about this event is physically painful. After a few seconds have passed I ask John if I can include the incident in the book. 'Yes,' he responds, with his wonderful smile returning to his face, 'the shame of that moment has long since passed.'

*   *   *

While the rest of the battalion later departed in preparation for the Sicily landings, John remained behind in North Africa and wouldn't see active service again for almost a year. Eventually he was posted back to the 8th Army, which by this stage was making slow progress up through Italy, and on the voyage from Algiers to Naples he met an old friend who was about to change his life.

'By one of those flukes that happen in life, I was having a pre-dinner drink on that first night on board when another officer walked into the bar and I immediately recognised him as Peter Glass, a chum with whom I had been at prep school many years earlier. Over the next three days I explained how my Army career had suffered because of events which had nothing to do with me, and he said, "Why don't you join the special forces?" I had never heard of any such organisation, but the more their role was explained to me the more fascinated I became. I thought, "That's what I want to do, that will be a new beginning," but I had absolutely no idea as to how I was going to achieve it.'

John arrived in the chaos of Naples in March 1944 with thousands of other soldiers during the midst of the battle for Monte Cassino. The operation consisted of four costly battles fought by the Allies against the Germans with the intention of breaking through the enemy defences and seizing Rome. The battle last four months and one day, with more than 65,000 German and Allied casualties. It remains one of the most contentious battles of the Second World War and has often been described as a 'hollow victory'.

John was initially stationed at the infantry depot hopefully awaiting posting for a front-line unit. The camp was a foul, dirty, unpleasant place, full of soldiers and officers with little or no combat experience but who were only too keen to act as if they were war heroes to a man.

Almost immediately John fell foul of the adjutant after borrowing an army truck to go and search for his equipment, from which he had been separated.

When he eventually found his kit, he discovered that someone for some unknown reason had placed a green tin marked 'Eating Chocolate' inside his bed roll. On opening the box, John discovered that it was full of demonstration booby traps. Although fascinating, the training aids were of no use to John; so, with some trepidation, he decided to give them to the depot training major, a man with a fearsome reputation. The officer had created a sort of museum of battlefield paraphernalia to help in the training of new officers.

'I knocked on the door on which was the sign "R. Hamilton, Major. Training Officer", and there was this almighty roar: "Come in!"'

'Major Hamilton was one of those officers who had served on the front line in the First World War but was now deemed to be too old for combat in this war and so decided to make everyone else's life a misery. I walked in and he looked at me as though I was the lowest form of life. He shouted: "What do you want?" The major was sitting with a pot of tea in front of him, eating a slice of cake, and he was clearly angry that he had been disturbed.

'I held the box out in front of me and said, "Sir, I have something which might interest you."

'Well, what is it?' responded the major. John handed over the green tin, and on opening the lid a smile illuminated the major's face like that of a child at Christmas. 'Do you think I could have one or two of these things for my museum?' the major asked, hesitantly.

'They are no use to me,' answered John. 'I thought you might want the whole lot to use on the courses you run for new officers.'

John immediately became the officer's 'dear boy' and was fed a healthy slice of cake and a much-needed refreshing cup of tea.

'Now tell me,' Major Hamilton asked with the air of a kind uncle speaking to his favourite nephew. 'Do you have any problems I could help with?'

'Well, I am rather keen on getting into the special forces.'

'Yes, I can see that,' said the major. 'You're just the type. I can help you with that. Finish up and we'll take a visit to the depot postings officer. I'll see what I can do.'

Outside the postings office was a long line of young lieutenants and captains all waiting for a brief minute with one of the busiest officers in the depot. The training major ignored the queue of tutting officers, knocked on the door and marched straight into the office.

'Bill, I've got a brilliant young officer who would make a superb candidate for the special forces; speaks Italian like a native.'*

'Well,' said Bill, 'I know the adjutant of No. 1 Demolition Squadron, otherwise known as Popski's Private Army. It could be right up his tree. I'll send a wire straight away.'

Three days later John was sent on a mountain course as part of the depot training programme. Over two days he learnt the basics of navigation and climbing. He was starting to wonder if the wire sent by the training officer had been ignored when, on the second day of the course, he was told to pack his kit and be ready to report to No. 1 Demolition Squadron's headquarters, located a few miles away from the depot training area. An hour or so later an officer appeared, wearing a black beret with a cap badge the like of which John had never previously seen, and whisked him off in a jeep along the road to Naples.

'We soon arrived at the bar of the San Carlo Opera House in Naples, which had become the British Officers Club. There I met Jean Caneri, a French Corsican, the second-in-command of the squadron, who made me feel very welcome and told me to call him Jean.'

★    ★    ★

Popski's Private Army, or No. 1 Demolition Squadron, became operational in December 1942, with the aim of attacking and disrupting Field-Marshal Rommel's fuel supplies ahead of General

---

* John learnt Italian while serving in North Africa.

Montgomery's advance at El Alamein. The organisation's founder was the then Major Vladimir Peniakoff, a Belgian born to Russian parents. Having previously served in the First World War as a private soldier in the French artillery, he volunteered for active service in 1939 and was commissioned as a Second Lieutenant into the Libyan Arab Force in 1940 at the age of 43. Peniakoff had lived in Egypt before the war and had learnt Arabic. Prior to forming PPA he created the Libyan Arab Force Commando and operated behind enemy lines for several months in 1942. After the unit was disbanded he briefly served with the Long Range Desert Group and was subsequently awarded the Military Cross for his numerous successful desert operations. It was during Peniakoff's service with the LRDG that he came to be called Popski. Legend has it that LRDG radio operators gave him the nickname because it was easier to say than Peniakoff.

Lieutenant-Colonel Shan Hackett, who was responsible for coordinating the various 'special units' which existed within the 8th Army some time later gave Popski the opportunity of creating another independent unit. Popski was having trouble deciding on a name. He wanted something short and memorable but that gave no clue as to its nature. During a meeting in Cairo, Shan Hackett, who was becoming increasingly exasperated with Popski over the naming of the group, said: 'You had better find a name quick, or we shall call you Popski's Private Army,' at which the Belgian said, 'I'll have it.' In the end the new unit's official name was No. 1 Demolition Squadron, PPA.

Popski had very strong ideas on how his new force, which then numbered around 20 men, would be run. PPA, he decided, would be run along similar lines to the LRDG, which he so admired. There were to be no strict forms of military discipline, no saluting or drill, and all ranks were expected to act in a professional manner at all times; those who were found unsuitable were returned to their units forthwith. Popski was also convinced that the unit would achieve success if it remained small and mobile but was capable of delivering a very heavy punch. Hence Popski set about selecting men who were self-reliant, intelligent and fearless. Like the major-

Noreen Riols

Jimmy Patch

Corran Purdon

Mike Sadler

John Campbell

Leonard Ratcliff

Bill Towill

Fred Bailey

Harry Verlander

John Sharp

ity of the special forces groups that fought in the desert at the time, PPA used a variety of vehicles, which were stripped down to the bare essentials, for speed and manoeuvrability, with the main armament being either Lewis guns or twin gas-operated .303 Vickers machine-guns.

Following the 8th Army's success in North Africa, PPA began preparing for the invasion of Sicily, but its role in the operation was cancelled. In September 1943 PPA arrived in Italy and following a string of successful operations was authorised to increase its size to 80 all ranks. The organisation was now based around three patrols: P (for Popski, later renamed R), B (for Bob Yunnie) and S (for South Africa, after the South African officer Lieutenant Reeve-Walker), each of which consisted of 18 men in six jeeps fitted with .50 and .303 Browning machine-guns. The unit also consisted of a tactical HQ patrol known as Blitz as well as the HQ element.

Every member of the patrol was trained to used all the various machine-guns and was equipped with a tommy-gun or rifle, a .45 semi-automatic pistol and a fighting knife.

The unit was trained in parachuting, mountain warfare, amphibious landings, intelligence gathering, demolition, counter-demolition and reconnaissance, and everyone who joined had to revert to the most junior rank – private for soldiers and lieutenant for officers.

★　　★　　★

When John arrived in San Gregorio, where PPA were now based, Popski was away somewhere else, and during that time and he and Jean Caneri became very firm friends.

'I think he immediately took to me and I recognised a kindred spirit. I began to feel quite comfortable and almost, after all this time, that I had finally found a place in the Army in which I felt at home.'

John settled into life in San Gregorio with his new family and felt sure that he would be accepted, but when Popski arrived John's dreams were crushed.

In his book *Popski's Private Army*, Peniakoff described the meeting as follows: 'One evening I came home from a trip to Caserta and found waiting for me a young captain, John Campbell, who had come from the Infantry Reinforcement Training Depot to offer his services. For the occasion he had put on his best clothes; apart from the hair which hadn't been cut in six months, he looked neat enough in a tunic, trews and rather dainty shoes. Tired, hungry and a little short in temper, I was not impressed; Campbell was tongue-tied, said the wrong things and I turned him down. Caneri took me aside and said: "I think you should give him a try. I have talked to him this afternoon and he seems all right. You have frightened him."

'I looked again at the big awkward lad in his tight clothes and told him: "We have an exercise starting in an hour's time. Without going into detail now, it involves finding your way across country with a companion and walking about 60 miles carrying 40 pounds in a pack and your weapons. The trip has to be done in record time, as it is by way of being a race. Go on the exercise – if you come back in good time I shall take you in PPA."'

John was now faced with the realisation that his Army future and happiness hung in the balance. Illness in the desert had affected his fitness and he was about to face the toughest physical test of his life so far.

'Luckily for me, I was teamed with Jock Cameron, a Scottish gamekeeper, and another chap called Sam Cowperthwaite, but my main concern was my physical fitness, on which my various illnesses in the desert had taken their toll. I hauled my pack on to my back and set off, with Jock leading the way. After 100 yards I was already breathing heavily and doubted I had the strength to complete the task. But Jock managed to pick a route which kept us high in the mountains and we rarely dropped into the valleys and so saved both time and energy. After four days we arrived back at the headquarters in first place and I felt sure that I would be accepted into the unit.

'But my achievement had absolutely no effect on Popski, who I think was hoping that I would fail. When Jean gave him the results and told him that we finished as one of the first teams, Popski said, "I still don't want him." But Jean again was insistent: "You can't make him take a test and when he comes first say, 'I don't want him.' You can't do that, Popski, you must reconsider." Popski must have known that he was in the wrong and, rather like a chided schoolboy, he said, "Well, all right then."

'And that was that. I was in, and I immediately became the adjutant and I was absolutely delighted, but I still believed I had to prove myself to Popski, who I think still had his doubts. I think I impressed him, before I became a patrol commander, by becoming a first-class scrounger. At that stage my battles weren't fought against the Germans but against quartermasters, who wanted to hang on to kit and equipment rather than distribute it to the men doing the fighting.'

Popski's force had no allegiance to any specific army formation and answered only to 8th Army Headquarters. An unintended consequence of such independence was that PPA was often short of equipment, weapons and spares. By the autumn of 1944, following the initial success of D-Day, virtually all forms of equipment – from uniforms to rations and even ammunition – were in short supply in the Italian theatre of operations because the main effort went into supporting the breakout from Normandy. But equipment shortages were often imposed by quartermasters operating in the safety of the rear echelon, miles behind the front line, who, according to John, had plenty of kit but for some peculiar reason believed that stores should be stored rather than being issued to men.

'I developed a reputation for getting stores and extra kit which we needed, such as spares or replacement wheels or even new jeeps, if one had been damaged. The Italian campaign had become a bit of a backwater and everything was being sent to Normandy. I developed this routine whenever I visited the 8th Army Headquarters. There was one occasion where 12 jeeps were destroyed during a failed amphibious mission, Operation Astrolabe, when a landing craft got stuck on a sand bar and had to be blown up. I went to different quartermasters with the same story and replaced the 12 jeeps twice over. The vehicles were all lined up, gleaming and brand new, outside the headquarters when Popski returned from the failed mission.'

As in the North African campaign, a jeep was worth its weight in gold. It was, according to John, a 'go anywhere and do anything' vehicle. PPA, like other units who used them, would modify vehicles to meet the demands of the terrain. In Italy, PPA jeeps were fitted with a snorkel over the exhaust which allowed them to drive through rivers.

'As far as we were concerned it was our secret weapon. The driver sat on the left and on the other side was the .50 calibre heavy machine-gun. We also had extra fuel, radios, first aid, masses of ammunition, rations, water and vehicle spares.'

The standard jeep capacity was 5cwt, but PPA jeeps were fitted with modified suspension and carried 20cwt (1 ton). Each jeep was also usually modified to take two spare wheels at the back, making them immediately identifiable as PPA vehicles.

'We wore whatever made us comfortable and there was little attention paid to wearing the correct uniform. I tended to wear a beret and battledress, but it would often depend on the weather. I always carried a pistol and had a tommy-gun nearby too.

'I was extremely enthusiastic about life when I was in Italy with PPA, and I soon managed to put my calamitous start to the war to the back of my mind. I tried not to actively think about it, but it was always there, I suppose, hanging over me.

'I was enjoying working in the headquarters, but what I really wanted to do was to take command of one of the patrols and see some action; after all, that was why one joined the special forces.'

In the summer of 1944 John finally got his wish and took command of S Patrol after its former commander was injured. Reeve-Walker was wounded in the stomach after shooting wildly at something he thought he had seen and was hit in the stomach by a ricochet. He was later court-martialled for refusing to obey an order after being ambushed by the Germans. The incident left him crushed, and he never fully recovered from the blow. After the war he committed suicide.

Commanding a PPA patrol was a steep learning curve, but John quickly grew into the job. Largely thanks to his loyal second-in-command Sergeant Bill O'Leary, who was the epitome of the tough non-commissioned officer and gave him able support, John's confidence was starting to grow and he was becoming increasingly bold.

John soon realised that detailed intelligence work, good reconnaissance and planning were vital for special forces operations, but so was luck. A whispered word by a pro-German villager who had noticed a PPA patrol in the area, or a dog barking after picking up the scent of a reconnaissance patrol, could have a profound effect on the outcome of an operation.

Popski would always try and keep two patrols conducting operations at any one time, with the third resting or re-equipping. The rugged terrain meant that the jeep took a fearful battering almost every day, and after a two-week patrol would have to undergo extensive maintenance. Although it was relatively rare for the patrols to become involved in contacts with the German troops, the stress of operating up to and beyond the front line, always at risk of ambush or air attack, would also take its toll and the patrol members would often return to their headquarters physically and mentally fatigued.

\*    \*    \*

By the winter of 1944 the 8th Army had become drastically overstretched through casualties suffered while pushing deep into the north of Italy. On paper, the 8th Army still consisted of the same number of divisions, but those divisions were so reduced in numbers, especially in infantry troops, that they were effectively brigades. The 1st Canadians Corp was particularly badly hit, and one infantry battalion which John came across consisted of just 90 soldiers. With the situation desperate, many cavalry and armoured car regiments were forced to dismount their troops to hold the line.

At the beginning of November 1944 PPA became part of 'Porterforce', a group of small units based around the 27th Lancers and led by Lieutenant-Colonel Andrew Horsburgh-Porter. The force also included elements of the 28th Garibaldi Brigade of Italian partisans, who were mainly communists, and quickly developed a reputation for being robust fighters.

The force was based in the Pineta di Classe pine forests on the Adriatic Coast, south of the town of Ravenna. The aim was to hold a three-mile front – had the Germans known that the front was held by such a small force it is likely they would have attempted to break through the British line.

'The only way I felt we could really have any effect was to try and give the impression that we, that is the British and the Canadians, were a much larger force than what the Germans thought was there. So I set about charging round the woods leaving tracks all over the place so that any spotter planes would report back that there was lots of movement. We also had one self-propelled artillery gun, which left track marks and sounded like a tank and, we hoped, gave the impression that there was a lot of armour in the area.

'Our days were spent very much doing our own thing, a law only unto ourselves. In the night we would set up camp somewhere in the forest, unknown to the enemy and therefore quite safe. But the weather was cold and wet and after two weeks I think we were all getting a bit fed up. We had hoped that with all of our firing and movement, those Germans closest to the front line might think twice and withdraw to safer positions, but there had been no sign of any such movement. Then, on the day of my 23th birthday, we discovered that our plan seemed to have worked.

'We had been in the area before but had been fired at by the Germans; this time however, it was quiet. We crossed the canal in a small rubber boat and discovered that the area was empty. We pushed on further to a large farmhouse occupied by Italians who informed us that the Germans had abandoned one of their posts that very morning. So, pleased with our plan of bluff, we sat down and tucked into a lavish supper of garlic sausages and red wine.

'In another house the following day we discovered that the Germans based there had also evacuated their position in a hurry, leaving behind a couple of legs of mutton, some ammunition and a rifle. The mutton provided another first-class feed, after which I attempted to contact B Patrol, who were to our left. After having travelled just a few yards from our house, the front left wheel of my jeep was blown off by a mine. We worked for an hour to put on a spare before moving off again, this time with me walking ahead looking out for mines. After about 100 yards the jeep struck another mine. Being blown up twice in one night was enough for anyone, so we gave up and returned to the house on foot. When we returned the following day to repair the damage I saw my large footprint just an inch from another mine. That night the engineers built a bridge over the canal, which was immediately called Popski's Private Bridge. We crossed the following day and took up position in a farmhouse, with two jeeps positioned in front of the house with guns ready to fire in the event of an attack.

'But within a few hours the Germans had spotted us and artillery shells were landing close by, so I moved my jeep to the rear in the belief that it might be safe.

'That afternoon a forward observation officer from the artillery regiment in support of the Lancers came up to use our farmhouse as an observation post to fire off a few rounds, and after he had done so departed. Almost immediately after he had gone, a German 88 fired off several rounds, one of which came in through one of the upper windows, flew down the stairs, burst through the door and smashed into my jeep, which had been positioned there for reasons of safety. After being blown up three times in the space of 24 hours, I acquired the nickname "Bulldozer".'

S Patrol, like the rest of PPA, were itching for a bit of action, and John was keen to experiment in some 'cloak and dagger operations'. A German outpost, a farm called La Favorita, was holding up Porterforce's advance, so John set about formulating a plan to capture it. Guerino Ravaioli, one of the partisans attached to the force, who had become a good friend of John's, conducted a series of reconnaissance trips around the farm by posing as a milkman. Every morning the partisan dressed in civilian clothes and, unarmed, would walk up to the farm and sell the Germans some milk. In doing so, he managed to gain detailed intelligence on the enemy's strength and routine, as well as secure routes through the marshes and minefields. He discovered that at night nearly all the Germans were on guard, but during the morning they would wearily return to the house leaving just one man on guard.

'Every half-decent army in the world always "stands to" in the minutes before dawn in expectation of a first light attack, and the Germans were no different. The British did the same, and I knew that wonderful sense of relief when no attack was mounted. I decided to exploit this weakness and wait for the Germans to be relaxed and at ease, enjoying their breakfast, before striking.

'Guerino said that he had found a route which would allow us to creep down behind where the Germans took up their guard positions and then hide up until full daylight. I also knew from intelligence we had gleaned from partisans that the house behind the German post was empty and did not have any windows facing the German lines.

'I explained the plan to Popski and told him that success was certain because of the mistakes the Germans had made in choosing their position. He was reluctant at first because we knew that there would be at least ten Germans in the house, and if they put up a half decent fight the raid might fail or, worse, we might lose men, which we could ill afford, but in the end he relented. His only stipulation was that there should be no firing, which meant that we had to take all of the Germans prisoner.

'I briefed S Patrol and everyone was really excited and itching to do some real special forces work. The mission took place on 13 November. The patrol carefully moved into position following a route proved by Guerino. We moved into position and waited for the tell-tale sign of smoke coming up through the chimney which meant they would be preparing breakfast. I gave them a little extra time to relax and then we stormed through the front door.

'Bill O'Leary went in first and we all went in behind him. Our hearts were racing and the adrenaline was pumping, but I had great faith that this operation was going to work without a shot being fired. As we burst through the door there was this look of disbelief on their tired faces and one of them shouted out in German, "Don't shoot, don't shoot!" I have to say that they were so terrified that we felt sorry for them. Bill rushed upstairs and came face to face with a Jerry armed with a machine-gun. He knocked it out of his hands and rushed into another room where some of the Germans were still asleep. It was a very brave act because he was on his own.

'We rounded them up and took them away pretty sharpish. We tidied up everything so there didn't look as if there had been any sort of attack or struggle. We knew that a ration party was coming up later that day and we wanted it to appear as if these 10 Germans had just disappeared.

'Popski was waiting 400 yards away and he was delighted, because capturing 10 Germans like that was quite unusual.

'For me the real success of this operation was the effect I believed this would have on the Germans' morale. I often wondered what the ration party would have thought when they arrived at the farm and the place was empty. The impact on the high command must have also been significant too, because they probably thought the whole post had deserted, and that would have filtered down to other troops in the area.'

For his actions Corporal O'Leary was awarded the Military Medal, while another member of the patrol, Dennis 'Hodge' Hodgson, Bill's best friend from the Parachute Regiment, was mentioned in dispatches.

The operation worked wonders for the morale of the entire PPA, resulting in the two other patrols also wanting to get in on the act, such was the competition within the unit. Some two weeks later Popski asked John and S Patrol to begin planning a similar mission to capture a German unit based in a customs house and tower complex at the mouth of the Fiumi Uniti. The tower provided the Germans with great visibility along the coast and also guarded the left flank of the enemy force in Ravenna.

John eagerly agreed but also immediately realised that this next mission would be an entirely different undertaking from La Favorita.

'The building, the Caserna Dei Fiumi Uniti, occupied by the Germans was situated about one hundred yards from the mouth of the Fiumi Uniti, the river surrounding Ravenna and around 4,000 yards from our location.

'During the recce we had to cross some very marshy land. I stepped into the swamp and began to sink and sink – and only stopped sinking when the water reached my neck. We crossed the swamp and moved on to a thin strip of sand and then up into a scrubby forest, where we saw a house about 90 yards from the fort. We crawled up to the house, which was full of civilians; at which point they, the Italians, spotted us and one came over, I suppose to find out who we were. We knew they would be friendly but they could have also exposed our position.

'I stood up to chat to him from behind a wall. I was wearing my beret, which had a distinctive silhouette, and Bill was furious and said, "Get your fuckin' 'ead down." But instead I leant over the wall and took off the Italian peasant's hat and put it on. I couldn't help laughing but Bill couldn't see the funny side and was fuming.

'I started chatting away in Italian, trying to get as much intelligence from this chap as I could as quickly as possible. He explained that the barbed wire which I could see in front of the post ringed the entire house, which, he estimated, was occupied by around 20 soldiers. He also divulged that a German four-man patrol would walk down to the beach at around midnight and that their morning routine consisted of washing by the pump at around 8am.'

John and Bill monitored the movement at the customs house for the next 48 hours before returning to their lines to discuss the operation with Popski. Clearly impressed with the intelligence gathered, he told John that he wanted the mission launched the following evening. Everyone in the patrol was fully aware of the risks – the reconnaissance, although successful, provided an incomplete picture of the German position and, to add to their worries, the night would be lit by a full moon.

Briefing began early. The patrol cleaned their weapons, checked radios and primed grenades. John and Bill decided that it would be best to move in light order, but that each man should carry extra ammunition.

'The following night we set out around midnight and rowed along the canal in a couple of rubber boats while Lance-Corporal Monty "Tich" Reece moved along the bank reeling out a telephone line which would provide our communications back to Jean and the headquarters.

'We knew the area was mined and the ground was soft, so the last thing we wanted to do was to either set off a mine or leave lines of footprints.

'When we arrived at one of the checkpoints, a small house, we rested for a few hours while we waited for the German patrol to come and go. At around 3am we moved off and followed the Germans' footprints. As we moved forwards towards the German lines, the fort came into view, so we crawled for about 100 yards and then began to move on a course up to the cowshed. Had the Germans being watching the area closely they might have spotted us, but we made it to the cowshed without a problem. We climbed in through a window and prepared for an attack, which fortunately never came. As we settled in everybody seemed to start coughing, and I mean everybody. It was a terrifyingly tense time, and I think for me possibly the most frightening I had experienced during the whole of the war. The shed was only about 30 feet from the house and I was utterly convinced the Germans would hear us.

'Around dawn, a door opened and an Alsatian was let out – and I thought that's it, the dog will smell us immediately and begin barking and the game will be up. I could see us fighting our way out and taking lots of casualties, but after 10 minutes or so the door to the customs house opened, a German soldier leant out and whistled, and the dog ran back inside wagging its tail.

'The relief inside was tangible – for me it was probably the greatest relief I have ever known. It was then a case of waiting for the smoke to appear from the chimney – my breakfast theory. At around 8.30am we leapt through the window of the shed and formed up outside the front door before rushing in with tommy-guns at the ready.

'We burst through the door and shouted "Hands up!" in German. Jerry was absolutely terrified and I think at that point they thought we intended to shoot them all. Some of them were having breakfast while others were still lying in their beds. They shouted "Don't shoot, don't shoot!" – which of course we didn't. There was a great sense of confidence and jubilation at what we had achieved, because once again we captured them without a shot having been fired.'

The Germans were searched and corralled into a corner of the farm, at which point John made it clear that they did not intend to kill them but they would be taken prisoner and treated well.

'Once the area was secure we sent the coded message "Send chocolate" over the radio which was the signal for Jean to come to us in the DUKW* and collect the 18 prisoners.

'R Patrol (its name had just been changed from B Patrol) came in and occupied the house and we returned to our headquarters feeling immensely proud of what we had achieved. The entire plan had gone like clockwork and there were no casualties. But to our utter amazement the Germans kept coming. An orderly came along with an officer's greatcoat, which had been repaired, and he was nabbed. Then an hour or so later someone came to look for the orderly and he never returned.

'A patrol came up some time later and they were captured. A few hours later, a German officer, Leutnant Jung, arrived to find out what had happened to his men and he was also taken prisoner. By the time the post was abandoned around 70 Germans had been captured.'

The German forces were so disheartened by the day's events that all similar posts south of the river were withdrawn.

Both operations were heralded as a great success, and for planning and executing the operation John was awarded the Military Cross. After the trauma of being labelled a coward in the desert, John, for the first time since the war started, felt pride in his achievement.

The following morning, the jeeps were loaded on to the DUKWs and R Patrol entered Ravenna together with the Canadians, while S Patrol pushed north to Viserbo. Fighting had

* Designation for a US amphibious vehicle, colloquially known as a Duck.

turned much of it into rubble, like many of the towns, villages and hamlets, but it served as a good headquarters for the patrol while they rested after spending weeks living in the forest of Ravenna.

On 9 December 1944 Popski was seriously injured when the Germans launched a counter-attack in the Ravenna area. A small unit from the 27th Lancers found themselves surrounded by the enemy and reported that the situation was becoming increasingly desperate and would probably result in their surrender by the evening. Popski decided that urgent action was required and led a party of five PPA jeeps. The Germans numbered some 200, but Popski was undeterred and with covering fire from a troop of tanks 600 yards away pushed up to within 30 yards of the enemy, who were well dug in on a canal bank, and opened fired. The five jeeps blazed away for 50 minutes, firing some 25,000 rounds. The Germans fled, leaving 80 dead, but Popski had been seriously injured. He had been hit by a bullet in the right hand and his left had been all but severed by a rocket-propelled grenade.

'Popski's report of the incident barely mentioned his role in the battle but we later discovered from Charlie Burrows, another member of the unit who witnessed the incident, that Popski was magnificent and fought off 10 Germans single-handedly with a pistol and a bag full of grenades. Charlie also told us that Popski did not stop firing until the Germans had fled. Popski was evacuated for treatment and I later met up with him when he had recovered from his injuries. He had been given a hook as a prosthetic limb, which of course he loved because it all added to the Popski mystique.'

\*     \*     \*

By April 1945, as the war was drawing to a close, John and S Patrol found themselves approaching the small town of Vigonovo, which is situated directly east of the ancient city of Padua, around half an hour west of Venice.

On 29 April the six jeeps of S Patrol were cruising along a deserted road when the air exploded with the sound of artillery fire.

'At first we thought we were coming under attack, and then we realised that it was the sound of an artillery battery very close by. It was an absolutely colossal roar. We knew straight away that it must have been German. We pushed on a little bit further until we could see the battery was composed of 88-millimetre guns, which, although we didn't know it at the time, were firing on British troops just outside Padua. We had managed to approach the battery from the rear, and if they had any guards posted they hadn't seen us, so the element of surprise was with us.

'I turned to Bill O'Leary and said, "What do you think we should do?" And Bill replied in his own inimitable way, "It's not up to me to say. It's your fucking decision." He was right, of course. There were two options. I could report the position of the battery and withdraw, or we could attack. So I said something like, "Right, we're going to drive in all guns blazing." Everyone did exactly as they were told. They simply said, "OK, skipper!' For me it wasn't really that much of a choice. We were soldiers in a war and we had found some enemy, so we attacked.

'We turned to our right, positioned ourselves so that we were in line abreast and charged in across country with all our machine-guns firing at the full rate. It was a hell of a fire-power − 12 machine-guns, six .30 calibre Brownings and six .50 Brownings. We had very long belts of ammunition so we could just carry on firing.'

'S Patrol tore across the open countryside firing burst after burst into the German position, creating panic and mayhem.

'We charged in guns blazing not really knowing what we were getting ourselves into. But the .50 cal can put down a tremendous weight of fire and I think we just took the Germans by surprise. We were firing directly into where they were concentrated, and they must have thought we were at the front of a very large attack because they simply packed up and surrendered. It all happened very quickly. The Germans' morale had been totally crushed by our surprise attack because they thought they would have been as safe as houses. It was our most spectacular success of the entire war because we managed to capture 300 Germans. I later discovered that a cousin of mine, Charlie Price, was entering Padua at a time when this fire was coming. And he later said that it stopped, and that was probably due to us.'

John handed over the care of the Germans to the partisans, somewhat reluctantly. There had been stories of partisans murdering German POWs, but John secured an assurance from their leader before heading off to Padua. In reality he had no choice. John's patrol numbered only 18 men, and had the German POWs decided to attack their captors there would have been little they could do. On arrival in Padua, John discovered that the partisans had risen up and captured the German force within the city.

Six days later news broke that Mussolini had been captured by partisans as he tried to escape to Switzerland. His body was later taken to Milan and hung from a lamp-post in a public square.

The following day Hitler committed suicide in his underground bunker in Berlin as the Soviet forces closed in.

As the final stages of the war drew near John, who was awarded a bar to his Military Cross for the action outside Padua, was faced with a situation which was potentially damaging to the trust and integrity that existed within the patrol. Everyone knew the war would be over in a matter of weeks, and stories had begun to surface about some soldiers making fortunes from selling goods on the black market. One day the convoy of vehicles in which John was travelling stopped outside a village and word soon spread amongst the locals that British troops had truckloads of tyres.

'There were two trucks – one was full of diesel and the other was full of tyres, and the tyres as far as the Italians were concerned were beyond value because they were so difficult to get hold of. Slowly, over the course of an hour or so, a large number of Italians turned up with bags full of lirae and offered to buy the trucks, but I refused. I got the chaps together and I said, "Look we have been very good friends, we have come through quite a lot in our time together and I don't want to spoil it. If we take the money we will start to quarrel." I knew our relationship would have been destroyed. I also knew that some of the chaps in my patrol would be going home to very little and that money could have come in very handy. I didn't doubt the integrity of any of my men, but I admit it was a very tempting offer and clearly other soldiers had been doing it. But instead of taking their money we let them have the trucks – their need was greater than ours so we handed them over and everyone just accepted it.'

On 7 May 1945 the German high command agreed to the unconditional surrender of all German forces to the Allies. S Patrol moved up to Austria for a while, but for PPA it was all over and on 14 September the organisation was disbanded. By the end of the war 250 soldiers from all ranks had served in PPA. Two officers and 10 other ranks had been killed, 17 men had been wounded and one member of the unit had been captured.

Popski remains a controversial figure to this day. He was an enigmatic and at times controversial character who divided opinion. David Lloyd Owen, who commanded the LRDG in North Africa, had little time for the Belgian. In his book, *Providence Their Guide: The Long Range Desert Group, 1940–45*, Owen describes Popski as 'a character who later created for himself a considerable reputation, based more, I think, on his strange behaviour rather than on anything that he ever achieved'. He went on to add: 'He was certainly a colourful character and his personal courage was never in question; but I found he had such a muddled mind that I am afraid I became very impatient with him and his procrastination.'

Whatever his detractors thought, however, he managed to create a fighting force which, by the end of the war, had destroyed thousands of tons of enemy fuel, captured hundreds of POWs and won a DSO, six MCs, one DCM, 10 MMs and 14 MiDs.

★　★　★

Today John lives near Leominister in Herefordshire and is now PPA's last surviving patrol commander. Despite the winning of two Military Crosses and being described by Popski as 'the most daring of us all', the accusations of cowardice which were made during his service with the 7th Battalion, The Argyll and Sutherland Highlanders, were still painful some 70 years later – even though he had also received the best possible vindication for his conduct on his first patrol.

'Some time after the war I met up with Lorne Campbell, and by that time he had won the Victoria Cross and the Distinguished Service Order and bar, so clearly he was a very brave man. We chatted about the night of that very first patrol, and he told me that he would not have been able to shoot the corporal who had run away and would have probably done exactly the same as I had done, which was to just get on with life. I found that very comforting, especially coming from him, a man whose bravery was beyond question. I later thought about what he said and when it would be acceptable to shoot one of your own men who was demonstrating clear cowardice and by doing so jeopardising a mission and risking the lives of others. The only time that such a terrible thing would be acceptable would have been during the absolute heat of battle, and this was not the heat of battle, the firing had already stopped, so such an act would have been completely unacceptable. Had I shot the corporal at that moment, I don't think I would have been able to live with myself.'

John Campbell left the Army as an honorary major and then served as a District Officer of the Colonial Service in Kenya from 1949 to 1961, gaining an MBE in 1957. He followed this with a long and distinguished career in the Diplomatic Service, as did many special forces officers, serving in Canada and Italy, and rising to Consul-General in Naples from 1977 to 1981. John was made CVO in 1980 and advanced to CBE in 1981. Since retiring, John has become chairman of the Friends of PPA and went back to Ravenna and Venice in 2005 to lay wreaths at the graves of some of the men that he fought alongside. He oversaw all fundraising for the PPA Memorial which was unveiled in 2008 in the Allied Special Forces Grove within the National Memorial Arboretum in Staffordshire.

# CHAPTER 6

# The Moonlight Squadrons

### *Leonard Ratcliff on Flying the SOE and the SIS*

*'Look for me by moonlight, watch for me by moonlight, I'll come
to thee by moonlight, though hell should bar the way.'*
ALFRED NOYES, 'The Highwayman'

No. 161 (Special Duties) Squadron, which had previously existed
during the First World War, was re-formed in February 1942 and
tasked with parachuting or landing SOE agents into Nazi-occupied
Europe. It was a mission that came with enormous risk and an
exceptionally high casualty rate – by the end of the war the entire
complement of the squadron had been lost three times over. Yet
despite the risks and the losses there was always a steady stream of
volunteers ready to risk all.

Those chosen either were, or had the potential to become, expert
pilots and aircrew, but the key quality each pilot required was being
able to improvise under conditions of extreme pressure. The pilots
who tended to blossom in this secret world were men who showed
an entrepreneurial spirit, and were of independent thought.

Wing Commander Leonard Fitch Ratcliff, DSO, DFC and Bar,
AFC, Légion d'Honneur, C de G, flew with and later commanded
161 Special Duties Squadron, one of the two so-called 'Moonlight'
squadrons,* the other being 138 Squadron. Both units were based at

---

\* So named because missions were flown in the light of the period moon to
assist navigation.

RAF Tempsford in Bedfordshire, a covert air base whose secrets only became public in 1998. By the end of the war hundreds of secret agents and tons of equipments had been either dropped by parachute or flown in to secret rendezvous across occupied Europe from RAF Tempsford.

I learnt about the Moonlight squadrons in 2009, when I was visiting an RAF base and noticed a painting of a Lysander aircraft landing at a secret rendezvous in France and dropping off a female agent. A member of the officers' mess began to explain that the agents were ferried to their RVs in a variety of different aircraft by a very special breed of pilots. That was the first time that I had heard of Leonard Ratcliff's name.

★   ★   ★

Leonard and I met on a sunny summer's afternoon in the garden of his house near the town of Saffron Walden in Essex. He had only agreed to talk to me on the grounds that I didn't 'puff him up', as he put it. 'There are plenty of people who seem to think they won the war on their own – I'm not one of them. My squadron was a team effort – we were wiped out three times. A lot of good men died.'

Leonard's life plan had been to enter the family farming business and perhaps become something of an entrepreneur, but the war, at least temporarily, changed all of that.

'The international situation was beginning to deteriorate rapidly, and when Prime Minister Chamberlain came back from a meeting with Hitler, waving a piece of paper claiming "Peace in our time", it appeared to me that war was inevitable. I hated the idea of trench warfare, the Royal Navy didn't appeal, so that left the RAF.'

In February 1939 Leonard was accepted into the Royal Air Force Volunteer Reserve at Southend-on-Sea as a pilot under training with the rank of Sergeant U/T. Still only 19, he was fired with stories about the Red Baron and his chivalrous and courageous approach to air warfare. Like many young men at the time, Leonard was desperate to emulate his German hero and become a fighter pilot, but his rush to serve his country was met with frustration.

'We were all terribly enthusiastic, but nothing happened. There was no infrastructure, no training, no uniform and certainly no aircraft, and that pretty much remained the case right up until the start of the war in September 1939. I rushed home from playing golf on the day that war was declared and almost immediately received a telegram telling me to report for active service at Southend airport by noon the following day. Well, I thought, fantastic, this is it. I shot off the following morning, leaving my mother in tears, only to find that the airfield had been completely overwhelmed with dozens of other would-be fighter aces. I was fitted with a uniform and sent on immediate leave, returning home for tea feeling like a complete and utter fraud.'

It would be nine months before Leonard learnt how to fly Tiger Moths at No. 4 Elementary Flying Training School (EFTS) in Brough, Yorkshire, on the banks of the Humber. Two months later and with 51 hours of flying under his belt, and rated 'above average', he was posted to No. 10 EFTS at Ternhill in Shropshire, where he learnt how to fly a two-engine AVRO Anson. With the award of his wings, Leonard made it clear that he wanted to go into fighters.

But Leonard's superiors had other ideas. They regarded him as a natural leader and felt that he would be more suited to leading a bombing crew in a multi-engine aircraft. Leonard was promoted to pilot officer and because he had shown a flair for navigation – a skill which would stand him in great stead later in the war – he was posted to No. 2 School for Advanced Navigation.

By July 1941 Leonard was a skipper with his own crew flying a Handley Page 52 Hampden twin-engine light bomber with 49 Squadron at Scampton in Lincolnshire. The war had entered a much more aggressive phase with the RAF launching nightly bombing raids over Germany, and, tragically, casualties had become part of daily life.

Leonard, like many of the pilots and crew, was married and the wives would often spend the nights together while their husbands

*Leonard Ratcliff*

were away on ops, offering each other support and company and hoping desperately that their husbands would make it home.

'It was a difficult time because a lot of people were getting killed. There was this one awful morning. A great friend of ours called Brenda Wilcox, who was married to Squadron Leader David Wilcox, known to us as "Daddo", came to stay at our house while David and I were away on ops. It had been a night of very heavy casualties. In the morning the two wives looked outside the window and saw the vicar walking up the path to the house, which only meant one thing. They looked at one another and wondered which one of them was going to get the bad news. Brenda's husband was never heard of again.

'The most emotional thing about it all was that it was right on top of us. I came home and he didn't – so you can imagine how it must have been for the wives. If you let it worry you, you were no bloody good to anyone, so you had to accept that every time you took off there was always an element of doubt as to whether you were going to come back.'

Night raids over Germany, which claimed the lives of thousands of Allied aircrew, became a lottery of survival. Some of the best pilots and best crews were killed because they were simply unlucky.

'When you were going on a bombing raid to the Ruhr in Germany, you were at the mercy of night fighters, flak, searchlights and the hazards of crashing into one another because you were all heading for the same target. Fear was with us all the time, and you never became hardened to it but you did overcome it. But for some very brave men the fear simply became too much. We all only had a certain amount of courage and for some it ran out more quickly than others, but I think if you were continually on ops anyone's courage would have eventually run out.

'There was the well-known expression Lack of Moral Fibre – and as I say the "well of courage" is different for everybody – but when you are in a crew and somebody is LMF he will be putting the whole crew at risk. I can remember only too well a member of my squadron, an Australian who out of the generosity of his heart had given up his career in Australia and had volunteered for the RAF, because he wanted to fight against the Nazis. But the stress got the better of him, so I rang up the postings officer and said, "This fellow has volunteered to serve with us and support us, but he is now suffering from terrible home sickness for Australia. Couldn't you find him a posting back home?" – and they did. Strictly speaking, of course, he was no good to anybody on ops – it was far better that he was home doing something useful.

'By far the worst thing for me on ops was being caught by three or four searchlights. The searchlights were tracked by radar and when they got a fix on the aircraft you immediately became illuminated, isolated and vulnerable – and by God, do you feel naked. You are up there weaving about trying to get out before you are spotted by the night fighters. When you were in that searchlight beam, naked as the day you were born, you couldn't see anything because you were blinded by the light, you were then attacked by the night fighters – don't let me overdo it – but it was pretty terrifying.

'There was one day in my life when I didn't expect to make it back. It was when the two girls were at home together and I just thought that I wasn't going to make it back – there was something in the back of my mind telling me that my time was up. A mate of mine had just got it and I thought, "I'm next." That was the only night really that I felt somebody was stalking me. But we had our way of dealing with fear. We used to throw tinsel out of the aircraft to try and confuse the radar, followed by an empty beer bottle. I doubt they did much good, but bottles made a loud whistling sound as they fell to earth, and that made us feel a bit better.'

Leonard's prowess as a pilot and navigator was obvious, and in the autumn of 1941 he was promoted to deputy flight commander with the rank of flight lieutenant. His crew was also selected to train for a special low-level operation on the Knapsack power station near Cologne in Germany, which supplied power to a large part of the industrial Ruhr. The operation, as Leonard said, 'was not without considerable risk'. The power station was defended like a fortress and was heavily protected by barrage balloons and anti-aircraft guns. To counter the balloon threat, the Hampdens were fitted with special cable cutters on their wings, the idea being that the barrage balloon cable slid down the wing and activated a cartridge which cut the cable. In theory it was a straightforward exercise, but the reality was that the technique required an inordinate amount of skill and steady nerve, both of which Leonard possessed. Nevertheless, when the operation was cancelled there was a collective sigh of relief amongst the crew.

It was at this stage that Leonard acquired a new navigator – Wilbur Wright. Everyone in the RAF at the time who had the surname Wright immediately attracted the nickname 'Orville' or 'Wilbur' after the cross-channel pioneers.

'Wilbur was a perfectly good navigator but was a complete bag of nerves before every flight and was always hoping that the op would be cancelled, which could be quite irritating. But once we were airborne he was perfectly fine and would just get on with the job of navigating the aircraft to the target, which he could always find without too much difficulty; it was just his way of handling the pressure and stress. Everybody was affected in some way; some showed it, others didn't. I always took a camera to record the accuracy of the bomb blast. It was a way of judging our own accuracy. In order to do this you had to fly straight and level for two minutes with the flak bursting around you – and it seemed like a very long time.'

In April 1942, after he had completed 29 sorties, Leonard's operational duty came to an end. He was due a period of rest and was sent to No. 24 Operational Training Unit in Honeybourne as an instructor and deputy flight commander under Squadron Leader Bob Hodges, who was later posted to 161 Special Duties Squadron at RAF Tempsford. Leonard threw himself into pilot training with his characteristic gusto and at the age of just 24 became the squadron leader in charge of eight pilot instructors.

Operation training units had effectively become pilot training factories, and the production of and the demand for formed air crews was phenomenal – a reflection of the casualties being sustained by bomber crews. The unit received a new course of 16 crews every month and the course lasted eight weeks. 'Operational training was vital if Britain was to keep up the pressure against the enemy, and for my efforts I received the Air Force Cross, but after 14 months I was itching to get back to ops.'

Through the RAF grapevine, Leonard learnt that 161 Squadron had suffered heavy casualties. In just two days three squadron leaders had been killed. One of the casualties was Tony Walker, the deputy flight commander at 24 OTU, at Honeybourne, who had been posted to 161 Squadron but was tragically killed after just a few operations. Leonard, who had already decided that the time had come to move back into operational flying, decided to offer his services.

'I rang [Bob Hodges] and said, "Bob, I'm terribly sorry, you've had a lot of bad luck, but I'm ready to come back to ops and I'd very much like to work with you again." And he said,

"That's a jolly good idea, I would love that," and he rang up the personnel people and two days later, on 24 June 1943, I arrived at Tempsford.'

\*     \*     \*

In the summer of 1943 RAF Tempsford was one of the most secret bases in Britain and the major staging post for SOE agents entering occupied Europe. The base was located in the Bedfordshire countryside near the hamlet of Tempsford. Most military bases, especially RAF stations, were heavily guarded to protect against acts of sabotage by German agents, and RAF Tempsford, tucked away at the end of a road closed to the public, was no different.

Whilst the location of the base was known to the local population, its operational activity remained top secret. 'None of the locals asked any questions, not even in the pub, the Anchor and Wheatsheaf. If someone came in who didn't know the form, they were simply told the work was secret and that was the end of that.'

The base was home to two Special Duties Squadrons – 161 Squadron, which consisted of Halifaxes,\* Hudsons,† Havocs‡ and Lysanders,§ and 138 Squadron, with Halifaxes and a flight consisting mainly of Polish crews. Both squadrons were under the command of Group Captain Edward 'Mouse' Fielden, a highly experienced pilot and former commander of the King's Flight.

RAF Tempsford was a hive of activity throughout 1943. An almost constant convoy of trucks and cars delivered agents and equipment on a daily basis. The agents would receive their final briefing in a building known as Gibraltar Farm Barn, which had been disguised to look like a barn but was in fact a secure compound within which SOE agents would receive any final instructions, hand over any documents that could give away their real identities

---

\* Handley Page Halifax – four-engined heavy bomber.

† Lockheed Hudson – twin-engined light bomber.

‡ Douglas A-20 Havoc – twin-engined light bomber.

§ Westland Lysander – single-engined observation aircraft used in clandestine missions.

and receive their so-called 'fatal pills', which they were under orders to take rather than face capture. As well as transporting agents, the two special duties squadrons also dropped containers and packages containing all the equipment a resistance force would require to remain operational. Rifles, Bren guns, Sten guns, pistols, hand grenades, high explosives, detonators, clothing, radios and even skis and bicycles were carefully packed into containers at a secret location and driven into the base.

In France bicycles were a rare commodity and could only be purchased on the black market. But dismantled they could be dropped by parachute. An agent riding around the Dutch or French countryside on a bike was far less likely to arouse the suspicion of the authorities than he would travelling in a car. A bike also allowed agents to reconnoitre dropping zones by using footpaths and small tracks. Between 1941 and July 1945, when it was disbanded, 161 Squadron conducted 13,500 operational sorties in support of the Resistance in Europe, landed 324 agents, parachuted in 1,500 agents and picked up 593. Such was the secrecy surrounding RAF Tempsford that its true role was only publicly revealed in 1998.

The role of the agents was to organise the Resistance into a secret network of fighting units. It was difficult and dangerous work and the risk of betrayal was ever present. One of the key roles was to identify landing sites, so that agents could be covertly flown in or picked up, and to maintain radio contact with the London headquarters. The landing area was usually a field, a good distance away from enemy forces. It was flat, capable of taking an aircraft such as a Lysander or a Hudson, and devoid of any obstacles such as ditches, fences or power lines. Once the landing zones had been identified, map references would be sent back to Air Intelligence (AI2C) at the Air Ministry in London. An aerial reconnaissance flight would take photos of the designated area and, if everything was in order, final approval for a sortie would be given.

'When I arrived at 161 Squadron, pretty much the first thing I had to do was learn how to fly a four-engined plane, which I hadn't done before. Bob gave me an hour's familiarisation and then over the next few days it was up to me to get a grip on things.

'My flight consisted of 10 Halifaxes, two Havocs and three Hudsons, which were used for missions to support the resistance forces from Norway down through Denmark, Holland, Germany, Belgium and France. The Halifaxes were used for long-distance missions in the occupied countries, while the Havocs were used for radio telephone (RT) intelligence gathering with contacts and agents.

'Each mission usually consisted of a several destinations or dropping zones (DZ). Sometimes we found ourselves operating in several different countries on any one night. One aeroplane could do three drops. The critical factor in such a flight was the selection of the crews. Everyone was selected on the strength of their character and working on their own initiative. We looked for people with an entrepreneurial spirit. I would say that was the single most important characteristic. If we were dropping agents we had to approach the target at around 600 feet, so most of the missions were flown in the moon period. The height of 600 feet was critical so that the agent's parachute could open.

'The Squadron could pretty much accommodate any destination in any of the occupied countries, but it was not possible to send a Halifax into Germany because the Germans didn't have any four-engined aircraft. It was very easy to tell the difference between a two-engine and four-engine plane, so if you flew over in the latter you were immediately advertising the fact that you were the enemy and in all likelihood dropping an agent, and you were likely to be attacked by fighters or shot down. When flying into Germany, the Hudson was always used.'

By this stage of the war Leonard's wife Bet and his one-year-old son Rupert had been installed in a furnished home a few miles away from Tempsford. It was a relatively comfortable existence, but the stress on the pilot's families was tremendous. Aircraft would often return riddled with bullets, or with bits of trees trapped in the undercarriage. The casualty rate would often fluctuate from being relatively low to periods of greater attrition when the squadron was losing up to one crew a week.

Although all the pilots were fully aware that they were dropping agents into occupied Europe, the identities of the agents were never revealed and contact with the crew was kept to a minimum. This was some of the most secret work undertaken by Britain during the war. Establishing a network of agents across Europe would only succeed if security was absolute.

'We had a separate compound known as "the Barn" at Tempsford where the agents received their final briefings. It was very secure and well away from other parts of the airfield and out of bounds to all pilots and aircrew. I would go to the Barn and talk to the agents and ensure that they were correctly looked after.

'The various flight commanders would also take it in turns to be in charge of the control room for the whole night during the course of a mission, so if there were any problems, such as mechanical failure, flak damage or the failure of a reception committee to turn up, we would be at the end of a wireless and available to offer advice. We knew SOE existed, of course, but we were kept separate from it and had no actual interaction with it as an organisation. That was all done through liaison officers, such as a chap called Major Tice, who was an SOE officer but lived on the airfield and was essentially one of us.'

Within a few days Leonard had managed to assemble a new crew, including navigator Philippe Livry, a 49-year-old Free French officer, who had joined the RAF after the collapse of France.

'Philippe was a very capable and brave man. He had already been decorated with the Croix de Guerre avec 13 Palmes and counted Charles de Gaulle amongst his many friends. But at times of high stress when flying he had this extremely annoying habit of breaking into completely unintelligible French. The full crew of my Halifax, callsign X for X-Ray, consisted of a pilot, navigator, wireless operator, rear gunner, engineer and dispatcher. Part of the engineer's job, given that I am a bit short in the arms and legs, was to give me a shove at the appropriate time so that I could reach the necessary throttles on take-off. The dispatcher looked after the Joes, as we called the agents, and made sure that they were kept informed of the flight's progress. Prior to jumping, he checked the agent's harness, opened up the hole in the floor of the fuselage and dispatched them at the appropriate time – the Green Light. He was also responsible for making sure their personal kit also followed them too, as well as dropping containers and packages.'

On 12 July 1943 Leonard and his new crew took part in their first operation to Belgium in a Havoc; two days later the crew flew in a Halifax to France, and on 16 July they again flew in a Havoc to Belgium, all of which missions were completed successfully.

'On 17 July we set off again, this time to find a rather obscure field in the Burgundy region of France to deliver two urgently needed agents. This was the period of the most danger for both the crews and the members of the Resistance. If the Germans got wind of what was happening they could capture an entire reception committee, who would in all likelihood be tortured and executed, and there was every chance they would capture us too. On this particular mission we flew low across the Channel to Cabourg, and when we were in sight of the coast we climbed to around 4,000 feet in order to avoid coastal defences, but on this particular mission something went wrong. The starboard engine packed up, suggesting that we must have been hit by some light flak. We managed to drop the agents successfully but, because of our reduced speed from flying on three engines, there was no way that we were going to make it across the Channel before daylight, which meant that we would be easy pickings for enemy fighters.

'The best course of action was to fly to Algiers where another special duties squadron was based. We flew directly to the Spanish border and over the Balearic Islands. We were all a bit concerned because we weren't 100 per cent sure of the exact location of Algiers and fuel was getting low. Then we had two strokes of luck. Our navigation equipment gave an accurate fix, and the Germans launched a huge attack on Algiers. This seemed to illuminate the whole sky above Algiers which seemed to be alight with tracer fire, so we simply followed the lights. By the time we came to the North African coast that part of the battle was over and we managed to find the Blida aerodrome just as our fuel was almost spent.

'We travelled all that way in pretty difficult circumstances and the only casualty we suffered was when Joe Corner, the rear gunner, jumped out of the turret and broke his leg when he landed. A few days later we were ready to return but with one additional passenger – a member of another crew who had been badly injured and needed brain surgery. We took him with us, got him back home and he survived the war. On the return trip we also stopped off in Gibraltar and loaded up with sherry and other goodies.

'As a young fellow of 22 or 23 I was in charge of my own destiny and the destiny of the people under me – many people flew with the special squadrons but apart from me there isn't anybody who did all the jobs, who flew all the different sorts of aircraft to Denmark and Norway and did the pick-up operations in the Hudsons and Lysanders, and it was incredibly rewarding.

'When it came to running the various flights and then the squadron and then both squadrons I found it incredibly easy to get people to follow what I was trying to get them to do. I think that came down to personality and experience. The day started at 10am and you met in the intelligence room with the commander of the station, Mouse Fieldon, a lovely fellow but a total autocrat. I loved that old man and he and I got along very well together, except on one occasion when he had the nerve to call me a conservative sod because I wouldn't alter my tactics to accept his strategy, and in the event I was proved justified. There was a tremendous camaraderie on the squadrons but everyone was an individual. Because we were doing special ops, we wanted people who were entrepreneurs capable of working on their own initiative. There's only a certain amount that you can tell a fellow when he has to take an aeroplane somewhere in Bordeaux. You can explain to him how to get there and what to do, but he's got to do the doing and take his own decisions.

'I set about recruiting people who I regarded as entrepreneurs. I had the good fortune to have trained a lot of Norwegians when I was in OTU. Many of them had made the journey from Norway to the Shetland Islands in a little boat known as the Larson Ferry. They were all wonderful chaps – absolutely solid stock and great personalities, like Per Hysing Dahl. They were all motivated by the desire to rid Norway of the Nazis, so when I approached them and asked if they would join, they all agreed.'

Through the summer and autumn of 1943 Leonard and his squadron continued with the process of picking up and dropping off agents in France and Norway. Eventually the ageing Halifaxes were phased out and the squadron was re-equipped with Stirling bombers, which had become obsolete because they could no longer reach the height needed for bombing missions.

In February 1944 Leonard volunteered to take part in an operation to pick up Henri Déricourt, a French member of the SOE, who was needed in London as part of an investigation. Déricourt had arrived in the Loire area of France in January 1943 and began to build a huge and successful Resistance network. But later that summer a number of SOE agents were arrested in a major crackdown by the German Sicherheitsdienst (SD), the intelligence agency of the SS. Some members of the Resistance who avoided capture would later claim that Déricourt had formed contacts with the SD and was working for both sides.

'A cloud hung over Henri Déricourt, who was suspected of being a double agent. Suspicion arose because after he arrived in an area of France where a number of SOE agents were working, several of them suddenly disappeared. He had been recruited by MI6 and went on to work with the SOE. So when suspicions began to arise, quite rightly the SOE wanted him to come back for questioning. The problem for the SOE was that if he was in fact a double agent then any crew sent in to pick him up together with a reception committee might be walking into a trap and would almost certainly end up in the hands of the Gestapo, and we all knew what that meant.

'I had met Déricourt some time before when he had returned from France to give a briefing to the pilots at Tempsford on the role and the activities of the SOE. I found him to be very charming but it was clear that he had a huge ego and I understood him to be a man who was first, second and third for Henri Déricourt. But in spite of his rather egotistical outlook he was a remarkable man and he ran an extraordinarily prolific number of dropping zones and landing fields. He was totally dedicated to the Resistance movement and I found him to be a very impressive individual and I think most of us did at the time. He was a man of enormous energy and was very good at doing what he was doing. As far as I was concerned we were all in the same boat together and I was perfectly happy to ride in his boat. To me, he was a compatible character and I liked him.

'During that period of the war the SOE was a hive of suspicion. I think everybody realised or suspected that there was a mole in SOE but obviously nobody knew who it was and the identity of the mole remains unknown to this day. Some time later we received instructions from SOE stating that Déricourt needed to be picked up and brought back for questioning. There was a great deal of discussion as to how they were going to get him back to Britain so that he could face the allegations that had been made against him. I was quite happy to go and get him, because I believed in him and didn't think that he would let me down. The plan which was originally formulated was for me to fly to France, capture him and bring him back under duress. But I thought this was nonsense and I said, "No way!"

'Instead I suggested that the best course of action was to take another member of the SOE, Major Gerry Morel, to try and persuade Déricourt to return to England. I explained that as the pilot I alone couldn't sit in a aircraft in a foreign environment waiting to take off at the same time as trying to persuade a suspected spy to climb on board and face the allegations in Britain.

'SOE couldn't actually inform Déricourt that he was being brought back to Britain for interrogation because of the risk that he would disappear. There was already a plan to extract around 12 agents, all senior members of the Resistance, from the Angers area of the Loire so it was decided we would use that extraction to try and get him out.

'I told SOE that I wouldn't capture Déricourt but that it was up to Morel to use his powers of persuasion to convince him to come back. Déricourt at the time was head of the reception committee, and the plan was effectively to spring it on him when we landed.'

The mission was codenamed Operation Knacker and took place on 4 February 1944. Leonard and his three-man crew flew their Hudson to a large riverside meadow located at the junction of the Loire and a tributary south of Angers. Illuminated by moonlight, Leonard's crew had little difficulty navigating their way to the landing zone.

'The reception committee set out four hand torches in the normal L shape to guide us in. An agreed recognition signal was given, which was very important and was really the final assurance that you weren't flying into a trap. No recognition signal, no landing. I landed on the side of the L without any problems and taxied back to the first torch and turned the Hudson into the wind so that we were ready for take-off if an emergency occurred.

'Morel climbed out and was greeted by Déricourt and the rest of the reception committee together with the agents we were planning to take back with us. Morel explained the situation to Déricourt, but he reacted very badly and was furious when he was told that he would have to come back and clear his name, and so were the rest of the agents. Déricourt said, "No, I can't come at this moment. It is impossible, I have things to attend to, I have a wife at home, I can't leave her without making arrangements." But he added that if Morel was to return at the next full moon he would return to Britain.

'Those discussions became very fraught and I think it developed into a bit of a brawl and a few punches were thrown. While all this was going on, I was sitting in the plane shouting at them out of the window to hurry up. When you fly into a landing zone you don't want to hang around. If possible you want to be on the ground for just a few minutes because you are extremely vulnerable. As soon as the Germans heard a plane they knew it had something to do with the Resistance and would soon be out scouring the country-side looking for people.

'Morel didn't really have any option at that stage so he had to accept Déricourt's word. We flew off with the 12 agents and amongst that bunch were Bob Maloubier, who was only 19 at the time, Robert Bendist, Philippe Liewer, Henri Borosh and Madeleine Lavigne.

'Déricourt returned as he promised at the next full moon and was flown back to Britain, where he was interrogated by SOE, but nothing was ever proved. He spent the rest of the war in SOE HQ in London and was never allowed to go back into the field.'

Suspicion hung over him for many years. At the end of the war evidence emerged that appeared to prove that Déricourt was indeed a traitor whose actions had led to the deaths of eight SOE agents.

Déricourt was arrested and tried in France in 1948. During the trial, Nicholas Bodington, an SOE staff officer who 'ran' Déricourt, admitted that he was aware that Déricourt was in contact with the Germans but that no important information had been revealed. Although there was a great deal of circumstantial evidence suggesting he was a traitor, the prosecution lacked hard facts and he was acquitted.

'My view of Déricourt is that I think he was a very cute negotiator and he walked along a very tight rope. The allegation was that he had handed names over to the Gestapo, but who am I to know? Who is anyone to know that? Nobody could prove it and everybody blamed everybody else. I'm damn sure that he had a foot in both camps but it was never proved. I fought against him being condemned as a double agent for years. These people lived a very shadowy existence – it wasn't black and white but very murky. He had a very chequered career after the war and became a smuggler in south-east Asia and it is reported that he was killed in a plane crash in Laos in 1962 with a gold bar strapped to his leg.'

*        *        *

During the early spring of 1944 the United States Air Force allocated a Liberator* Squadron to assist the Resistance movement in Europe. The squadron was based at Alconbury in Cambridgeshire, north of Tempsford. Leonard was approached by the USAF squadron colonel and asked if he was prepared to help the American pilots with some operational experience. Leonard's crews were very accommodating and over a period of about four months took many of the US pilots as passengers on Halifax missions across occupied Europe.

'Over this period we became good friends with the Americans and they were very grateful for our help. At the end of the training period a party was thrown to say farewell and the colonel came up to me and as a demonstration of his indebtedness gave me an Auster† plane. He wrote out a chit and I collected the Auster the next day and used it as my own little runabout for the remainder of my time at Tempsford. One cannot just imagine a gesture like that coming from the British side, primarily because our resources were so stretched – and the auditor of public accounts would have gone berserk.'

On 9 May 1944 Leonard took part in one of the most unusual and daring raids in the history of 161 Squadron. Codenamed Operation Mineur, the mission was to fly into a field near Vierzon Ville, in the Touraine region of France, with six SOE agents and return to Britain with eight agents who were needed for debriefing. Ordinarily such an operation would only require a single large aircraft, but for this particular mission the only suitable landing zone in the area was a field just large enough to take a Lysander.

After much deliberation, Leonard decided that the best way of conducting the operation was to fly three Lysanders into the area at 10-minute intervals. Lysander operations always had a certain element of risk because the pilot had to fly the aircraft and navigate at the same time – all by the light of the moon. The other danger

---

* US B-24 Liberator four-engined USAF heavy bomber.
† Single-engined observation aircraft.

was that flying three aircraft into the same area tripled the chance of alerting any Germans garrisoned nearby.

Given the dangers associated with the mission, Leonard decided to lead it himself and chose Flight Lieutenant Bob Large, a former Spitfire pilot, and Lieutenant Per Hysing Dahl, a Norwegian whom Leonard had helped train.

'The three of us set off from Tangmere, our forward base, and flew over to Cabourg, which is in a little inlet on the coast near Caen. When carrying out missions in a Lysander it was vital that you stuck to your plan and flew to the checkpoints, such as rivers or towns. If you followed the rules but were flexible enough to adapt to the circumstances and could think your way out of problems and luck was on your side, then you would stand a fighting chance of coming home. All the pilots knew most of the routes fairly well and the location of the danger points, especially the night fighters, who could really ruin your day. I would keep in regular contact with Bletchley Park, whose code-breakers knew where the night fighter squadrons were going to be flying. The squadrons often moved around, which meant that our bombers couldn't always avoid them, but we nearly always seemed to know where they were going to be, so we kept a sensible distance.

'The three aircraft took off without any problems and after reaching the Loire we flew on to Vierzon Ville. The Norwegians don't have a V in their vocabulary and they pronounce every letter in a word so Vierzon Ville became Wierzon Willie. There was a very accommodating German in the town who had a searchlight, and if you went too near the town he would switch on the searchlight and from there you would set a course from the searchlight to the landing zone some 30 or 40 miles away. The plan was to fly to an RV and for us to circle there until we were all in the area, then fly on to the landing zone in quick succession.

'I arrived first and made contact with Per, but Bob had got a bit lost and turned up terribly late – which sparked a very funny conversation between Bob and Per. Per said to Bob, "Where the hell have you been?" and Bob said, "I've been having my hair cut," and Per said, "But you can't have your hair cut in the company's time," and Bob said, "Well, it grew in the company's time." Per said, "But not all of it." Bob answered, "Well, I didn't have all of it cut off."

'We all had a chuckle and then we had to get back to the serious business of dropping off the agents. As I flew over the field I could see the torchlights below and flew in and landed. The reception committee came to meet me, we exchanged a few words and I dropped off my two agents and three packages, turned the aircraft into the wind and picked up three agents and four packages. It was a terrible squeeze to get the agents inside and the flight must have been pretty miserable. It was awful for the passengers. You couldn't speak to them or communicate with them in any way, because the Lysander is a single-seater with a compartment up front for the pilot, while the passengers had to almost squat in the rear compartment, which is shaped like a tube.

'With my cargo on board, I took off and Bob Large landed, dropped off one agent and five packages and departed with two agents and four packages, and lastly Per dropped off three agents and picked up three agents and two packages. Everything went like clockwork and we managed to fly in and land at 10-minute intervals.

'The mission worked very well. Looking back I think it was the height of impossibility to have three fellows with a map strapped to the knee flying 500 miles and landing in a field in the middle of France in torchlight and doing it in unison and arriving at the same place and arriving home – it was jolly nearly impossible, and we did it with 100 per cent success. Before we left I knew it was going to be tricky to pull it off. I knew Per would be all right, but I knew Bob was a bit of a scatterbrain but was the sort of fellow you would choose in a tight corner because you knew that despite his scatterbrain he would not let you down.

'At the time I knew that it was a virtually impossible mission but we just didn't think about it in those terms. It came up as a treble operation and we thought, "Well, this is going to be a bit tricky." There was a sense of immense relief when we all landed and we three shared a bottle of Champagne, given to us by the reception committee. It was a nice trophy and there was always a message on the bottle – Good Luck.'

On the morning of 6 June, just before the D-Day landings began in Normandy, the Halifaxes of 161 Squadron were given the task of flying low over the Channel, just above sea level, to simulate an approaching fleet in the Dover-Calais area. The aircraft circled in ever-widening circles to confuse enemy radar.

'I don't have any idea if the tactic was successful or not, but history tells us that many German divisions were held back from the Normandy beachhead, allowing the Allies to get a precious foothold.'

'A few days later, Per Hysing Dahl was dispatched to France with three agents and a bag containing 11 million Francs to pay the Resistance fighters, but he was shot down by our own forces and was forced to ditch his aircraft into the sea. Per survived* with a broken arm after being rescued by a US cruiser, but failed to save the cash and tragically one of the three agents was killed.

On 8 October 1944 Leonard was posted to the Air Ministry Intelligence Department in Horseferry Road, London, as the wing commander in charge of AI2C (Air Intelligence). AI2C was part of the Deputy Directorate of Intelligence commanded by Group Captain John Palmer.

The department had originally been established to coordinate the various clandestine operations taking place across Europe. Leonard, aged just 24, was responsible for all operations of 138 and 161 Squadrons. He also had to brief the Chief of the Air Staff (CAS) every morning on all operations involving the squadrons and all Resistance activity.

---

* George Bush Senior, the former US president, was a member of the cruiser crew which shot down Per Hysing Dahl's aircraft. The two men met many years later when Per was the Chairman of the Political Committee of Nato. When the two men met in Washington, Per said, 'Not only did you pick me up but you were probably the blighter that shot me down.' George Bush immediately commissioned a plaque to record this amazing coincidence and presented it to Per.

'I also received copies of communications between the various Allied world leaders, including Prime Minister Winston Churchill, President Franklin D. Roosevelt, Stanislaw Mikolajczyk, the Polish Prime Minister in exile, and Josef Stalin, the leader of the Soviet Union. Other department heads, nearly all senior officers of Air Commodore rank and above, also attended the morning briefing and gave their account of operations in their particular area of operations.

'I knew exactly what was going on in Europe during that period. There was no need for me to buy a newspaper because I was getting all the information I needed right from the horse's mouth – it was an incredibly fascinating and privileged position to have. The days were very long while I was at the air ministry. I would get the tube every morning from my bedsit in Lancaster Terrace and arrive at 7am when it was still dark and prepare for the morning briefing. If time allowed I would try and get a bit of fresh air and get outside and walk across Green Park to the RAF Club for lunch or go to the Churchill Club in Westminster, but more often than not I was confined to the office, well below ground. I would then leave the office around 7pm, and so for almost three and a half months I hardly ever saw any daylight.'

The majority of Leonard's work was dealing with the requests of the SOE and the Secret Intelligence Service (SIS), who were often at each other's throats because they were always competing for the same resources. SOE recruited people like Bob Maloubier and Peter Churchill for their ability to sabotage lines of communication or for their ability to organise the Resistance, whereas SIS wanted intelligence-gatherers and wouldn't sully their hands with the work of the SOE.

'There was always some sort of row going on between SIS and SOE. Both organisations had the ear of Churchill. Major-General Colin Gubbins,* the head of SOE, was a blue-eyed boy of Churchill's – he did no wrong – and C, head of SIS, was in direct touch with the Prime Minister, as his equivalent is today.

---

* Executive head of the SOE.

'In order to minimise the stress between the two it was decided that 138 Squadron would give priority to SOE and 161 Squadron would give priority to SIS. I don't remember a single occasion where that priority existed. There were never too few aeroplanes to do the jobs that needed to be done. The animosity was at the top, never at the bottom on the ground where people were operating at Tempsford. I didn't feel any pressure, I thought it was a bit of a joke. I didn't care whether they fought with one another, it didn't make any difference to me. It was just egos.'

One of Leonard's primary roles while working for air intelligence, apart from briefing the CAS, was to approve all of the landing sites for the delivery of agents into occupied Europe.

'It was my responsibility to approve all the landing grounds to be used by Lysanders and Hudsons, which was quite an onerous task and was far more complex than an agent on the ground assuming that a field was "suitable". When a request came in from an SOE or an SIS agent the first thing we would do was to send up an air reconnaissance aircraft, usually a Mosquito, to take some photographs of the site so that the air intelligence people could check for obstacles, like fences, pylons and ditches. Such safeguards were absolutely vital so that the pilot could have complete faith in the "chef de reception" or the individual responsible for the landing site.

'My stint at AI2C coincided with the Siege of Warsaw. As the Russians began their advance westwards from Stalingrad, the Resistance fighters – there were about 30,000 of them who were never subdued – were urged to rise up in an attempt to divert German resources away from the eastern front. The Ghetto would need to be re-supplied if this task was to be achieved with any reasonable degree of success. The task of re-supplying the Ghetto was given to 138 Squadron, which had a Polish flight, composed entirely of volunteers.

'The supply drops were a monumental undertaking which resulted in the loss of tremendous numbers of pilots and crews. It was impossible for crews to fly all the way to Warsaw, drop their supplies and fly back to Britain in one night without refuelling, so the crews flew on to Brindisi in Italy, where the Blida squadron had established a forward operating base, to conduct operations in Yugoslavia.

'The fighting in the ghetto at the time was incredibly fierce, and in some areas the opposing forces were only 20 yards apart. It was vital that supplies of ammunition, weapons, food, radios, medicines, everything the Poles needed to stay alive and to continue fighting, ended up in their hands and not the Germans'. At the time, the only way you could ensure that this was to happen was to fly at around 600 feet – but that makes you very vulnerable and a lot of aircraft were blown out of the sky and the net result was that the squadron was decimated.

'A great friend of mine, David Pitt, who was the CO of 138 Squadron at the time, did a couple of trips. It was pushing your luck to do one trip, let alone two. Look at the logistics: you went across to the Baltic and you went in north of Berlin, through to Warsaw, then through all the mountains of the Balkans, down to Brindisi – even today it's a mammoth undertaking. Everybody was after you. You went over hostile country, over Denmark, north of the Kiel Canal, over Prussia, Warsaw, and the length of the flight and the hazards were just tremendous. When the crews landed they had a short rest, refuelled and rearmed, and then flew back to Warsaw where they dropped more supplies and then returned home to Tempsford.

'The main problem we faced was the refusal of the Russians to allow our aircraft to land and refuel in their territory. There was a hell of a row about it at that time. Churchill, Roosevelt and Mikolajczyk all pressurised Stalin to try and get permission for our aircraft supporting the Warsaw uprising to land in their area, but the Russians refused, so there was no other choice but to go to Brindisi. The reason for this was that the Russians wanted the Germans and the Poles to annihilate each other. As the Russians approached Warsaw, Churchill urged Stalin to relieve the siege, but he refused and stopped his forces 20 miles short of the city. The Germans killed 10,000 Resistance fighters and there was a hell of a row about this. I actually wrote a speech for the air minister to deliver to the House of Commons to explain the circumstances at the time

– and I was fortunate to go along to the Commons and actually hear the air minister read my speech, which is quite something.'

During Leonard's time a film was made about the SOE called *School for Danger*, in which Leonard actually played himself. The film can be found on YouTube. It was during this period that London and other cities were being hammered by Hitler's V1 and V2 rockets. 'It was amazing how these bombs could fall without any warning – which I suppose is why they were so terrifying. You could be walking down a perfectly quiet street and then there would be this huge explosion, after which you were either all right or not.'

Four months later, in February 1945, Leonard was back at Tempsford but arrived to find that morale within the squadron was quite low. Two squadron leaders had been killed in quick succession, adding to an already high attrition rate.

The complement of aircrew in both 138 and 161 Squadrons was 200 men, but the casualties during three and a half years of operation amounted to almost 600 – which effectively meant that both squadrons had been lost three times over.

'The casualty rate was much higher than other squadrons. Those who volunteered didn't really know the risks they were taking when joining. An awful lot of the casualties resulted from pilots straying off the straight and narrow. If you flew over a German-occupied airfield you expected to get shot at. But if you went five miles to the south of it the Germans wouldn't shoot at all. Survival depended on your ability to do your homework and to pay attention in briefings and to listen to experienced crew members – if you didn't stray off course there was a good chance you would survive. Some of the places in Belgium and the fringes around Paris were very difficult to navigate. You were aiming for a pin point, a particular field, which was maybe 10 miles from the nearest town, and if you were circling to look for the target you could inadvertently stray over the wrong outfit, such as the coastal defences. One couldn't spend too long searching for a target because you might run out of fuel, so the ability to navigate expertly would also help keep you alive.

'I would brief my pilots as much as possible, often individually to make sure they had everything squared away. You would tell them about the met situation, where the German defences were, to be careful of that area because that's a red-hot spot – that sort of thing – so it was incredibly personal. I would talk to them and advise them on the way to do it and advise them on which route to take because, after my experience, I had a pretty good under-standing of the routes, what to avoid and where the good land-marks were.

'When Bomber Command were sending 1,000 bombers to Cologne it was a huge collective operation and there was safety in numbers. It was unlikely that all 1,000 were going to get lost. But my 10 fellas in their Halifaxes were all going to different areas, perhaps one to Norway, a couple to Denmark, two or three to France. I used to fly at about 2,000 feet and I advised my people to do the same. When you were going from the UK into France, or anywhere else, one of the things you had to get over was the coastal defence, so you always went up to 4,000 feet in order to cross the coast. That's the level at which light ack-ack [anti-aircraft fire] falls off before it gets to you. At 4,000 feet you were usually safe, but forget to do that and you were in trouble.'

The last mission in which Leonard took part came after Germany surrendered on 9 May 1945. His 161 Squadron had been given the role of dropping leaflets to the remote parts of Norway informing the population that the war was over. The leaflets were dropped over towns all the way up to the Arctic Circle. But one of the aircraft flying in the northern part of Norway developed engine trouble and was forced to land on the German-controlled airfield at Trondheim. Just before the aircraft landed, the radio operator managed to send a message back to Tempsford explaining that they were being forced to land.

'I decided to get a crew together and a spare engine, engineers, together with Per Hysing Dahl – after all it was his home country – and we set off for Trondheim in a Hudson. Before leaving, I sent a signal to the German commander explaining the situation and saying that we were on our way.

'It was 10 May when we arrived, and shortly after we landed a German officer appeared with a message stating that the German commander in the region wished to surrender all of his forces to our senior commander. I sent a message back explaining that although I was the senior officer he must surrender his forces to Captain Per Hysing Dahl, who was a Norwegian. He agreed to this, fortunately, and so together the two of us took the surrender of all German forces in Scandinavia, a total of 60,000 officers and men.'

Two days later the 'official' surrender was taken by the captain of a Royal Navy Cruiser, Captain Ruck-Keen.

'I flew back to home and left Per behind to oversee the repairs to the aircraft. By this time Per had telephoned his school-time sweetheart, Dagny, in Bergen, who immediately travelled up to Trondheim, where they were married by Captain Ruck-Keen, who lent the newlyweds his cabin for a honeymoon.

'When the Hudson was repaired, the crew together with Per's wife set off back to the UK. I received an urgent message from SIS stating that there was a woman on board one of my aircraft who was suspected of being a Quisling and as a consequence they were going to arrest her on landing. I radioed the plane and changed the airfield of arrival and met Per and his wife before driving to SIS HQ. I went inside and said to the duty officer, "Here are the two you were going to arrest. I vouch for them and you will arrest them over my dead body." They relented.'

On 11 June 1945 Leonard was appointed Station Commander in charge of 161 and 138 Squadrons – but his major ambition now was to get out of uniform and get on with his real life.

In six years of war Leonard flew 71 missions, 42 of them with 161 Squadron. He had been awarded the DSO, the DFC and Bar, and the AFC. He was also subsequently decorated by the French, who appointed him Chevalier de la Légion d'Honneur and awarded him the Croix de Guerre avec Palme.

After the war, Leonard returned to the family business, which he built into a highly successful agricultural company in Essex. In 1988 he was appointed the High Sheriff of Essex and dedicated much of his time to charity work and fund-raising for a wide variety of causes.

# CHAPTER 7

# Jungle Warfare behind Enemy Lines

## *Bill Towill with the Chindits*

'There was a man of genius who might have
become also a man of destiny.'
WINSTON CHURCHILL after the death of Major-General
Orde Wingate, the creator of the Chindits

The largest of the Allied special forces, the Chindits were a military
unit which was raised to fight deep behind enemy lines in the
Burmese jungle after the Japanese Imperial Army had swept
through south-east Asia. It was a brutal guerrilla war where little
quarter was given by either side. In a series of desperate battles and
daring raids the Chindits, also known as the 'Special Force', helped
destroy the myth of Japanese invincibility. Captain Bill Towill was
one of their number.

The fighting in Burma was at close quarters and casualties were
high, with many men succumbing to tropical diseases. Bill witnessed
the appalling brutality of the Japanese at first hand and saw men die
not only from the enemy's bullet but from a broken will, such were
the terrible strains of jungle combat. Those dreadful memories have
never left him.

I tracked down Bill Towill through the Burma Star Association,
an organisation which represents the interests of men and women
who served in Burma during the Second World War. When I met
Bill at his home in Surrey his health was poor, he was housebound
and cared for by his wife, but his mind was as sharp as ever. He was

eager to talk, and showed undying love for both the Gurkhas, a unit in which he served, and the Chindits.

★    ★    ★

It is fair to say that until war intervened Bill Towill was looking forward to a comfortable but quiet life as a solicitor, possibly in Paignton, Devon, where he was born, writing wills, drawing up contracts and carrying out the odd conveyance. A naturally gentle man in the truest possible sense, in time he hoped to marry and raise a family, and there was always the possibility that he might one day establish his own practice.

But as another European conflict loomed, Bill, like many of his generation, realised that his life and plans for the future would change irrecoverably.

Bill was different from many of the young men eager to prove themselves in battle: he was a pacifist and a member of the Plymouth Brethren, and his faith meant that he would not take up arms. However, he was still determined to do his bit and so he joined a local Territorial Army Royal Army Medical Corps unit.

In May 1940, Bill, then just 19, was part of the British Expeditionary Force,[*] serving with 11th Casualty Clearing Station stationed at a quiet little village called Pernois, not far from Amiens, France. It was the height of the so-called 'Phoney War', when morale amongst the troops was high. This was a period of false optimism which would only last until the Allies felt the full effect of the Nazis' brilliant Blitzkreig.

Using this strategy, German commanders made a feint attack into Belgium, drawing in the Allies, but their main thrust was around the northern end of the much-vaunted Maginot Line[†] and through the Ardennes forest, which the French had quite wrongly deemed impossible for tanks. German forces encountered very little resistance as they thundered towards the Channel coast, sweeping the

---

[*] A force of over 300,000 troops sent to France at the outbreak of war.

[†] A line of concrete fortifications running along France's border with Germany and Italy.

*Bill Towill*

Allies before them and forcing the bulk of the British Expeditionary Force towards the Belgian coast and the town of Dunkirk.

'During one night, on the Belgian coast to the east of La Panne, I spent a miserable night wading up to my chest in icy cold water, carrying stretchers shoulder high and loading the wounded on to boats to take them to ships waiting offshore.

'La Panne was the Army HQ and they set up their hospital in the casino, right on the sea front, but under heavy shell fire had to move into an underground shelter next door. On the morning of Friday 31 May I came off night duty to find my unit on parade and about to move off towards Dunkirk, about 11 miles further along the beach. A call was made for volunteers to stay behind and look after the injured, and the order was given – "Volunteers, one pace forward, quick march; volunteers stand fast; remainder dismiss!"'

Far more volunteered than were needed and the order was given a second time, followed by a third. Eventually five volunteers were left, of which Bill was one. They were joined by 20 men from other medical units and sped around the beach picking up the wounded and giving them what treatment they could.

As night fell, the medical orderlies worked by the light of the bursting shells. Time and time again great shards of shrapnel sent plumes of sand towering into the air around them, but almost incredibly not one of them was wounded.

The following morning at around 3am all British troops had long since passed by on their way to Dunkirk.

'Our officer, Major Lovibond, led a few of us into the casino, which had been turned into a morgue. Scores of bodies lay in orderly rows around the walls. There was no opportunity to give the men a proper burial, but Major Lovibond did the best he could by reading the burial service over them. It was pitch black and quite eerie. The only light came from the major's small pocket torch as he read from the Book of Revelation in his prayer book:

> And God shall wipe away all tears from their eyes; and there shall be no more death, neither sorrow, nor crying, neither shall there be any more pain: for the former things are passed away.

'For the previous few days we had been surrounded and almost submerged with pain and suffering, and these words of hope brought enormous comfort to a 19-year-old lad.

'Shortly afterwards, the major called us together. He told us that the Germans were now just down the road, and there was no need for all of us to stay. He put 25 pieces of paper in his hat and eight of them had a number on them – if you picked a number you would remain behind, look after the wounded and be taken prisoner. But those who drew a blank would be given the chance to escape.

'This simple act was one of the most important things I had ever done in my whole life. I picked a blank; but had I not done so, how very different my life would have been.

'The rest of us moved off quickly along the coast and came to a line of trucks backed out into the sea, to make a sort of quay, over which troops could scramble to board boats. We rested a little while and then saw a fighter plane coming towards us from over the sea but couldn't tell if it was enemy or friendly. Then we saw little lights sparkling along the front wings of the plane and in a trice we were in a hail of machine-gun and cannon shells, but mercifully none of us were injured. We moved on further into France, tried unsuccessfully to launch some beached boats and eventually came within sight of Dunkirk. It was a truly appalling scene. Petrol storage tanks were on fire, there was a great thick cloud of black oily smoke covering everything. There was heavy shelling, mortaring, strafing and machine-gunning going on. But the most fearsome were the Stuka dive-bombers, making a terrifying screaming noise as they attacked ships laden with troops. Many would have thought that now they were on board a ship they were safe and on their way home, only to be sunk by a Stuka, and the losses were horrific.

'Later that night we lined up to go on to the wooden Mole, attached to the outside of the harbour wall, in the hope of embarking on a ship. Access was by a concrete walkway, to the left of which and about 20 feet below was a canal, alongside which were the bodies of several British soldiers, and they all had the same injury. The tops of their skulls had been taken off as if by a can opener and it was obviously not a very healthy place to be. We never got on a boat that night, so we went back to the beach and dug a hole for ourselves near the Mole. We had a horrible night and on three occasions we were almost killed by bombs and we had to dig ourselves out.

'Eventually, very late on the evening of Sunday 2 June, all the shelling, strafing and bombing stopped, as if by a miracle, and we were able to clamber out of our holes in the sand and make our way quietly along the Mole and on to a ship. We didn't know it at the time but the Royal Navy had determined that this would be the last day of the evacuation, codenamed Operation Dynamo, so it was indeed a very close run thing.

'We hadn't eaten or had anything to drink for some days and were truly exhausted. It was at that stage that my pacifist views were eroded away. I had seen for myself the truly vile face of our enemy, how they had mercilessly strafed the pitiful columns of refugees and their violence at Dunkirk, and I was determined that if I ever got off that beach I would hit back as hard as I could. I had become fully convinced that the use of arms to prevent such atrocities was more than justified.

'We arrived at Dover early the next morning and were welcomed by a Guards drill sergeant, complete with pace stick, red sash and boots, bulled so that you could see your face in them, bellowing at us to pull ourselves together and did we think we'd been on a Sunday school outing? I was full of rage and wanted to punch in his smug face, but I then realised that his attitude was right, even if proclaimed too provocatively – I felt a strange pride that I was part of an army which could take such a beating yet still hold its head high. I have very few mementoes from the war, but one that I still treasure is a small pewter hip-flask from Major Lovibond with a note saying:

> Pte Towill. To commemorate some thirsty hours spent together on Dinkirk beach, 1 and 2 June, 1940.

'As we made our way north by train, crowds cheered us to the echo, which at first I found difficult to accept, since we'd run away like a dog with its tail between its legs. At stations where we halted, wonderful women plied us with sandwiches and beakers of tea.'

★　　★　　★

Later that year Bill was recommended for a commission and was sent to Bellerby Camp in Yorkshire, where he saw a notice asking for cadets to serve in the Indian Army. He had no idea what was involved but thought it interesting and so put his name down.

The Indian Army volunteers eventually sailed via the Cape of Good Hope to India. After arriving in Bombay they were divided into groups and were sent to the three OCTUs for training. Bill was sent to the Indian Military Academy in Dehra Dun, the Indian equivalent of Sandhurst.

It was during Bill's period of officer training that Japan entered the war. On 8 December 1941 they attacked Pearl Harbor, destroying much of the US Pacific Fleet, and on the same day they invaded Hong Kong. Two days later two major British warships, HMS *Repulse* and HMS *Prince of Wales*, were sunk in a Japanese air attack off the coast of Malaya. In January 1942 the Japanese armed forces invaded Burma and the Dutch East Indies and captured Manila and Kuala Lumpur. On 15 February, Singapore fell to the Japanese and 130,000 Allied troops became prisoners of war, the largest surrender in British military history. By this stage the Japanese army was already advancing in Burma, sweeping all before them. Rangoon, the country's capital, fell in March and the Allies were in full retreat, finally reaching the Indian border in May 1942. By this stage of the war the Allies' morale was all but broken, and many believed, not surprisingly, that in the Japanese army they faced an invincible enemy.

But that notion was not accepted by Brigadier Orde Charles Wingate, who arrived in India in March 1942 with the aim of launching guerrilla operations against the Japanese in Burma. Wingate had won a reputation for being an unconventional but effective commander who had achieved considerable, if controversial, success in carrying out guerrilla operations in Palestine and Abyssinia.

The unconventional brigadier began to reconnoitre the terrain in north Burma with a view to operating behind the Japanese front line with a force supplied by air. He explained to General Sir Archibald Wavell, the Commander-in-Chief of British forces in India, his belief that formations of specially trained troops, which he called columns, could operate for long periods behind enemy lines. The column's strength was to be about half the size of a battalion with supporting groups, and would be supplied by air, and although it was a significant departure from normal battalion structure Wingate believed the column was large enough to inflict heavy

casualties against the enemy but small enough to flit away afterwards. Wingate called this strategy Long Range Penetration.

Wingate appreciated that the British defeat in Burma had cata-
strophically damaged morale. If his plan of long-range penetration
was to work, he would require a special breed of soldier. He
wanted men similar to those who had fought with the SAS and
the LRDG in the North African campaign; soldiers who embraced
his unconventional tactics and had the mental fortitude to push
themselves to the very limit in some of the most arduous terrain
on earth; men with real grit and determination, who perhaps even
saw themselves as being slightly superior to the rank and file. A
small dose of arrogance is no bad thing in military units providing
it can be backed up when the going gets tough. A similar mental
attitude exists within many of the elite formations of Britain's
armed forces today. Those who volunteer to serve in either the
Parachute Regiment of the Royal Marines, the SAS or the SBS
do so, in my opinion, because they want to be part of something
special, something different. The hard training and the selection
process create a strong *esprit de corps* and huge self-belief, which in
the heat of battle can often mean the difference between success
and failure, something which is as relevant today as it was in 1943.
Wingate understood this better than anyone, and although he
pushed his men almost to the brink in training he also knew that
those who met his exacting standards would carry the name of the
Chindit with pride – a vital quality when fighting in the jungle
against the Japanese.

Soldiers from a variety of units were drawn together to form 77
Brigade and underwent an intense period of training, and many
failed to meet the exacting standards. Wingate's men needed to be
able to march for days on end through some of the most challenging environment on earth, often short of food and water, where the
humidity was 100 per cent and the temperatures were well into the
90s and sometimes above. The troops would be under constant
threat of attack and the stress of knowing that capture by the
Japanese would mean torture and possibly execution, or at best a
stay in one of the enemy's appallingly brutal prison camps. Those

who were injured and too sick to walk, Wingate ordered, would be left behind.

The training took place in the Indian jungle during the rainy season. Soldiers carried anything up to 120lb of equipment. The kit included personal weapons and ammunition, spare ammunition for the heavier weapons, hand grenades, mortars, rations for seven days, spare clothing and a ground sheet.

The new unit became known as the Chindits – the name deriving from the Chinthe, the mythical winged, lion-like creature found guarding the four sides of Buddhist temples.

Half of the troops came from the King's Liverpool Regiment, while soldiers from the Bush Warfare School formed 142 Commando Company, with the remainder of the force being drawn from the Burma Rifles and the 2nd Gurkha Rifles.

The first Chindit operation began on 8 February 1942 and was codenamed Operation Longcloth. Troops marched into Burma from Imphal, in Assam, and over the next three months fought a series of ferocious actions against the Japanese. Of the 3,000 Chindits who took part in the operation, 818 men were killed, captured or died of disease, and of the 2,182 soldiers who returned, more than 600 were too weak or ill to continue with further military service. The majority of those who survived had marched around 1,000 miles.

The success of Operation Longcloth still divides opinion today. The main Burma north–south railway line was cut in 70 places, yet it was up and running again within days. But the chief effect of the operation was to raise the morale of British troops by demonstrating that the Japanese could be defeated and were not the invincible enemy which many had believed them to be. Wingate's exploits also, crucially, won the support of Winston Churchill,

In August 1943, less than a year before D-Day, Churchill, Roosevelt and the Combined Chiefs of Staff met at Quebec to discuss the future Allied strategy, and Churchill insisted that Wingate accompany him. During the conference Wingate presented his plans for the use of Long Range Penetration Group as part of another expedition into Burma, but this time involving many more troops. The Americans supported the plan and promised to provide air support via what became known as the First US Air Commando, a force comprising bombers, fighters, transport aircraft and gliders. Given that the Allied invasion of France was already close at hand, obtaining such a formidable air armada was a quite remarkable achievement.

While plans were being hatched which would help to turn the tide of the war in the Far East, Bill Towill and the 3rd/9th Gurkha Rifles, as part of 4th Indian Infantry Brigade, 26th Indian Division, had since the early part of 1943 been based in the Arakan on the west coast of Burma, where the unit took part in many clashes with the Japanese.

By this stage of the war Bill had completed his officer training and was now the intelligence officer of the 3rd/9th Gurkha Rifles. His battalion had spent many months training in preparation for the inevitable battle with the Japanese. But in January 1944 the battalion received the surprising news that it was being withdrawn from the division and was to become part of the Chindits.

'The move to the Chindits came out of the blue for us and we were initially puzzled, but when we met Wingate we were all immediately mesmerised by his charisma and oratorical powers.'

Wingate's second expedition, codename Operation Thursday, would involve inserting a force behind enemy lines, consisting of six brigades: the 16th, 77th, 111th, 14th, 3rd and 23rd. With around 10,000 troops, the force was far larger than the first operation and its objectives were more ambitious, as they would be preparing the way for the retaking of Burma.

All of the brigades would land by glider and Dakota, except 16 Brigade which was to march into the Indaw area of Burma, a route over unknown mountainous country. The training began in earnest at Gwalior in India, where once again the soldiers spent days on end marching while carrying back-breaking loads. They also learnt how to survive and fight in the jungle – the skills required by the guerrilla fighter.

But not everyone was so adequately prepared for deep penetration operations.

'We didn't really do a great deal of specialist training, because we didn't have the time, only about eight weeks between our joining the force and flying in. Wingate trained the Chindits almost to the point of destruction but we missed almost all of it. All of the unfit and older people were weeded out, leaving only the very fit. But the Gurkhas were very fit because of their extremely arduous home conditions.'

Bill's battalion would form part of 77 Brigade along with 3rd/6th Gurkhas, 1st King's (Liverpool) Regiment, 1st Lancashire Fusiliers and the 1st South Staffordshire. The Brigade was commanded by Brigadier Mike ('Mad Mike') Calvert, an officer already famous for his personal courage who had previously served under Wingate in Operation Longcloth and had been one of his column commanders.

On Sunday 5 March 1944, Bill along with hundreds of other young soldiers, some anxious, others excited, were about to fly into Burma from the Lalaghat airfield some 70 miles west of Imphal in Assam as part of Operation Thursday.

'It was a couple of days before the full moon, carefully chosen so that the landings, due to take place over five consecutive days, would have the light of the moon. Along the runway of the airfield were about 80 large Waco troop-carrying gliders, two abreast in a long queue. Carefully laid out in front of them were all the nylon tow ropes, ready to be hooked up on to the Dakotas, gathered around the edge of the airfield.

'We were in about the fifth pair of gliders, waiting to board, but I wasn't feeling very nervous. I was only 23 and full of fight and vigour, and I was very excited by the prospect. There had been all of this preparation, and there comes a point when you just want to get on with it. Looking around the airfield, I knew that many of my colleagues who were about to be flown deep behind Japanese lines into Burma would not return. But it wasn't a solemn experience. We were aware that we were all taking part in something historic, something of great worth.'

Operation Thursday was at that point the largest operation of its kind in the war, only three months before the great invasion of

Normandy. The troops were due to land on three landing grounds, codenamed Broadway, Piccadilly and Chowringhee, and to establish 'strongholds'. These were to serve as bases from which columns could strike deep into the heart of Japanese-occupied Burma. But just before H-Hour, the Piccadilly operation was abandoned after reconnaissance flights revealed that the landing ground had been blocked with tree trunks. Instead 77 Brigade led the way and went into Broadway.

'I formed part of an advance party along with my commanding officer, Lieutenant-Colonel Noel George, and a few riflemen. I was utterly convinced that we were on a course to victory; I think that was the feeling of us all – we never doubted that we would succeed, whatever the cost. Although we had only been with the Special Force for a few weeks we had become completely caught up with Wingate's zeal and enthusiasm. He was a tremendous orator, who could speak to you for just a little while and you were like putty in his hand.

'Eventually we wheeled our glider forward as each pair took off, and shortly after 7pm it was our turn. Our advance party clambered on board and soon we were trundling down the runway. The noise was deafening – from the groaning glider as it was dragged along and also from the engines of the Dakota – but then almost suddenly the bumping and groaning stopped: we were airborne. I was sitting behind the pilot and almost immediately realised that something was wrong. He was wrestling with the controls and trying to trim the glider and keep it stable, while at the same time the glider on the starboard side was swinging dangerously towards us. He must have assumed that we were going to collide. I then saw him reach up and punch the lever to release the tow cable and we were away. I looked out of the window and I could see, lit by moonlight, the paddy fields racing up below. I saw the pilot brace himself and he yelled "Hang on!" We had no seatbelts but I grabbed the struts alongside and shouted to the others to do the same. We must have hit the ground at around 70mph and we bounced along the paddy fields for what seemed like an eternity before coming to a halt. Although we were a bit knocked about we had survived, and the most seriously injured amongst us had only sustained a broken arm. We radioed the airfield and fired a few Very lights and were soon picked up by transport and taken back to the airport, ready to try our luck again.

'But it was all stopped by a message from Brigadier Calvert who was leading the advance. He and Wingate had arranged messages that could be sent uncoded. If things were going well they would signal "Pork Sausage", which was something the troops loved, and if things weren't going too well they would send "Soya Link", which meant sausages made from soya which the troops didn't much like.

'About 3.30am the message "Soya Link" came through – nothing else – meaning to stop all flying from the airfield. A real sense of gloom descended on us, because at that stage no one had any idea what was happening. Then at 6.30am came the message "Pork Sausage" which, to everyone's immense relief, meant that flying could be resumed.'

The delay had been caused by a number of gliders piling into each other on landing. Of the 61 gliders which had been dispatched, only 34 had arrived. But there had been sufficient men to form a work party able to prepare a rough airstrip which could receive the Dakotas that same night. Bill and his party eventually arrived at Broadway that night, as did Wingate, following his practice of always leading from the front.

'He called us all together, and we gathered round. He congratulated us and wished us luck and expressed his sympathies for the deaths sustained, but added, "You can't make an omelette without breaking a few eggs." Though obviously saddened by the deaths, he still managed to radiate this confidence. He was dressed in his crumpled bush jacket, dirty ammunition boots, with a Lee Enfield rifle slung over his shoulder and his traditional Wolseley sun helmet.

'Then behind us what seemed to be a battle started up, with grenades, mortar bombs and machine-guns all going off. It emerged that a glider had crashed very high up in the trees. All on board had been killed, but the bodies could not be extricated from the tangled wreckage, and so the glider was turned into a macabre funeral pyre.'

When Wingate left, Brigadier Calvert led Bill's party across the airstrip into the jungle. After marching for about 100 yards they came across a very shallow valley with a clear stream running through it. The location was the perfect position for a stronghold, on the fringe of a mature teak forest. The thick canopy inhibited undergrowth and made walking through this area quite easy. Bill's team began laying out the general area of the stronghold, so that as the rest of the battalion flew in over the next two nights they could be moved directly into their assigned areas.

'As soon as the rest of the battalion arrived they began digging in. We dug without let-up. I personally dug all the way through the night because we knew that the Japs would attack soon and we all wanted to make the stronghold impregnable. By the time we had finished, each of the individual foxholes had interlocking arcs of fire. The foxholes had roofs made from timber and were covered with earth and afforded great protection from mortar fire. Once the foxholes were dug, we enveloped the whole stronghold with triple Danert barbed wire entanglements. Over the next few days we continued to improve the defensive position – it was always a work in progress. As we worked through that first night the aircraft continued to come in, one after the other, hour after hour, at the rate of about one every three minutes, and it was exhilarating in the extreme to see this happening.'

By the end of the sixth day of Operation Thursday, 78 glider and 660 Dakota sorties had been flown: 9,052 troops had been landed, along with 1,360 pack animals and 250 tons of supplies. Casualties were 121 men killed or wounded, all associated with glider landings.

Life at Broadway continued at a frenetic pace for several days, with troops either wholly embroiled in reinforcing their new home or conducting patrols. Bill meanwhile began establishing his own briefing area. Having found a glider wing, hauled it back and lashed it to two trees, he pasted one-inch and quarter-inch maps on it and nailed some perspex glider windows on top of them, which could readily be marked up with chinagraph pencils to show Chindit and enemy locations.

'My little fiefdom gradually became a meeting place for officers who wanted to be able to read the daily sitrep [situation reports]. We also got reports of enemy movement from the local Kachin tribesmen, who were very friendly and would happily tell all to our Burma Rifle troops.

'We all knew that soon we would be attacked, and the first came on 13 March, when about 20 Zero* fighters attacked and strafed the airfield and the stronghold. Five Spitfires took off against the Japs, shooting down four enemy planes with the loss of only one of our aircraft. Another attack followed three days later but this time the Japs used medium bombers. On 20 March we were attacked by a much heavier bomber force which, with hindsight, was the prelim to a full battalion-sized attack which was just about to hit us.'

By this stage Calvert had already departed from Broadway with the remainder of the brigade and marched south-west to establish a road and rail block. It was during one of the attacks that Calvert personally led a bayonet charge to clear the enemy from an area known as Pagoda Hill. The enemy held the top of the hill and Calvert could be heard shouting, 'Come on, boys! One last effort and we'll have them on the run.'

During the ferocious combat which followed, Lieutenant George Cairns of the South Staffords had his arm severed by a Japanese officer wielding a ceremonial sword. Before the officer could deliver the fatal blow, Cairns shot him dead with his pistol, picked up the sword and set about dispatching several more Japanese soldiers before collapsing and dying from loss of blood.

The block became known as 'White City' because of the numerous parachutes which hung in the trees. White City was to become the scene of many fierce battles in which the Japanese suffered huge losses. The first attack took place on 17 March, when two companies of Japanese infantry assaulted the position. The majority of the enemy force was killed within the first few minutes of the

---

* Mitsubishi A6M Zero long-range fighter.

attack. But the losses served as no deterrent and over the next three days the Japanese attacked time and again. The siting of the block was almost perfect and it became a terrible killing ground for the enemy. It was reckoned that at any one time there were upwards of 1,000 Japanese bodies hanging in the wire. It was said that the pilots didn't have to navigate to White City – they just followed the stench of the dead.

Although enemy attacks against the Chindits were beginning to gather pace, the real test of Special Force's fighting spirit came on 24 March, when the aircraft in which Wingate was travelling crashed in bad weather, killing everyone on board. Every member of the force felt the sense of loss. In many of the soldiers' eyes Wingate *was* the Chindits, and he was widely regarded as being irreplaceable. Perhaps one man capable of filling the role was Calvert, but instead Brigadier Joe Lentaigne of III Brigade was appointed commander of Special Force; John Masters, the then brigade major, took command of the elements of III Brigade which had managed to travel west after landing at Chowringhee, while the remainder travelled east on to the Mytkyina front and were commanded by Jumbo Morris, who took the rank of brigadier.

Bill and many others within the Chindits did not regard Lentaigne as a suitable replacement. He was not generally in tune with Wingate's ideas and lacked his charisma and strength of character.

Wingate's death would also result some two months later in the control of the Chindits being passed to General 'Vinegar' Joe Stilwell, who was known to have what was once described as a 'pathological hatred' of everything British. Under his command the Chindits were to suffer their greatest number of casualties.

'One night we heard the peculiar sound of men marching from the airstrip and someone was shouting commands, "Left right, left right, left right – right turn", in English, but we knew they couldn't be our men, because they wouldn't be out there. Then they screamed "Charge!" and came at us, shouting our password which was "Mandalay". But we held our fire till they hit the wire and then we let them have it. Hardly any got through, but I remember seeing one who had done so. He crawled through the wire but a grenade exploded under his chin. It didn't blow his head off but splayed his jaw out and made him look frog-like.

'Around the northern edge of our clearing, D Company, commanded by Major Irwin Pickett, was operating beyond the wire as a sort of floater company. I don't know what his orders had been, but following Chindit protocol he should have remained loose and so free to strike at any enemy forces who attacked the block. But instead, each of his three platoons dug separate defensive positions, denying themselves any mobility.'

The first attack took place around 10.30pm when a D Company sentry opened fire after hearing enemy movement in the forest. This was met by a flurry of grenades from the Japanese. The ensuing battle lasted about 40 minutes, and as each platoon position was overwhelmed by superior force they fell back on to the company HQ. A grenade landing in his lap mortally wounded Major Irwin Pickett. It was vicious hand-to-hand fighting in the pitch darkness where almost everything was used as a weapon.

'Despite our hatred of the Japs we could not help but admire their bravery and how lightly they managed to travel. When we searched through some of the kit of the dead we found that their rations consisted of a sock full of rice and some raw brown sugar, wrapped in brown paper. During that first attack we lost around 12 men dead and 40 injured, but we believed that the Japs suffered many more casualties. They seemed to have such a disregard for their own lives or for varying their tactics – they would just charge full-frontal and be cut down.

'On the second night of the attacks there was a hellish electrical storm with lightning and thunder and the rain was coming down like a waterfall. I thought the Japs would come through for certain, so I went to see how my men were getting along. I was crawling along a narrow slit trench and I just put my head up to see what I could, when two mortar bombs exploded simultaneously either side of the trench and close to my head. It was like being cuffed across the back of the head by a giant hand. I couldn't stop vomiting and retching, and I had the greatest trouble to get control of myself and it took me many seconds to do so. Had I lifted my head half a second earlier I would have been a goner, because I would have met the full force of those two mortar bombs.

'On 31 March we finally managed to get air support. Our fighter bombers queued in a taxi rank, as we called them, and we identified the enemy's position with coloured smoke bombs fired from our 3-inch mortar, which they then bombed. Once the bombing had finished, we climbed out of our trenches and moved into the jungle, ready to mop up any surviving Jap troops. In front of one of the Japanese positions I saw something which filled me with rage and despair. There lay the bodies of seven of our men who had been captured earlier. Their hands had been tied behind their backs and the Japs had butchered them and then stacked them up like a pile of logs.

'These men had been posted outside the perimeter to guard the Spitfires. When the Japs first attacked they had sent back a runner to say that they would hold out for as long as possible. Later, on patrol around the perimeter, we often came across one of our men, body on one side and the blackened putrefying head on the other, where a Japanese officer had done a bit of sword practice. Gradually the attacks subsided and the battalion continued with its mission of holding the stronghold and securing the area by patrolling. It was around this time that the two RAF pilots attached to the battalion managed to get a couple of light aircraft flying through their mechanical ingenuity.

'One day the brigade major came up to me and said, "Bill, I've got a great idea. Let's fill our shirts with grenades, go up with these RAF chaps and drops the grenades on the Japs." Despite having grave doubts about the plan, I could hardly refuse the brigade major, a man of great charm and much senior rank, and so we set out. We didn't find any Japs but we found a group of our own men. We dived down vertically, in the RAF equivalent of a *feu de joie*, and the troops below scattered, and I'm sure they didn't appreciate the spirit of the greeting. It was also too much for my stomach and I vomited. The brigade major was fine, and as we flew side by side and he waved cheerily at me and I responded as gallantly as I could, but, after that the RAF never invited us back into their aircraft.'

In early May, Bill's regiment suffered another morale-sapping blow, which hit many of the officers and men particularly hard. The battalion's popular commanding officer, Lieutenant-Colonel Noel George, fell ill and had to be evacuated. It later emerged that he had contracted polio. An officer unknown to the battalion, Major Alec Harper, a cavalry man from the famous Indian regiment the Royal Deccan Horse, was sent to replace him.

Harper had been commissioned in about 1930 and had volunteered to serve with the Special Force to see some action. One of his first actions was to sack the adjutant, who he thought was a bit nervy. He then called all the company commanders together and asked them for their opinions on who should replace him, and they all said Bill Towill – so he became adjutant.

White City, despite all of the fighting and sacrifice, was abandoned on Stilwell's orders. He wanted to move the troops further north to the area of Hopin, in support of his own force and III Brigade, who were establishing a new block. Almost immediately after Harper's arrival the battalion received orders that Broadway too had now achieved its purpose and should be abandoned. The new orders were to head north for Railway Valley and await further instructions.

'Over the next few days all excess equipment was dispatched on Dakota aircraft. Officers were issued with a US M30 carbine, which was semi-automatic and held 15 rounds, was much lighter and a great improvement on the Lee Enfield, although it didn't pack the same punch. I also traded my .38 Smith & Wesson revolver for a .45 semi-automatic Remington pistol belonging to a US pilot.

'During that very busy period we had to get our personal equipment in order and picked up five days' supply of the US K-ration, three cartons per day marked Breakfast, Dinner and Supper. Breakfast was a tin of cheese incorporating small bits of ham, together with instant coffee and powdered milk; dinner was tinned cheese, biscuits, chocolate and lemonade powder, and supper was effectively the same but with powdered soup instead of lemonade. The rations also contained four cigarettes, which did wonders for the morale of smokers. The rations were only meant to be consumed in an emergency but they quickly formed all our diet.

'Early on 13 May the battalion silently left Broadway via a gap in the north-east corner of the wire. We went past Irwin Pickett's grave and saw, just to our left, an area about a yard square tightly packed with the most beautiful butterflies. In a long, snaking single file, we headed for the Gangaw Range. Initially, in the cool morning air, because we always started out just before dawn, the 60lb loads each man was carrying seemed bearable, but when the energy-sapping, steaming jungle heat arrived a few hours later, most of the exhausted soldiers could think of little else but the five minutes' rest at the end of every hour.

'The straps from the packs cut into our shoulders and at times it seemed that it was all you could do to stand upright. When the column stopped for some reason or other the men would bend over to relieve the pressure on their aching shoulders – we called it "the Chindit stoop".

'Every night we would move into a special harbour location which had to be carefully positioned. The routine was to stop and then move from the track straight into the jungle for four or five hundred yards and locate a readily visible point, such as a huge tree. Then as the rest of the battalion came in, three companies were sent out on 120-degree bearings, so as to provide all-round defence, keeping one company in reserve. We would turn it into a rough defensive position as best as time would allow. The signals section would set up their wireless and get in touch with base and also start the "chore horse" generator to charge the batteries.

'Accompanying us were the indispensable mules, truly valiant animals, which carried radios and battery chargers, Vickers machine-guns, 3-inch mortars and other heavy gear. As the column moved deeper into the jungle and closer to the Gangaw Range the weather broke and the rains came, turning the jungle paths into thick, cloying tracks in which men and often mules became stuck fast. The distance we covered each day would be totally dependent on the ground; sometimes it might not be much more than five miles. We sometimes had to hack our way through the jungle, which was slow and gruelling.

'I later heard a story about how mules behaved from another Chindit, who told me that his party came to a steep downward slope, which a loaded mule couldn't negotiate. The troops had to off-load the mules, take all the loads down below and then reload them. To help, this chap was carrying his men's rifles, three on each shoulder, and as he followed his feet begin to slip. He was steadied by a strong grip on his right arm and, looking round, he found it was the mule that was preventing him from falling. Believe it or not, he assured me it was true. They really were quite the most remarkable animals and most of us were very fond of them.'

On 4 March the battalion arrived at the village of Lamai, high in the Gangaw hills, where the exhausted soldiers waited for a supply drop. News arrived that the battalion was being transferred to III Brigade, at a new road and rail block, codenamed Blackpool. But the change in the weather, the misty conditions and high mountains meant that the Dakotas bringing supplies could not always fly low enough to see the dropping zone. Always under heavy physical strain, the soldiers weakened, having used up all their reserves of energy. Their health rapidly deteriorated and they became shadows of their former selves. There came a stage when British soldiers began to die of no apparent illness.

'I simply couldn't understand it. I had never seen anything like that before, so I asked a medical officer, "Why are these chaps dying like this?" and he said, "They've had enough, they can't take any more and have just given up."'

After six solid days' marching, the column arrived at Blackpool and it was immediately clear that the block had been the scene of very intense fighting. They had arrived late in the evening, too late to enter the security of the compound, and had to spend the first night beyond the wire.

'Blackpool was located on a hilltop, about 300 feet up, and its various features had been allocated cricketing names. The central spine where Brigade HQ was located was called the Wicket, with Keeper to the west and Bowler and Umpire along the spine to the east. Beyond Umpire was a place to be avoided at all costs. It was known as the Deep, and it was at the bottom of a very slippery slope ending in a waterlogged swamp. The Pavilion was on a hill to the right of the Wicket above the Deep. Clockwise from Pavilion was Cover Point, followed by Silly Point. To the north of Wicket in a clockwise direction were Fine Leg, Square Leg and Mid On. So if you understood cricketing terms it helped you to move around.'

Turning Blackpool into an effective block had been a difficult task. The soldiers who had established the block knew that the enemy would attack very soon. During the heat of the day they toiled for hours on end building the defensive position, unable to fully rest at night because of the threat of attack. When the Japanese did attack, it was at first in little more than platoon strength and each attack was a suicidal failure, but the Japanese were unrelenting, and the effect was beginning to take its toll on the embattled troops. On 20 May Bill and his battalion moved into the block and took up their positions on the perimeter, but many fresh enemy troops had arrived in the area and were preparing for a concerted attack against Blackpool.

'We didn't have anything like the strength that we needed to hold the block against the Japs, and the men that we did have were suffering from extreme fatigue. We could see that the morale of the men we had come to support at Blackpool was at rock bottom. They had not received a visit from the new general and they felt abandoned. It was a situation I felt sure would have never been allowed to exist under Wingate. There was a horrible desperation about Blackpool. The whole area stank of decomposing human remains and excreta. The earth had been churned up into a sticky, muddy mess. One soldier was found on his own sitting upright in his slit trench. When called he made no reply and when tapped on the shoulder he rolled over, stone dead. What was so alarming was that he had just been left there by his own comrades. No one seemed to care.

'The area between the double wire entanglements had been sown with booby traps, which made entering and leaving the block very difficult and on more than one occasion led to our own men being killed. The trenches we took over had been poorly prepared and offered little protection, and although our men were exhausted from a terrible march through the jungle there was no time to rest. Instead we set about reinforcing our position.'

Over the days that followed the frequency and ferocity of enemy attacks increased, as did mortar and artillery fire. Anti-aircraft guns began to take their toll on the Dakotas trying to resupply the Chindits, and a sense of inevitable doom began to descend on many of the men.

'We lost control of the airstrip and even air drops had to face anti-aircraft fire. Everyone now knew that the injured could not be flown out, and when the time came to abandon Blackpool, the seriously wounded faced a terrible fate.'

As if to heap more misery on to their already wretched existence, the rains came, turning Blackpool into what Bill described as 'a hopeless quagmire'.

'We were running short of food and ammunition, and the following afternoon three Dakotas flew in at the suicidal altitude of around 50 feet. The Japs fired at them with everything they had, but the pilots heroically held a steady course, dropping the life-saving supplies. Then one of the planes was hit and I watched in horror as it crashed in a ball of flames. Despite the pilots' valiant efforts many of the parachutes fell outside the perimeter, and by the time we had collected them all, the supplies amounted to little more than a meal per man and ammunition for another 24 hours. It was a shattering blow, because we knew that there was no chance whatever of receiving any further supplies.

'After the supply drop, the artillery started up again and a man standing right in front of me was literally cut in half by shrapnel. I will never forget the stench of fresh human blood and guts. It was truly appalling. That night, the 24th of May, was terrible. The Japs came at us time and again. They took everything we could throw at them but still returned. We lost a lot of men, but their casualties must have been horrendous.'

On 25 May the enemy attacked in strength across the airstrip and began to overrun a number of positions. The situation was now desperate and the commander of III Brigade, John Masters, decided that the only real course left open was to abandon the block.

'If we stayed we knew that we would have to fight to the last man and we would face certain death. I think we were all of the view that we would never be taken prisoner because the Japanese would enjoy devising the slowest, most painful and humiliating death for us that they could. We never really understood why the Japanese were so brutal and barbaric. But within the Japanese army itself life was very brutal and their seniors routinely beat soldiers for the slightest offence. A prisoner of war was the very lowest of the low as far as they were concerned. No one could sink lower than allow himself to be taken prisoner.

'Then of course we came to the wounded. Those who could walk or had any chance of survival we took with us. There were about 60 severely wounded whom we took with us and about 100 walking wounded. At the regimental aid post there were around 18 who were dying or were very close to death. These poor fellows had terrible injuries and would not have survived much longer. The only real option was to put them out of their misery, and this was done by a bullet to the head by one of the medical team. It was heartbreaking, but it was the right thing to do.'

The unthinkable prospect of having to shoot injured soldiers, some of whom were both colleagues and friends, was a reflection of how desperate the situation had become. Having witnessed the brutality of the Japanese at close hand, the Chindits were utterly convinced that the injured would be tortured before facing a terrible death.

*          *          *

One of those who suddenly found themselves having to kill a fellow British soldier was Lieutenant Bill Smyly, an Irishman who was the Animal Transport Officer serving with the 3rd/9th Gurkhas. He was a friend of Bill Towill at the time when Blackpool was abandoned. I spoke to Smyly, one of the few surviving soldiers who took part in both Chindit expeditions, and he too recalled for me the tragic withdrawal from Blackpool.

'As we began to move out I looked ahead along a track and I saw two stretcher-bearers running along or walking very quickly with a very seriously injured soldier, and suddenly he rolled off. The two soldiers stopped and put him back on the stretcher. I told them to hurry up because the Japanese were closing in. They looked around at us and simply left this poor fellow by the side of the track. When I got to him moments later I could see that his left arm and shoulder had gone. He had either been blown up or hit by machine-gun fire. But either way he was very badly injured. I saw another young officer close by, so I called him over and the two of us carried him away. By this stage the Japanese were bearing down on us, they were herding us out of Blackpool. We could see their flags on sticks, as they were moving through the long elephant grass, and they could have only been 20 or 30 metres away. We could actually hear them talking.

'The young officer and I – in fact we were both just 19 or 20 – were carrying this badly wounded soldier, and when we got to the bottom of the hill it became obvious that we were not going to get out if we tried to take him with us. I don't know which one of us said it first, but one of us spoke out: "We can't do this!" We both agreed.

'I knew there and then that we were going to have to shoot him and I took it upon myself to do it. I don't want to say what his name was, because he may have some family still alive today.

'He had lost an arm and a shoulder and he was in a kind of trauma where the injured don't feel much pain. He was conscious, and when I talked to him he seemed to acknowledge what I was saying. We all knew before the operation started that the badly injured would be left behind. That was the case on the first show,

*Bill Smyly*

but after that we tried to take as many as we could whenever we abandoned a position, but we could only really help the walking wounded. It wasn't as if there was a hospital a few miles away. We were in the middle of the jungle, with the enemy minutes away. I stroked his hair and tried to make him feel comfortable. He was a Scottish soldier and seemed at that point to be very content. I withdrew my service revolver from my holster and looked at the other officer, who seemed to be very shocked and he turned away. I knelt at the head of the stretcher and talked to the injured Scotsman. I asked him where he came from and he told me, and I said, "You'll be back there soon enough." He seemed to be at peace, in a state of what you could describe as contentment.

'As the Animal Transport Officer it was my job to shoot injured mules, and what you'd do is shoot in the middle of the forehead, aiming for the spine, so that it goes down a series of vital structures. I did the same thing to this poor chap. I pulled the trigger and his head shot back and I closed his eyes and left him at peace. I stood up and the other chap, who was very clearly shocked, said, "You are a better man than me." I didn't say anything.

'Afterwards, thinking it over, I wished I had left him alive, because we learnt that the Japs did take prisoners, but we didn't know that at the time. I think possibly he would have been taken to hospital, but how much chance he would have had of surviving I don't know. I suppose also I could have ignored him and pretended that I hadn't seen him, but I didn't think that was the sort of thing an officer ought to do either.

'There is a very strong bond with the injured amongst service people and you want to do anything you can to look after them. The idea of me getting up and saying, "Well, mate, goodbye!" is not something you can do. The reason why I never volunteered the story in the past is because I question it. I question my actions, but I do so as an afterthought. Then, at that time, in battle it was custom-ary to get on and do the next thing that had to be done. I couldn't leave him, so I shot him. We had orders that we should shoot the injured who couldn't be moved, that we shouldn't leave them to the Japanese. That was a mistake, but it was the instruction.

'It hasn't been difficult to live with, it's part of me. One doesn't know what the next life will be like, but I think he'll be waiting for me and I'll say hello!'

As Bill quickly walked along the track, with the Japanese just 30 yards behind, he came across a scene which has haunted him ever since. As the brigade scrambled to make good their withdrawal, some of the most badly injured soldiers had simply been aban-doned by the side of the track.

'There were abandoned stretchers with soldiers lying on them all along the track in the grass; some were still conscious, just lying there, and I was overcome by a great sense of shame. One soldier, a Cameronian,* who was sitting up on his elbows, looked me right

---

* The 1st Cameronians served in 111 Brigade during Operation Thursday.

in the eye and I felt very ashamed and I couldn't look at him. I wish we had had some sort of drill where we would salute them or something, but we didn't have anything. On another occasion a Gurkha who was abandoned because he was badly injured insisted on shaking hands with everyone as they marched past. He was left with a tommy-gun, and after we marched past we heard a burst of machine-gun fire and he had shot himself. That seemed to me a much better military end than just walking past and not doing anything. But I suppose there was nothing we could do. You are not going to joke with a man who is facing death with his eyes open. If I'm honest I have to say that one was almost irritated with them for being wounded and asking the impossible of you. Their condition, their wounds, asked you to do something, but there was nothing you could do and they knew there was nothing to be done and that made the whole experience even more traumatic.

'It was a dreadful end to a hellish period and we all found it very difficult to talk about. You possibly heard one officer say rather despairingly, "I had to shoot one of my men," and someone else might mumble something, but more often than not the conversation would be about how good the bully beef tasted, anything really to avoid the subject that was preying on our minds.'

★        ★        ★

Like his friend Bill Smyly, Bill Towill was among the last to leave Blackpool: 'With the battalion headquarters, I was one of the very last to leave that hell-hole. As we moved down a shallow nullah [gully] we came to an open area about 100 yards across, on our left. I saw some of our men moving across the open ground, neglecting the cardinal rule to always use all available cover when you move. All of a sudden, in a well-coordinated ambush, several enemy machine-guns and mortars opened fire, and what had been a tranquil scene was immediately one of carnage, with men dead and wounded lying all around the place.

'About 30 yards out was our cipher sergeant who had been seriously injured. The CO and I went out under heavy machine-gun and mortar fire, and when we got to him he said, "Leave me, sir,

I'm done for." We ignored him and, each taking one of his arms around our neck, dragged him back to safety where our men made a stretcher out of a groundsheet and bamboo and took him away. I saw him months later when we were back in India; he was hobbling but had almost recovered and was very pleased that we had not left him.

'I was left with a platoon of men to cover the evacuation and we took cover in the edge of the jungle, laid our grenades out in front of us and made sure our weapons were ready for immediate use. All was deadly silent. There was nothing except the sound of the rain falling in the trees, and after all the turmoil and tumult of the past few days it was quite eerie.

'The Japs did not attempt to pursue and, after a couple of hours, I reckoned that our men had had ample time to get away, so we moved out and followed their tracks for a couple of miles along a river bank and then up into the hills. There were no stragglers or any injured to pick up.

'The brigade had harboured further up the track and my battalion was acting as rearguard. We moved in that night and tried to rest. We were tired, wet and hungry beyond comprehension, and covered from head to foot in mud. We had no food; we'd given all that we had to the wounded. One of my comrades had a mug of hot water and he gave me half, and we sat, back to back, in the rain with a blanket over our heads, praying for the dawn to come.'

Bill's battalion marched through the jungle for almost a week and had been without food for five or six days when one of the officers, much to the horror of the Gurkhas, decided to slaughter one of the mules.

'We were starving and I suppose someone thought this was a good idea. But the meat was inedible. It was like chewing on an old rubber boot. I suppose if it had been cooked in a pressure cooker or stewed for many, many hours it might have been slightly more edible, but we didn't have either the time or the equipment. When I think we were very close to the end of our tether, we got an emergency supply drop of K-rations. Our prayers were answered. But tragically one of the soldiers was killed instantly when he was struck by a sack of boots which had been thrown out of an aircraft without a parachute – it seemed like such a terribly wasteful death given everything that we had been through. On another occasion another CO was nearly killed by a free-falling box of ammunition.

'We eventually got to the area of the Indawgyi Lake, which measured 15 miles by 5 miles at its widest point. After carrying our injured over horrendously steep hills and through the thick jungle for many days, arriving at the lake was something of a relief. It was here that the brigade RAF officer, Chesty Jennings, had the brilliant idea of landing flying boats on the lake to evacuate the wounded. We were allotted two old aircraft which came to be known as Gert and Daisy. We were all in a pretty poor way, but getting the wounded and sick out was a relief for all of us and did wonders for morale. In a few days we managed to evacuate 500 wounded and sick men and also received fresh supplies of food, new radio sets, ammunition, 3-inch mortars and Vickers machine-guns.

'After resting and being resupplied, the battalion was on the move once again, marching further up the valley, nearly up to our knees in mud and water all the time. Suddenly your leading foot would go into a void and you would go head over heels in mud and water and had to struggle to your feet again, with your heavy burden. Elephants had been there before us and made these big holes, and if you went up the slope a little you could see them in the distance. The mules struggled too, and often when a mule was stuck in the mud we would have to off-load all the equipment, pull the mule out and re-load it, before again moving off.'

Over the next few weeks the Chindits were involved in a number of operations which cost the lives of many men. 77 Brigade were ordered to march 160 miles north to the area of Mogaung to bring pressure on the Japanese opposing General Stilwell's force of Chinese troops. The march was marked by a series of bloody encounters with the enemy, and when they arrived at their destination they soon discovered that Stilwell wanted the brigade to capture the stronghold of Mogaung on their own. The enemy force was estimated at 4,000, while 77 Brigade's number had dwindled from 3,500 men to 2,000. Mogaung was finally captured on 27 June, but the brigade suffered 50 per cent casualties. During the fighting two Victoria Crosses were won by Captain Michael Allmand and Rifleman Tul Bahadur Pun, both in the same company of 3rd/6th Gurkhas.

In the meantime III Brigade were ordered to capture a hill known as Point 2171, which was on top of a ridge leading directly down to the road and railway and so had been turned into a stronghold by a force of well equipped Japanese.

'The march to Point 2171 was exhausting and by the time we arrived we were hardly in a fit state to fight. We stayed on the lower slopes while we waited for air drops and during that period we faced almost constant shelling. The plan was to attack on the morning of 9 July. B Company of the 3/9 Gurkhas under the command of John Thorpe would attack up through an existing trail on the right; Major Frank "Jimmy" Blaker and his C Company would make a left hook. It was also decided that there would be no covering mortar fire, because once the attack was under way the thickness of the jungle would prevent pinpointing our own troops.

'On 9 July I was ordered to recce one of the routes, so I went off to find Jimmy Blaker to see if he had any particular orders for me and I found him eating his rations by torchlight. Before setting off we had a chat about what we were going to do after the war. Jimmy wanted to qualify as a doctor and I wanted to become a solicitor. We knew by that stage the war was coming to an end. We got reports of how well the Normandy invasion was going, and it seemed impossible that Germany would be able to kick the Allies out of France. In Burma, the Jap advance on Imphal and Kohima had failed and things were looking up.

'I set off on my patrol just before dawn, moving up the right-hand track, although it was hardly a track at all. Some of the time my men and I were reduced to crawling on all fours. As I rounded one bend quite a way up the track, to my horror I saw a Jap squatting behind a machine-gun, pointed straight at me. I leapt into cover and when I peered out I saw that he was quite dead. His head hung on his chest and his hands hung by his side, but instead of falling over he had just sunk into this squatting position behind the machine-gun. I decided that I had gone far enough and had probably reached the perimeter of the enemy position and so returned back and reported to John Thorpe. I think my patrol was actually counter-productive, since it meant that John's company would be able to move quite quickly up to the position of the dead Jap, whilst C Company would take longer to reach their attack position, so preventing both companies from assaulting simultaneously, as planned.

'John's attack went in and by this time I was at the bottom of the hill with the CO, when one of B Company's platoon commanders, Jemedar Yem Bahadur, was brought down on a stretcher. He had been badly wounded by a bullet which had shattered the femur bone in his leg. The stretcher was awash with his blood, and as he stopped to report to the CO, Alec Harper, his blood sluiced out of the front of the stretcher. After he told us what was happening he lamented the fact that he had not been able to set about the Japs with his kukri. By this stage John Thorpe had also been injured by shrapnel in his knee and had a bullet wound across the top of his back, but he remained in the thick of battle.

'While this was taking place, C Company fought their way through the most difficult jungle, across numerous gulleys and ridges. When they arrived, they came under heavy Japanese machine-gun fire. Jimmy Blaker, as always, was at the very front of his men and, seeing his company were already taking casualties and risked being pinned down, he charged the machine-gun post alone. But he was struck in the abdomen by a burst of fire and fell back against a tree, mortally wounded. As he lay back dying he still cheered his men on and they pushed forward, following his example, and took the position. His second-in-command, Captain Sweetman, came to his aid but Jimmy's concern was not for himself but only to ensure that the position was consolidated and he ordered Sweetman to link up with B Company. Captain Sweetman was reluctant to leave his dear friend, knowing that he had but minutes to live and wanting to be with him as his life passed away, but Jimmy added, "That's an order." With a heavy heart, Sweetman said goodbye before pushing off up the hill and linking up with B Company and securing the hilltop. It was the last time he saw his friend alive.

'The enemy were soon counter-attacking and there was no opportunity to bury Jimmy. Instead his body was dragged into the jungle and covered with leaves. His remains were later identified by his dog tag and were buried.'

For his courage and leadership under fire Major Blaker was awarded the Victoria Cross. He was aged 24 when he died.

'Before that he had won an outstanding Military Cross in 1943, when the battalion was at Taung Bazar in the Arakan. A villager told him that there were some Japs resting up about 1,000 yards ahead of him in a nullah. Jimmy took two of his platoons and, approaching very cautiously, saw that the Japs had only one sentry, armed with a light machine-gun. One of Jimmy's sergeants crawled up to him, distracted him by throwing his hat to one side then leapt on him and slew him with his kukri. Then Jimmy attacked and chased the Japs for two miles, killing 16 of them and capturing three, which included the very first Jap officer to be captured in the Arakan, and his only losses were two killed, one by a sword stroke, and a few lightly wounded. Up to that point many soldiers were scared of the Japs, so that made a very good impression.'

Bill's battalion remained on top of Point 2171 until 11 July, when they were relieved by the King's of 30 Column. The battalion returned there on 15 July and remained until the 17th. 'During the period we occupied the hill we were under almost constant attack. The Japs had several 81mm mortars, a 77mm gun and a 105mm gun, which caused us a lot of problems and casualties. The attacks worked like clockwork and we were always well prepared. There would be an artillery barrage and then the Japs would attack, supported by machine-gun fire. That would last about half an hour. Then there would be a short break and they would attack again, to remove their dead and wounded. But despite the ferocity of their attacks they never breached our wire.

'We had a couple of machine-guns sited on either flank of our front to lay down enfilading fire to catch the enemy as they came up the steep hill. On one occasion, right in the middle of an attack, one of our men came up to me and reported that one of the guns had jammed. There was a spare Vickers just a few yards in front of my trench, so I jumped out, ran and picked up the Vickers with its tripod and, cradling it in my arms, dashed through all of this heavy artillery and mortar fire, replaced the working gun and got it firing again. The fire coming down on us was tremendous, but I wasn't hit – it was one of those very lucky days, I suppose.

'One day, at the bottom of the hill, I was ordered to take a patrol around the left-hand side of the hill to see if there was any enemy activity. There were no spare troops so I just had to take some fairly inexperienced men, ones from battalion headquarters. They were a bit edgy, so I thought I had better give them a lead myself and became point man, which is the most dangerous position in a patrol.

'We came to a little stream, and the path ahead was straight for 200 to 300 yards before turning around to the right. It was about a maximum of five feet wide, hemmed in on either side by very thick jungle. I took a very careful look up the track and then moved up it, and about half-way along, to my horror, a Japanese sniper opened up on me to my left. He reloaded and fired a second shot and again missed. I heard the bolt action on his rifle as clearly as if I had been standing behind him on the rifle range, so he was just feet away, not yards. I don't know how he missed me because, though emaciated, I was six foot two on a big frame. I put it down to someone "up there".'

Bill's brigade eventually withdrew on 18 July, with his battalion, the 3rd/9th Gurkha Rifles, acting as the advance guard while 30 Column acted as the rearguard.

'We had about 100 wounded with us and had to hack our way through the jungle with the Japs hot on our tail. The following day we met up with the Black Watch from 14 Brigade who were on their way to relieve us.

'Stilwell had insisted that we continue fighting, but Lentaigne had argued that we had reached the end of our tether. A compro-

mise was reached and it was decided that all the survivors of 77 and
III Brigade would be medically examined and those found to be
fit would continue fighting. The examinations found that of the
2,200 men only 118 men – 7 officers, 21 British other ranks and 90
Gurkhas – were classed as physically fit. I was one of those declared
fit even though my weight had fallen by about a third. But the
colonel refused to release me and so I went out with the others.
When I eventually was flown back to India I was in hospital for five
weeks, recovering and trying to beat a fever which was never
diagnosed.

'For us it was all over. We just had to march to Mogaung, be
towed on the rickety railway to Mytkyina and then flown out to
India. On the way to Mogaung we rested by the roadside. Troops
from 36 Division, led by their general, came marching down the
road in the opposite direction to take over from us. They looked so
splendid and fit compared to us gaunt, scruffy, ragged lot. But we
had done our job, and perhaps all the five months of pain, suffering
and great hardship had been worthwhile.

'Even now, after all these years, I cannot repress a feeling of pride
at the mention of Chindits. For just a few moments in our lives,
Wingate had made us greater than ourselves.'

Bill had two more years of soldiering, including clearing
Sourabaya in Java of the rebels who had taken over from the
Japanese. He also saw active service in Khota Bahru in the extreme
north-east of Malaya. By the time his demob leave had run its
course, he had served a total of seven years and one month.

After the war Bill returned to Britain and he joined British
Petroleum, a job which he said he 'hated'. He eventually became a
solicitor, as he had always intended, with his own practice in
Surbiton, a suburb of south-west London.

Like many Chindits, Bill could not forget the horror of the
events he witnessed in Burma and of the battles fought. 'I was one
of the few who weren't wounded, but I was scarred mentally. I
suffered from nightmares for many years and would wake up
screaming and shouting in the night.'

*        *        *

The Chindits were not the only special force to operate behind enemy lines in Burma. The fight against the Japanese was continued from early 1945, as the following chapters show, by the three-man Jedburgh Teams, who worked with local tribespeople and other resistance fighters, having first proved their worth in France.

# CHAPTER 8

# The Jedburgh Teams

## Fred Bailey in France and Burma

*'I believe that the Jedburgh operation was the most
decorated of the Second World War.'*
LT-COL. J.D. SAINSBURY,
Medals Section, Ministry of Defence

In early 1944, 100 three-man teams were trained by the Special
Operations Executive in a number of secret locations across Britain.
Their mission was to drop into occupied France in the days and
weeks before D-Day and to make contact with the French
Resistance. The codename given to the mission was Operation
Jedburgh. The work was dangerous and carried huge risk. The
chances of surviving more than six weeks were estimated at 50 per
cent. Some of those who survived working behind the lines later
volunteered to serve in Burma as part of Force 136, where they
fought against the Japanese Imperial Army.

Among them was Fred Bailey, who by the end of the Second
World War had seen active service in France, Burma and Malaya.
He had come close to death on several occasions but had experi-
enced more adventures than he could have ever imagined.

★　　★　　★

'I was born in Clerkenwell in London,' Fred told me, 'but I had a
heart condition when I was young and was quite ill in my early
years. The family doctor advised my parents to move off the damp,

wet London clay to the dry, gravel soil of Hertfordshire. My parents took his advice and it must have worked because I'm still here.

'I went to Hemel Hempstead School and then went to work at the Colne Valley Water Company, where I more or less intended to make my career. In those days you chose what you were going to do very early in life and you stuck with it. I had done reasonably well at school and I jumped at the chance of joining the water company. I was 15 at the outbreak of war, but 16 in November 1939.

'I began studying for my professional qualification to become a chartered secretary, but my mind was really on other things. By this stage I was already an ARP warden messenger and a member of the Home Guard. I also carried out fire pickets at the water works just in case the place was damaged during an air raid. From the age of 16 I felt fully immersed in the war.

'The whole country had sort of been mobilised into the war effort, and what amazes me now is that we never thought we were going to lose. Even after the catastrophe of Dunkirk – although none of us realised how desperate the situation was – we never envisaged the Germans would invade Britain.'

Desperate to 'do his bit' and filled with boyish enthusiasm, Fred joined up on his 18th birthday in 1941 and volunteered for active service in the Royal Armoured Corps. His decision to serve was accepted by his parents with a mixture of pride and resignation, but also by Fred's insistence that it was far better that he volunteered and chose his unit rather than waited to be called up and dispatched to part of the armed forces in which he had little interest.

'By the time I joined up the war was going on in the desert, and I joined the Royal Armoured Corps. I suppose with my boy's imagination I thought I'd be out in the desert fighting in the war.'

Fred was posted to the Young Soldiers Training Regiment in Bovington, Dorset, where he trained to become a radio operator/gunner and was taught the basics of wireless operation and Morse code, skills which were to prove very useful in an altogether different military unit some months later. After six months' training he was posted to the 13th Battalion, The Green Howards, an infantry

*Fred Bailey*

battalion which had been converted into an armoured car regiment in Scarborough.

'When we received our posting orders I was pretty pleased – I had wanted to join a tank unit, but the war in the desert was pretty much over and I thought an armoured car unit was bound to see a lot of action.

'But the unit was pretty poor from top to bottom. I remember thinking that the series of commanding officers which I saw were a dead loss and the commissioned and non-commissioned officers, with few exceptions, weren't much better. As for the other ranks, they seemed more interested in getting their next 48-hour pass than getting stuck into the war.

'Four of us from Bovington had been sent to the battalion, and we all felt the same. From pretty much our arrival we decided that we would try and get into one of the special units. We started applying to become paras, commandos, glider pilots, anything to get us out of the Green Howards. I think we all thought we were prepared to fight and die in the war, but if we were going to get killed we wanted to die doing something useful. Even though we were 18 or 19, all four of us thought that if we went into battle with the Green Howards we would end up getting killed because of the officers' poor leadership.'

A few months later the battalion moved from Scarborough to a new base in Trowbridge, in Somerset, where it was due to begin training for the Normandy invasion. One morning, as Fred was preparing for another day's training, he was told by his friend John Sharp that volunteers were needed for a new unit.

'There was a call for volunteers for "special duties". I was told the training would involve parachuting and hazardous duty, and I thought, Right, that's for me. I told some of my mates, and four of us, the same four that trained at Bovington, applied to join.

'None of us really knew what we were applying for but as far as we were concerned it had to be better than staying with the Green Howards.

'In October 1943 we were all called for interview and testing at a place just outside Oxford. We later learnt that there was a demand for tank radio operators. In tanks and armoured cars, communications over the radio are in clear voice – no code – but you learnt Morse because you tuned in the sets within the troop and within the squadron by pressing the Morse key. The maximum distance for vocal communication was about 10 to 12 miles, but if you were beyond that you could communicate with the Morse key – that was why we learnt Morse. That was the skill the Special Operations Executive were looking for at the time, although we only heard that later.

'There were 40 or 50 RAC radio operators at the interview where, along with other things, our Morse skills were tested. We also had a medical and saw a psychiatrist, who mainly asked about family, and by that stage I had got some idea as to what I was going to be involved in.

'The psychiatrist was asking a lot of questions, some about the war, others were much more general. He asked me how I felt about the war and combat, what my fears were, whether I thought I could cope with stress. I suspect that he was assessing me and the other lads in some way which we were not aware of.

'But the interview went quite well and some time later we received our orders to report to Fawley Court* at Henley-on-Thames, a country house, which also served as SOE's wireless training centre. We turned up and felt a bit like being back at recruit training again, but we were very excited and the training began immediately. The main effort was to improve our Morse and we also learnt how to use the B2 radio set† – the set we were later to use in the field. We also did a great deal of physical training. The idea was to get us into shape for the next phase of training, which was going to be even more demanding.'

The days were long at Fawley Court but the majority of the new SOE recruits willingly accepted the arduous training programme. Even though the volunteers had already been through an extensive selection process, they remained under constant pressure to improve and perform to their maximum ability.

'The Morse training became harder and harder – several hours a day, the pace getting quicker and quicker. We learnt how to encode and decode very quickly, and it got to the stage where some people would dream about Morse in their sleep, but we had to be as close to perfect as possible – there was no room for error in the work we were going to do.

'We conducted various exercises, taking radios out into the field and communicating back to headquarters using Morse. There were also FANYs at Fawley Court, employed as radio operators, drivers, secretaries, etc., and they were learning how to operate base stations, so it was quite a nice atmosphere with the women around.

---

* Fawley Court was a country house which had been commandeered by SOE during the early part of the war and became the organisation's signal school, codename STS 54a.

† Type B Mark 11 radio set – a portable radio known as the B2 or Jed Set.

'It was at Fawley Court that we were told the nature of the mission. We received a briefing in which an SOE colonel explained that we would be dropped behind the lines prior to D-Day, the invasion of France – no dates were given. We also learnt that after our training was complete we would move to another establishment and would form up into three-man teams. Our role was to help co-ordinate the various Resistance groups in France prior to and in the aftermath of the invasion. I was tremendously excited and felt that I was going to make a great contribution to the war effort.'

Whilst at Fawley Court, Fred and his colleagues were told that they would form Jedburgh Teams. Although the operation may have been given this name randomly, there is also a suggestion that it may have been named after the border town of Jedburgh, in Scotland, from where in the 12th century Scottish warriors used to conduct guerrilla warfare against the English forces.

After two intensive months, those radio operators still in the programme were sent to Milton Hall, a stately home in Cambridgeshire used by SOE during the war for the training of the Jedburgh Teams. The main house, which dated from the 17th century, was used for administration, recreation and lectures. The grounds, extending to several hundred acres, were used for training and contained the soldiers' temporary accommodation, mainly corrugated-iron huts, and their dining facilities. Soon after their arrival the radio operators were promoted to sergeants.

'There were all sorts of people being trained at Milton Hall, and we were all sworn to secrecy, but obviously things leaked out a little bit. We were taught various coding and decoding devices and we learnt to use weapons, such as the US M1 carbine, the Colt .45 semi-automatic pistol, Sten guns and fighting knives. The physical training also continued and we learnt unarmed combat and various sabotage techniques. There were lots of lectures from civilians, and scientists would come in and talk to us about the most effective way of blowing up bridges and railways lines or how to kill someone quietly and quickly.

'The training took place at all hours, sometimes in the middle of the night, but it was great fun; we were all young and all in it together. Towards the end of the training I was able to set up my radio almost anywhere and send and receive coded messages very quickly. The training was becoming more and more realistic, and it was impressed upon me that I should spend as little time as possible on the radio when transmitting.

'It was at Milton Hall that we first met the French and American soldiers who, with us, would form the three-man teams. Most of us knew schoolboy French, but living with French NCOs very quickly improved our language skills. Despite the stresses of the training, we all got on very well and developed friendships that lasted for a lifetime. As well as training at Milton Hall, we also went up to Dunbar in Scotland, where we occupied an old school. From there we would send Morse messages back to places in Peterborough and elsewhere around the country. It was during our time at Milton Hall that the teams were chosen. The training gave us an opportunity to find out who you got on with. Everyone knew that we would be working behind enemy lines and that our lives would depend on each other. Trust was vital, but also just the basic ability to get on with someone and to make sure that there were no personal habits which would drive you around the twist.

'Every team had to have at least one Frenchman in it, and I was approached by a Captain John Smallwood and asked if I wanted to be in his team. The other member of the team was Commandant Pierre Bloc, a French Foreign Legionnaire, whose *nom de guerre* was Commandant Alcée. He was a regular who went back to the Legion after the war and was later blown up and killed during the Algerian War of Independence.

'By that stage I already knew Smallwood very well and was very happy when he asked me. In fact when I discovered who was in the team I was delighted because we all got on very well. I also spoke reasonable French, so I could easily communicate with Bloc, who didn't speak any English at all. Smallwood also spoke fluent French with an Oxford accent. Between the three of us we could communicate quite happily.'

The team's codename was Citroën, and in the field Smallwood's codename was Anne, Bloc's was Lens and Fred's was Retif.

Citroën formed up in February 1944 and from that moment on conducted all of their training together. A few weeks later the teams were sent to Ringway airport in Manchester for a fast-track parachute course.

'The first parachute jump was from a balloon, and that was a very strange sensation because there was no noise. There were six of us in this cage, which was being held aloft by a barrage balloon at 800 feet. I always remember the dispatcher, a flight lieutenant, who had other things on his mind rather than our safety. As we got in the cage he said, "Now, look. I've got a 48-hour pass. I don't want any buggering about up there, because as soon as we all land I'm off." The first one out was someone who had parachuted before, and I was second, but someone gave me a push to make sure I was going. We all got down and then the instructor came down on a parachute and disappeared off on a motorbike.

'After that we progressed to jumping from a very old Whitley* bomber, which had never seen active service. With the Whitley you exited the aircraft by jumping through a hole in the fuselage. Before you boarded the aircraft, you had to go and get your parachute from this huge hangar where members of the Women's Auxiliary Air Force were packing parachutes. They watched you come in, pick up a parachute and walk out of the other end. But if you didn't jump, you had to go through this walk of shame where you had to go back to the hangar and hand in your unused parachute. Every one of those women in the hangar, and there must have been over 100 of them, would have known that the person handing the chute back in had refused to jump because he was too scared – it must have been utterly humiliating – and there was one American NCO with us who did refuse to jump. Anyone who refused was out straight away, sent back to their original units. I suppose the parachuting was another part of the selection process, which was ongoing all the time. Every so often you would hear that someone

---

* Armstrong Whitworth Whitley twin-engine front-line bomber.

had been sent back to their unit, usually because they weren't up to scratch in some way or another.'

By the end of the training programme in March 1944, 100 three-man Jedburgh Teams had been trained and were awaiting orders. Of those, 15 were sent to Algiers in North Africa in readiness to parachute into southern France – one of those teams was Citroën, Fred's team. The Jeds boarded the *Cape Town Castle*, a requisitioned liner, at Southampton and 10 days later arrived in North Africa. For many of those on board the trip was the first time they had left the country.

It was while the Jeds were in Algiers that the teams received their final briefings on exactly what role they would play in D-Day. They were given details of contacts in the French Resistance movement and where the various underground headquarters were located.

'We were billeted in a French officers' cavalry school, essentially a large house situated in a grove of greengages, in a camp called El Riath, where we all lived together. It was a very comfortable, almost idyllic setting and we continued training as we waited for D-Day. We would spend days marching up in the mountains, sending and receiving messages, and we also spent a lot of time practising our unarmed combat skills – I think our commanders just wanted to keep us busy, because we were trained and eager to get on with the operation.

'We all knew D-Day was approaching, but only a few of the teams received their operational orders, whilst my team wasn't put on any sort of readiness. I was becoming increasingly agitated, wondering when we were going to be deployed. The frustration was beyond belief because we just wanted to get on with it, but we watched as D-Day came and went and I think we thought at some stage that we might not go in at all. We kept asking when we were going to be sent in, but there was no answer. We had several briefings at the SOE HQ in Algiers, but no one there knew either.

'We heard a rumour that we were going to be part of the invasion of the south of France, Operation Dragoon. Then, towards the end of July, we received our orders. It was a massive relief and I remember, as we climbed on board a truck that drove us to Bleda air base, hoping that I hadn't missed all the action. Our mission was to parachute into an area close to Apt in the Vaucluse region of southern France and make contact with the Resistance.

'The hours before we jumped were spent mostly checking our equipment, making sure everything was working. You are always trying to balance what you think you will need with what you can carry. The last thing you wanted was to land and to discover within minutes that you didn't bring enough of something or, worse, had forgotten it altogether. It was a case of checking everything against a list.

'When we arrived at the airfield we got measured up for a parachute and climbed onboard a USAF B-24 Liberator and off we went. I was excited more than nervous. I had been trained and trained for this precise moment in my life, and now the time had come. There were no fatalistic thoughts, and anyway you always think it's going to be the other chap to get killed and not you. Virtually all of my equipment was in a container, including my radio set, my personal gear and my clothing. My M1 carbine was also in a separate container, but I kept my .45 and fighting knife on me just in case I got in a bit of trouble before I could marry up with my kit. The aircraft took off, climbed to its cruising altitude and it was a case of waiting for the green light. You couldn't really talk to one another because of the engine noise, and I'm not sure what you would say – crack a few jokes? I don't think we were in the mood. Then after an hour or so my team was given a warning order and prepared to jump. The dispatcher checked us and our equipment and we waited for the red light and then the green light came on and we exited the aircraft via a hole in the fuselage. We were sitting one behind the other and once we started to go that was it – you went out. All the parachutes and containers were on static lines, so there were no concerns about having to open them.

'We were dropped at night and what we hadn't realised was that instead of being dropped at 800 feet, which was the plan, the pilot put the green light on at 1,800 feet. It was the Liberator crew's last mission before they went home and they had become a bit windy

– flak happy, if you like. Some of the crew even seemed to think that they wouldn't make it back to base. It transpired that the captain had decided that it was too risky to drop us at 800 feet because of the risk of being hit by flak. But without telling us he put the green light on at around 1,800 feet, which was putting our lives in danger. As I floated down I remember thinking, "We must be landing soon," but the descent just went on and on, and eventually I saw an escarpment and then the ground, and I landed in a disused brickyard. I could have quite easily broken my back.

'We later found out that the dropping zone was meant to be for supplies only, so we were quite lucky to get away without any serious injuries. Another Jed team, codename Monocle, also had similar problems. They were also parachuted in at 1,800 feet and the team was dropped over a wide area after the pilot approached the DZ from the wrong direction, and the American Jed team member was seriously injured.

'Once we landed we regrouped and began to search for our equipment. I found my pannier but it was a wreck – the parachute failed to open and the the radio set was completely smashed and useless. The frame on my rucksack was also badly mangled. Fortunately we also had another radio set, called the Jed set, which could be powered by a hand generator, and that was the one I used.'

Having found their equipment and then each other in the darkness, as dawn approached the three members of Fred's team headed for the rendezvous with the local Maquis leaders.

'We quickly learnt that dealing with the Maquis was always potentially difficult. Many people regarded them as being untrustworthy, and some definitely were, but others were very brave men. The Maquis in Vaucluse were reasonably well organised and supplied but they were very political. There were essentially two groups in our area; one, the Francs-Tireurs Partisans (FTP), was composed of communists, while the other, the Forces Françaises de l'Intérieur (FFI), were Gaullists. We were given the distinct impression that neither group was being too active and both were conserving their efforts and weapons so that they would be the most powerful force after the liberation of France.

'This is where Alcée [Bloc] proved to be invaluable; he managed to smooth over the politics and get the Gaullists more engaged. But it was clear almost immediately that we weren't really needed and so we moved to another little town called Pertuis, about 15 miles north of Aix-en-Provence.

'We decided to drive to Pertuis in a clapped-out front-wheel-drive Citroën, which I for one wasn't sure would make the journey. We drove it across a ford and it stopped in the middle. The wheels kept turning but nothing happened, so we all had to get out and stand on the bumper to get the grip on the front wheels to get it over the ford. I was actually a little bit nervous because we weren't sure of who we could trust and whether the Germans had been informed about our presence. If we had been caught by the SS we would have been shot on the spot, which had happened in a few cases. If you were caught by the Gestapo or the Milice – the Vichy police – you were in for a very rough time, and you might finish up in a concentration camp or get shot.

'We were aware that we could never surrender. I knew that if things got difficult we would have to try and escape, and if there was no escape then we would fight it out to the end – there was no other choice. That was something impressed upon us very early in our training. We couldn't surrender, because we were in possession of all sorts of very important material, codes and cipher books, the names of agents and networks. Surrender was never an option, but the biggest danger was betrayal. We were regarded as terrorists by the Germans and there were rewards on everybody's head. A lot of the secret agents lost their lives because they were betrayed.

'By the end of that day we had arrived in Pertuis and immediately established radio contact with the headquarters in Algiers, and it was at this stage that we found that the Germans had started withdrawing.

'I was in contact with the HQ in Algiers usually twice a day, in the morning and the evening. I could set up my radio almost anywhere. I would quickly encode the message, then send it and wait for any response. The idea was to be on the air for as short a time as possible because the Germans had radio detector vans –

more in the north of France, but they were also present in the south. The general routine was to operate the schedules, which we called scheds, twice a day, but sometimes we wouldn't send any messages at all – it depended on what we were doing – so it was quite usual to miss a few without anyone worrying too much.

'During that period we received orders to ambush the Germans as they began retreating from the south. The team joined a group of Maquis who were following the German retreat in a bus, which had been commandeered and loaded with explosives and ammunition. The plan was to harass the Germans and try and ambush them as they headed north and east. While we were pushing north we came across a German tank, which was a surprise and a shock to everybody. I remember thinking it was about to open fire and everyone piled off and took cover in the verges either side of the road. I was waiting for the firing to start when a very brave young Frenchman ran up to the tank armed only with a Mills bomb, and dropped it through the driver's viewing hatch. The bomb exploded and the Germans inside were all blown to pieces; it was a right old mess. After that we scoured the area and we found another five German soldiers – a lieutenant, a sergeant-major and three private soldiers – whom we took prisoner, and I and some others escorted them to Pertuis, where there was a jail.

'By that stage Smallwood had pushed on past Avignon, while Alcée remained in Pertuis working with the Maquis. A day or so later Smallwood suddenly discovered that he had over-extended himself – finding himself in the middle of the German retreat, he got involved in quite a vicious firefight. He returned to Pertuis the next day feeling very pleased with himself.'

By the middle of August, Fred's team were working at full capacity. As well as leading recce patrols, the Jeds, especially Fred, had become a collecting house for all sorts of intelligence, some of which was good but a lot was very inaccurate. Then one morning Fred was told that a large German convoy was moving along the road from Grenoble to Lyon. This time the intelligence was spot on.

'I knew that we had to act quickly because the Germans weren't going to be on the road forever. I sent a coded message back to HQ in Algiers requesting an airstrike to attack the convoy. A series of Mosquito fighter bombers came in and destroyed the whole convoy. It was a scene of utter devastation, total carnage. There were dead Germans and body parts all over the place.

'I passed through the area a day or so later – the weather had been very hot and the German dead had begun to decompose very quickly. When I think about it now, I can still smell that terrible odour of death. Despite seeing lots of dead bodies, I didn't feel any pity. It was just war – and that was that. You really didn't have time to think about it.'

Within days of the airstrike Fred received some sad news. Sergeant Jess Gardener, a friend and fellow Jed, had been killed on the very first night his team, codename Veganin, parachuted into France on 9 June 1944. His parachute failed to open and he was killed instantly. The tragic news was kept from the rest of the teams awaiting deployment in Algiers, so as not to lower morale.

'A few days after Jess was killed, his OC and 2IC turned up at El Riath, and when we asked where Jess was, his OC made out that he was OK and had stayed on in France. But of course, with Jess being dead they couldn't operate, so they had returned, but that was kept from us.

'A few days after the airstrike I discovered that Jess had been killed and had been buried in a parachute container by the local Maquis somewhere near Lyon. I knew Jess pretty well; he was a lovely chap and wanted to become a schoolteacher after the war. I felt very sad, even though we all knew that not all of us would be coming home – casualties were a certainty. Three of us took it upon ourselves to find his grave. I wanted to be able to tell his mother that I had visited his grave out of respect, and I also wanted to make sure that there was an official record of where he was buried so that after the war, or when the time was appropriate, Jess's body could be exhumed and he could be given a full military funeral.

'I borrowed a jeep from an American unit nearby. I told them what I wanted to do and they really supported the idea. The three of us drove up to Lyon, made contact with the local Maquis commander, and they showed us where Jess was buried. They knew exactly where he was because they had buried him.

'I took a note of the grid reference and we then drove back via Lyon to Pertuis, and I sent a message to HQ explaining that I had established the location of Jess's grave. I felt relieved that I knew he wasn't just going to be forgotten. Some time later Jess was exhumed and given a proper military burial.

'Then, a few days later, all the Jed teams in the area were ordered to congregate in a hotel in Avignon because the war, for us, was effectively over. The Germans had been pushed out of our area, so there was no further need for the Jeds to work with the Resistance. The assumption was that we would return to the UK and more or less get posted back to our units, and no one I spoke to was very happy about it.

'While we were waiting at the hotel, a message came through with a request for three radio operators to fly to Italy for another mission. I didn't know anything about it, but along with two others I volunteered for the job – anything to avoid being posted back to a regular unit.

'We flew from Marseilles to Bari and then drove to an Italian town called Monopoli, where we had an interview with the local SOE colonel. I think right from the very beginning we felt that the mission just didn't smell right. The briefing was very vague, with the colonel saying, "We want you to go to southern Austria," and little else. Initially we thought, Fine, until we began asking some very basic questions such as, "What will we be doing and who's in charge?" The response wasn't very good – it was sort of, "We just want you to go there and we'll give you orders when you arrive." Well, I didn't like the sound of that at all and the colonel didn't seem to know what was happening. I had a chat with the other two and we were all in agreement and we refused to go. We tried to be diplomatic about it – SOE missions were often dangerous and we were all supposed to be volunteers. But the colonel got very huffy and his attitude was, "Well, if you won't go then you can stay here and rot." And in fact we were stuck there for several days, but by chance another group of Jeds came through and we asked them to tell Baker Street, our HQ in London, that we were stuck in Italy and needed to be reassigned to another mission. A few days later, the huffy colonel turned up and told us that we were being posted back to Britain. We flew to Cairo and got a boat in Alexandria on Christmas Eve and we eventually arrived home in January 1944.'

On returning to England, Fred headed straight for London and to the Baker Street headquarters for a full debriefing of his activities in France, after which he fully expected to be told that he was being posted back to the Royal Armoured Corps, something which he was dreading. To his surprise, however, at the end of a debriefing session one of the senior officers simply said, 'How do you fancy Burma, Fred?' The officer explained that Jedburgh Teams were needed in the Far East to work with Force 136.* The work would be similar to that which Fred undertook in France – essentially guerrilla warfare, but the conditions would be far more arduous. Fred jumped at the chance and, after two weeks' leave, took a train to Liverpool where he boarded a troopship bound for Calcutta.

'It took four weeks to get to Ceylon. The boat took us to Calcutta, then it was a five-day train journey down to the south of the country and a ferry over to the island. We did a little bit of acclimatisation training, and then I met up with my new team, Major Paddy McCoull and Captain Jimmy Moorhouse, a very nice chap and a good companion who liked a joke.

'Whilst we were in Ceylon we took part in a series of exercises to get us working as a team, and we were issued with our jungle equipment and obviously briefed on what our new role was to be.

'The plan was for us to jump into the Karen Hills in southern Burma and help mobilise, supply and co-ordinate the various guerrilla forces attacking the Japanese. The objective was to meet up with a force of around 200 guerrillas, including a detachment from the Burmese National Army,† who were now fighting with the

* Codename for SOE units operating in Burma and the Far East.

† Formed by the Japanese army to fight in the Burma campaign. Units within the BNA began switching sides between 1944 and 1945.

Allies, and capture the town of Thaton, situated mid-way between Rangoon and Moulmein. We were also tasked with attacking the Japanese using the main road between Rangoon and Moulmein. Taking Thaton was something of a gamble, obviously, because we had virtually no intelligence on the size of the enemy force in the town

'The new mission codename was Cow, and as usual my job as the radio operator – the communication link with the outside world – would be key.

'Mission Cow travelled by train to Calcutta in February 1945. We received our final briefings and were joined by two Burmese agents, of whom the chief, Kin Saw, spoke very good English and would act as our interpreter. We flew in a US Liberator but with a British crew and jumped at night. We jumped in fighting order, so we would be ready for any eventuality from the moment we hit the ground. The kit and equipment we were issued for the Burma operation was far superior to that which we had been given for the French operation. My most important possession was my rucksack, which was waterproof. This meant you could keep some of your personal belongings dry, and in the jungle that was a bonus. We also had canvas jungle boots, although we didn't expect them to last long.

'There was a reception committee waiting for us composed of around 20 or 30 guerrillas, and we were met by two members of Force 136, a Major Macadam, or Mac, as he was known, funny chap, and his radio operator. The drop went very well, even though it was pitch black and we couldn't see anything. I was the last out and it's a very strange feeling jumping into an operation because obviously you don't know what the future holds. You are sort of saying good-bye to one existence and joining another, but those thoughts quickly disappeared after I landed in some trees – for a moment I thought I was in real trouble, but they were only saplings and actually bent over to help break my fall.'

Fred and his two companions gathered their kit together, which took a while in the darkness, and eventually met up at a pre-arranged rally point. Although the three Jeds were deep behind enemy lines they all felt very safe. They were sheltered by the thickness of the jungle and unlike in France there was less chance that they would be discovered by a random enemy patrol.

'After we got our kit together we marched through the jungle for several hours to our new home, which was called Saw Bali Creek. During that march it occurred to me how much my life had changed since the war began. A few months earlier I was in France, fighting the Germans; now I was in the jungle, about to attack the Japanese. None of my friends or even my family had the slightest idea where I was or what sort of work I was doing.

'We eventually arrived at the creek, hot and tired, and I had a look around and thought, "Well, this is now home for a while." Mac had been there for a while so it was already quite well established. We occupied a few dilapidated huts, which we fixed up, and had quite a comfortable existence. There was a stream running through the creek, so we had plenty of water; the guerrillas drank it neat, but we had to use chlorine purification tablets.

'The huts we lived in were on stilts, with a bamboo floor, on which I spread my ground sheet and a lightweight blanket, and I hung a mosquito net, which was essential, otherwise you would have been eaten alive by mosquitos. We had some fresh rations and our K-rations, and after a couple of weeks I was fitter than I had ever been in my entire life – I had no body fat on me whatsoever – but that was a feeling which was not to last.

'I had a B2 radio, which operates off a battery, which of course runs out after a certain amount of use. But someone had developed a steam generator especially for charging B2 radio batteries. You lit a fire, boiled the water, set the alternator going and the batteries were charged – ingenious. Providing we had water and could light a fire I was always able to communicate with HQ. Whenever we needed something, such as new boots, rations, Mills bombs or ammunition, I would send a request to HQ, wait for an acknowledgement, which would also include drop time, and it would arrive in a couple of days.'

Fred and Mission Cow settled into jungle life pretty quickly and soon got the measure of the men they were dealing with. They discovered that the commanding officer of the BNA had been working with the Japanese forces until, as Fred put it, 'he realised he wasn't on a winner' and changed sides.

'When the Japs first invaded Burma they promised the Burmese independence and formed the Burmese National Army, but when things started going wrong for the Japs the BNA switched sides – we never really trusted them.

'We always looked upon the BNA soldiers as being in the war to see how they could benefit from it. Amongst the guerrillas there was a nucleus within that group of about 35 local levies (labourers who helped the British). Some of the levies were in a very poor state of health. It was quite a tragic thing to see. I thought I might be able to help and sent a message back to HQ calling for some medical supplies to be dropped in, and purely by chance I became a sort of doctor.

'One of the levies had an abscess behind his ear and was in absolute agony. He came to see me and I thought I would try and help. I got a scalpel, sterilised it and lanced this huge boil and cleaned it up and he got better. After that I would have queues of people coming to our camp needing medical help. It was taxing but it helped us bond with the locals – now more than ever they looked upon us as the good guys. The sick were mostly our levies but also some local people, mainly with foot problems; the Burmese always seemed to have terrible problems with their feet. Once their feet became infected the insects would eat away at the sores – terrible, and there was little they could do.

'I noticed that when the Burmese came across something they didn't recognise they would put a piece of the substance in their mouths to taste, obviously a bit risky. There was one occasion when one of the locals got hold of a stick of plastic explosive. He didn't know what it was and he tasted it, and it sent him off his rocker. He was thrashing about and I didn't know what to do with him. Nothing worked. In the end I gave him a capsule of morphine, hoping that it would calm him down, but tragically he died. We carried him for a day because he was unconscious, and then he died. I can only assume that the plastic explosive was poisonous and it killed him. I was only 21 at the time, and although it was shocking I had seen dead bodies before in France.

'As the local "doc", I would try and treat the wounds with different antiseptic creams that came in with the supplies, and I managed to help quite a lot of the Burmese, who thought I was this wonderful doctor – but I didn't really know what I was doing.'

Mission Cow had a delicate task. It was apparent that the Burmese had suffered greatly under Japanese rule, and although the majority were loyal to the British they had been fairly inactive as resistance fighters.

'A couple of weeks after we arrived, my CO very tactfully suggested to the Burmese elders that they should be doing a bit more killing of the Japanese. It was obviously a difficult subject to broach, because every time the guerrillas attacked, the local people would suffer reprisals from the Japanese, but they seemed to take our suggestions very well. Then one day early on, when I was on the radio, one of the levies turned up and came into the radio hut. He was saying "Freddy, Freddy", and I turned around and I saw a huge smile on his face, he was clearly very pleased with himself. I looked a bit closer and he raised his hands and was holding the heads of two Japanese soldiers – one in each hand. He was nodding his head, seeking approval. But I think my jaw must have dropped. I was just about able to utter "Well done" and then said, "Now for god's sake go and bury them."

'The mission was going very well, although life in the jungle was hard even when things were going well. There was always the threat that we would be discovered and attacked by the Japs, but what tended to get you down was the rain, heat, insects and food, which gradually started to run out. We became increasingly dependent on K-rations, which always contained some cigarettes so they were very popular, but you quickly grew tired of eating the same old processed food. I also found the leeches particularly difficult to contend with and never got used to them. We used to burn them off with cigarette ends. If you pulled the leech off, its head would be left buried in your leg, but if you touched it with a cigarette end it would drop off and you could kill it.'

The days in the jungle soon began to merge into each other and time passed quickly. Routine patrols were by now very frequent, as Mission Cow attempted to establish the whereabouts of the Japanese forces.

'During one recce patrol we discovered a Japanese transit camp on a road on the way to Moulmein. We always took guides with us wherever we went, otherwise we would have become hopelessly lost. In the jungle you are blind; the only thing you can really see is the area you are in.

'We watched for a while and took notes of the activity, that sort of thing, before withdrawing. When we got back to our base I transmitted the location of the transit camp back to the Ceylon HQ and we called in an air strike, which duly came and created quite a bit of havoc. The camp was situated on the main road, so it was fairly easy for this lone bomber to find. We heard the aircraft go in and drop its bombs, and there was a feeling of a job well done.

'But the success of the operation became something of a double-edged sword. After the air strike the Japanese were determined to hunt us down. Enemy commanders knew there was a covert group operating in the area – the supply drops from Allied planes were evidence of that.

'I suppose we suspected that the Japs might come after us, but we were a fair distance away. Our small base was actually only about five miles from the enemy – but five miles in the jungle extends to around 30 miles by the time you have threaded your way around swamps and through steep valleys, so we felt relatively safe.'

In the days that followed the air strike, Fred's team were told by the locals that there were a group of Indian soldiers in the area. In due course the Indian soldiers were escorted into Saw Bali Creek, where they were relieved to see British officers.

'They were a pretty sorry bunch led by a Sikh Havildar (equivalent to a Sergeant), who was armed only with a pistol. It seems that this lot had been captured and were POWs. They had almost been starved to death by the Japs, and had agreed to fight with them in return for food, but had escaped as soon as they could. The havildar showed me a picture of himself before the Japs had invaded and he was a splendid-looking individual, but when I met him he was in a rather sorry state, facing a very uncertain future because he and the others had fought alongside the Japs. He was very worried that even though he had spent many years in the Army he would be left destitute with no pension.

'The Indian soldiers swelled our numbers, which was welcome, but just after they arrived the Japanese attacked our position with around 120 men, and after that everything changed.'

The British team and their motley crew of levies, Indian soldiers and the increasingly unreliable BNA were no match for the well-equipped Japanese.

'The attack occurred in the morning about three weeks after we arrived in Burma. The first I knew of it was when a sentry opened up with a Bren gun. We knew immediately what was happening and my sole concern at that stage was to get the radio, the code-books, spare batteries and all our vital equipment packed away as quickly as possible. It was a bit of a panic because there was very little time. There was a hill by the camp and we sprinted to the top and waited until things died down. Once you were out of the immediate area of the camp you were in thick jungle, so we could sit and watch unseen at the top of the hill.'

As Fred and his comrades watched silently from the top of the hill, he was struck by a terrible realisation. In his eagerness to evacuate the camp, the steam generator, which powered the batteries for the B2 radio, had been left behind. Without it the radio would be useless within days. The only option was to wait for the Japanese to leave Saw Bali Creek and carry out a search.

'Once the Japanese soldiers had left, I went down into the camp with a guide to look for the generator – everyone knew that it was a vital piece of equipment. Walking down through the jungle at night on my own except for a guide, not knowing what was waiting for us, was pretty terrifying. Looking back, I think that was my most frightening experience of the entire war. But neither of us could find the generator; either it had been kicked into the jungle in the mêlée or the Japs had taken it with them. Either way we were in trouble, because although we had a radio the batteries were going to pack in pretty quickly. The following morning I resorted to desperate measures before the batteries lost all their power. I went on the air briefly and sent the message "Send Jenny" uncoded. Whoever was listening at the other end of the radio must have realised the seriousness of the problem, because a drop came in very shortly with a new generator.

'After that we set off marching as quickly as we could, with our guides leading us through the thick jungle. At first the Japs didn't seem interested in pursuing us, so we moved off thinking we would be able to relocate a few miles away, but that was a mistake. Within hours the Japs were on to us and chased us from arsehole to breakfast time for the next six weeks.

'As soon as the Japs attacked, the BNA soldiers took off with everything they could carry and we never saw them again. I suppose that wasn't unexpected, given how unreliable they were. We were left with around 30 levies and about 20 members of the Indian Army.

'From that moment on we were on the run for the next six weeks. The Japanese were close behind all the time. Sometimes they were several miles away, on other occasions it was just a few hundred yards. But it meant that being resupplied by air was virtually impossible, because we could never stay anywhere long enough to arrange a supply drop. From that moment on we were short of rations and we began to starve. We survived by eating boiled, unpolished rice and that was horrible. It was not just the three of us who needed food, it was the 50 other members of our party too.

'We had some K-rations to keep us going, but they soon ran out, and after that it was a case of buying or scrounging whatever we could, mainly chicken and rice, from the villages we passed through during our march. I think the Japs must have known that we were very short of food and that is why they constantly kept up the pressure of their pursuit. They knew that if we had to keep moving we couldn't be resupplied.

'The lack of food, the heat and the arduous conditions meant that our physical condition began to degrade very quickly. We understood this and knew that as we grew weaker we would succumb to jungle illnesses such as malaria, so it was vital that we took mepacrin anti-malaria tablets, which used to turn your skin yellow, but they must have worked because I never got malaria.

'My uniform at the time was basically a boiler suit, an all-in-one thing. I found that the most useful thing to wear. You could take it off and wash it and then put it back on again very quickly.

'We must have slept in a different place almost every night; it was utterly exhausting. We were circling, really, trying to get back on the road and throw off the Jap pursuit. What we wanted was to get back to the work we were supposed to be doing, which was harrying the Japs' retreat and organising the resistance. But the Japs must have been given information on our movements because they were always on to us, they were absolutely unrelenting.

'During that period, as we moved through the villages, I got a real insight into the brutality of the Japs. We heard stories of rape and murder. Old women were raped – it was unthinkable – and for some unknown reason they would enter a village and kill all the animals. It was just wanton cruelty, and I came to detest them; I thought they were savages. They were as brutal to each other as they were to everyone else – they were a vicious lot.

'As we moved through the jungle we always had people out looking for any sign of the Japs. The guerrillas who were with us were marvellous and could move around like the locals. Every time we got to one village we would recruit another guide to take us to the next village, and that's how we moved from village to village. They would supply us with intelligence, tell us the areas where the Japs were operating or the routes they used, and give us whatever food they could. Part of the reason for them helping us was the brutality of the Japs. Had the Japs treated them differently then perhaps they would have been more indifferent to us.

'One night we entered a village called West Milwin, where the locals quickly built some huts for us to sleep in. There were two villages, West Milwin and East Milwin, and as soon as we started to settle down for the night someone came rushing along saying the Japs were in East Milwin – which was just a couple of miles away. We were all exhausted and there was a bit of indecision as to whether we should take the risk and stay in the village for the night. In the jungle just a few miles can take a considerable time to cover, but despite our exhaustion we decided to move off again.

'At one stage we bought two elephants to try and carry our gear, but in fact while an elephant can pull and push enormous weights it can't carry much more than a good healthy mule can. We also learnt that an elephant needed a day's rest every three days, which was really no use to us as we needed to be on the move. Eventually the elephants got fed up with us and cleared off.

'After a few weeks of constantly being on the run, we managed to get back to the main road, which was being frequently used by the enemy, and it was decided that we should have a go at ambushing a Jap convoy. We knew the road was one of the main transit routes and we were desperate to get back to the job we were doing. The plan was to knock out the first vehicle with the PIAT* and then kill as many Japs as we could before making good our escape. We moved into position and everything seemed to be going well. The guerrillas and the Indian soldiers were armed with Sten guns – we had managed to get another air drop in to tool up the Indian soldiers – and we had our US carbines. Most of us had Mills bombs and we all felt confident and eager.

'We waited for the right moment to open fire with the PIAT, but the first round missed, so we tried again – but the second round missed. We were only about 20 yards away but the PIAT seemed to be hopelessly inaccurate. By this time the lead vehicle had stopped and we had opened fire at the trucks. The battle was quite ferocious, and initially for about half an hour we had the advantage, while the Japs were in disarray. But they gradually managed to sort themselves out and were forming up for a counter-attack, at which point we called it a day and disappeared back into the jungle – and once again they were after us.

'The hardest part of jungle warfare was coping with the conditions – the heat and being constantly wet through. But despite

---

* Projector Infantry Anti-Tank: a British hand-held anti-tank weapon, designed in 1942, with an effective range of 110 yards.

everything I always thought that we were going to get away with it. There were worries, though, and the real worry was the gradual degrading of our physical condition and the lack of food, combined with the fact that we were constantly on the move. There was always the prospect that you would wake one morning with a terrible fever, which could easily be the beginning of the end.

'I can remember the day the war ended in Europe in April 1945. We had no food and it had been pouring with rain for days. I was on the radio one day and a message came through which when decoded said, "Celebrate VE Day in your jungle camp." I was sitting there thinking, "Do those people at HQ have any idea what life has been like for us?" – and they probably didn't. But we had a good laugh about it. Despite everything our morale remained pretty high – we never really let the conditions get to us if we could help it. We all knew we had to remain cheerful, and we did. It was a bit of the good old stiff upper lip stuff, and it really helped.

'Over the next six weeks we lived from one day to the next. The aim was to stay ahead of the Japs and to remain alive. Then one day one of our Burmese agents was told of the existence of a camp with an airstrip, and we assumed it was British or at least an Allied base. We got a local guide to take us to the area and, right enough, the airstrip was where he said it would be. The camp had been built by Force 136 and was being run by Major Aubrey "Trof" Trofimov, who had a Russian name but was about as English as you could be.

'By that stage I was physically spent. For several weeks our daily rations consisted of a handful of rice, boiled in water with some coconut milk, if we could find a coconut. We were starving and not really in any fit state to continue. Trof gave us some food and we rested, but we realised that our mission was over. The main aim of taking Thaton had not been achieved, but we had caused the Japs a hell of a lot of problems and we left behind a well-motivated guerrilla force, so in that respect it had been a worthwhile effort.

'At that point we decided that the time was now right to close the mission. I set up my radio close by and sent a message to HQ requesting that they come and collect us, and two days later a

Lysander came in and flew us out. We flew to Calcutta and then returned to our HQ in Ceylon.'

★　　★　　★

Fred finally left Burma in June 1945, but not to go home. Before returning to Britain he undertook one last mission, this time in the jungles of Malaya. He and other members of the SOE were tasked with finding any members of the US Air Force who had been shot down during combat and taken prisoner. A month after he arrived, Japan surrendered.

'Some two weeks after the surrender the Chinese guerrilla forces came out of the jungle and set up headquarters in a police station in a village called Surrendah, just south of Kuala Lumpur. Two days later the Japanese mounted an early morning attack and we came close to being slaughtered. Fortunately there was a British colonel, with about a dozen Gurkhas, billeted in a hospital about half a mile away. They arrived in the nick of time carrying a Union Jack and persuaded the Japanese to cease fire. The Japanese CO claimed that he thought he was attacking a bunch of terrorists. Some weeks later I received a letter from Paddy McCoull saying that he had marched into Thaton after the surrender. I was sorry that I hadn't been with him.

'I eventually came home on my 23rd birthday in 1946, to a world that had changed. All the celebrations at the end of the war had come and gone. I was just another soldier who had been demobbed, and there were thousands of us. The public didn't want to celebrate any more, they just wanted to rebuild their lives.

'My parents knew that I was in something quite special, because I had to stop writing when I was in France and Burma, but they used to get letters from the headquarters saying that I was all right, so they knew I was up to something which was a bit hush-hush.

'When we returned home we were still subject to the Official Secrets Act and we weren't allowed to talk about what we had been up to. But back then a lot of people had been involved in some sort of covert activity. If someone asked what I did in the war I would say, "I was in the special forces," and the answer would often be

"Oh, how interesting," and that was about it. Very few people wanted to know any more than that. I then joined the Special Forces Association and then the Special Forces Club, and that was a great place to go and chat with former colleagues about our wartime activities.

'I went back to work at the water company on 1 January 1947. I suppose I could have stayed in the Army if I had wanted, but I wasn't interested in being a peacetime soldier, it just didn't appeal to me. I found the regular Army difficult enough to deal with during a war. SOE had been disbanded along with the Jeds, and there was no way I was going back to regular soldiering. I closed that chapter of my life and tried as best as I could to get on with civilian life. I realised that if I was to have any sort of career I needed professional qualifications and so I set about getting those. After I qualified as a company secretary I got a job with Portsmouth Water Company and stayed there until I retired.'

Fred Bailey has been a member of the Special Forces Club for more than 20 years. Although Fred only served in the Army for a little over four years, the period he spent in the Jedburgh Teams shaped the rest of his life. After the war the club became the venue of choice for Fred and many of his former comrades. These days Fred frequents the club less regularly, but its 'hallowed turf' still holds a special place in his heart.

# CHAPTER 9

# 'We weren't bloody playing cricket'

## *Harry Verlander in the Far East*

Harry Verlander was standing in the doorway of a twin-engine Dakota as it cruised above the lush, green canopy of Burmese jungle 600 feet below. As the aircraft approached the drop zone, an RAF dispatcher tapped Harry on the back – it was the signal to jump.

Leaning forward, he held his breath and threw himself into the void. Harry had jumped from an aircraft before – in France the previous year, when he dropped behind the lines to help mobilise the Resistance prior to D-Day, and at the RAF base at Ringway. In all the previous jumps, however, Harry had simply dropped through a hole in the aircraft's floor – good technique was not a necessity.

But jumping from a Dakota was different. As Harry exited the aircraft from a side door, he hit the slipstream with his legs apart – a basic mistake – and was spun like a top.

'I sensed straight away that I was falling too fast. I looked up and I could see the parachute rigging lines coiled like a rope. The canopy was streaming above me completely deflated, so I began kicking and pulling and doing a lot of swearing.'

Harry tugged away at the rigging lines and eventually pulled them free, allowing the canopy to form and slow his descent. But he was now way off course and, rather than drifting towards the cleared drop zone, he was heading for a steep wooded hillside.

'I kept my feet and knees together, covered my face and waited for the pain. I bounced off branches and ended up tumbling through bushes about six feet high. I landed on my right leg, it took my whole weight, and there was this great surge of pain which shot up my right-hand side. I fell backwards and whiplash sent pain searing through my neck, and at that stage I passed out, briefly.'

Harry regained consciousness and tried to stand but it was too painful to put any weight on his right side. His uniform had been ripped by thorns and one of the soles of his green canvas jungle boot had been torn off.

'Great start, I thought. I was hundreds of miles behind enemy lines and less than five minutes into the mission. I was injured and had become separated from the rest of the team. Then just as I was getting my bearings I heard a slashing sound from the jungle ahead.

'Japs! Can this get any worse, I thought to myself as I pulled out my .45, cocked it, removed the safety catch and was all but ready to fire when a young lad appeared carrying a machete. He looked at me, then the pistol, lowered the machete and smiled, and then I realised he wasn't a Jap but one of the Karen tribesmen who were helping the British push the Japs out of Burma.'

The young Karen could see that Harry was unable to walk unaided, so he offered his body as a crutch. Gingerly the two men moved towards the area where Harry assumed the drop zone was located.

As the two men moved along, an older man appeared, clearly European, dressed in green jungle uniform and sporting a grey beard.

'I'm Lieutenant-Colonel Cromarty Tulloch, the officer in charge of group Walrus [the codename for the area in which Harry was to operate], but you can call me Pop – everyone else does. There's no rank here. Anything broken?'

'No, sir, I mean Pop,' said Harry, still slightly bemused by the situation and unable to think straight due to the searing pain. 'I'm just a bit beaten up and I'm having a little bit of difficulty walking.'

'Well, we'll get some people to have a look at you, but you won't be able to make it to your base tonight. You'll have to rest in one of the caves and we'll come and get you in a few days' time – but don't worry, the locals are friendly and they'll look after you.'

*Harry Verlander*

Harry was taken up to a cave in a hillside and was soon joined by the two other members of his three-man Jedburgh team, Major Sandy Boal and Captain A. Coomber.

Harry was also reunited with his pack, which contained his emergency rations, water, ammunition, grenades, some spare clothes and, most importantly, cigarettes; and the four men ate a simple meal of rice and vegetables. After the area was cleared of any sign of activity, Pop and the two uninjured members of Harry's team said their goodbyes and left, promising to return in two to three days.

'As soon as I was hurt I knew that I would be left on my own somewhere safe. There was no other mode of transport, so if you couldn't walk you had to stay where you were. I wasn't at all bothered, I was armed, had my emergency rations, my cigarettes and some painkillers. I had a cigarette and settled down for the night in my makeshift bed, which consisted largely of my parachute, closed my eyes and went to sleep.'

★   ★   ★

Harry Verlander was 13 years old when the war broke out and was evacuated from the East End of London until he was old enough, almost, to volunteer and join the Army. By the time he was 16 (Harry had lied about his age) he had been in the Home Guard, volunteered for military service and enlisted into the King's Royal Rifle Corps on 19 March 1942 'for the duration of the war'.

But eight months later the regiment was disbanded and Harry joined the Royal Armoured Corps because it offered the best chance of seeing some action. It wasn't long, however, before Harry was to become disillusioned with life in the RAC.

'Our officers in the KRRC were always around, helping us, training with us, moulding us into a team. The morale was high and we all expected to serve together. But it was very different in the RAC. The only time we saw our officers was when we were in trouble, so I began to volunteer for everything going. I volunteered to train as a glider pilot and then to join the Parachute Regiment, the Commandos and even the Palestine police, but I never heard anything back.

'Then one day Fred White, who had also been in the KRRC, saw a notice on a board near to the orderly room inviting wireless operators to volunteer "for special duties which may include parachute training … and a knowledge of a European language would be an advantage".

Harry and Fred knew the work was obviously secret and both men decided to apply on the spot.

A few weeks later both Fred and Harry were in Oxford undergoing an interview at one of the colleges, where they signed Top Secret security forms and gave an undertaking not to repeat anything they had learnt during the day.

Through a series of lectures Harry and Fred were told of the activities of the Resistance in France and other areas of occupied

Europe and of the need for highly skilled radio operators who would keep clandestine teams in contact with their home base back in Britain. By the end of the day, following a series of tests and briefings, the number of volunteers had fallen from 400 to less than 100.

Once the familiarisation visit was over, those men who were still interested were told that they would be contacted in due course and informed as to whether their services were needed. Fred received his notification before Harry, who had assumed that he had not been chosen to undergo training. Then two days later Harry was told that he too had been called forward and his delay had been caused by an administrative error.

Training took place at Fawley Court in Henley-on-Thames, where Harry and 50 other volunteers spent weeks building up their Morse code speeds from sending 10 or 12 words per minute to 25. Training was long and arduous, requiring a great deal of concentration, which left most of the soldiers mentally exhausted at the end of the day.

As well as communications, the soldiers learnt how to parachute and were trained in unarmed combat, knife fighting and close-quarter battle and became proficient in the use of small arms, especially the Colt .45 semi-automatic pistol.

By Christmas 1943 all of those still on the course were told that they were to be promoted to sergeants and were now fully-fledged members of the Special Operations Executive, a force which had been created in 1940 on the order of Winston Churchill and whose mission was 'to set Europe ablaze'.

Harry and Fred also had a much better understanding of the type of work in which they would be involved. Each would be teamed up with two other members, both officers, one British or American and the other either French or from the country in which they were to be operational. Harry's mission was to take charge of the group's communications and to help train the Resistance fighters in the use of small arms, explosives and sabotage.

In the New Year those remaining were sent to Milton Hall in Cambridgeshire, where they were formed into Jedburgh Teams to undergo their final training.

In July 1944, Harry, aged 18, parachuted into occupied France, where he remained until November, killing Germans, blowing up trains and training and equipping the Resistance. The Jeds wreaked havoc in France and occupied Europe from before D-Day and beyond. In the hours before the invasion over 900 acts of sabotage were recorded. The northern part of the French railway system was badly disrupted by Resistance fighters, which meant in those first few critical days after D-Day vital German troops and supplies were unable to get to the beachhead. As a result it took some German reinforcements over two weeks to get to the front from other areas of France.

Then for Harry, who was having the time of his life, his war ended when a senior British officer came over to France to see them.

'We were in France and one of the chiefs arrived from the head-quarters in London and basically said that our job was now done, the mission was over and that we would be returning to England. He said we had a choice: go back to our old units, and for me that was a real no-no, or volunteer for more SOE work in the Far East, and straight away I said, "I'll volunteer."

'I didn't know what I would be doing, just that it was similar work. I left France on 23 November 1944, went to Paris and then by lorry and boat to the UK.

'But when I got back to Peterborough the brief had changed. Now I was told that somebody was needed to replace someone in Holland, so I said, "I'll do it. It makes no difference to me where I go."

'I got all my usual gear sorted out, then got a briefing as to what was going on. It was about 8 December. The final briefings were taking place in London, and because my family were there I was told that I could go home at night and wait for the date when I was to jump in. There were a few problems, and delays started to occur, and the date was pushed back and back.

'The Ardennes push was going on, and they were having a lot of trouble with bad weather, and they were having trouble making contact – that was the excuse anyway. All I had to do was to go to the local police station every day, ring the headquarters number and they would tell me whether to stay in London or return to Milton Hall. And that went on all over Christmas, and I had a hell of a Christmas because every day was going to be the last day. Then after New Year I was told that the Holland job had been cancelled and I would be going to Burma – again fine by me. Just change the kit for jungle warfare.'

The Jedburgh Teams had been regarded as a great success in occupied Europe, and the British high command took the view that, with the war drawing to a close in Europe, the Japanese occupation of Burma could be brought to an end more quickly if the Jeds could repeat in Burma what they did in France. So it was decided to send the teams into Burma to begin training, equipping and mobilising the Karen guerrillas.

'I got a ship from Liverpool in mid-February. It was a five-week trip all the way to Bombay and it was really enjoyable, very relaxing. After that I had to take a train from Bombay to Madras *en route* to Ceylon, where we were supposed to acclimatise, but in fact I spent most of the time on the beach.'

Once acclimatised, Harry went up to Calcutta, where he met up with the rest of his team and prepared to fly into Burma from Dum Dum airport. The monsoon season was approaching and a race was on to get Harry and his team fully embedded with Force 136, the clandestine SOE unit which had been causing havoc in the Burmese jungle under the codename Operation Character. The operation was launched in 1944 and its mission was to organise large-scale resistance amongst the Karen tribespeople.

The Karens were then, and still are, one of Burma's minority communities and inhabit the eastern hills of the country close to the border with Thailand and the Irrawaddy Delta region. The community had long supplied recruits to the Burma Rifles and were regarded by the British as deeply loyal allies. After the British retreat to India, many of the Karen tribesmen took their weapons and returned to their villages to await further orders. The Karens were formed into a guerrilla army by some British officers who remained behind and were resupplied by Force 136. At the height of the guerrilla war against the Japanese the Karen resistance force numbered some 8,000 volunteers.

*        *        *

That first night in a cave, as Harry rested his aching body, he thought of how much his life had changed since he first joined the Home Guard as a 15-year-old boy. Never in his wildest dreams could he have imagined that he would work behind enemy lines in occupied France or be parachuted into Burma, a country he knew nothing about. He also took some comfort from knowing that no matter how much planning you do prior to an operation, sometimes things just go wrong.

'When I dropped into France, my kit came down with the spare radio and bounced. The officer I was with couldn't even find his kit. We landed near a village which wasn't on the map and the RAF dropped us 20 miles from where we wanted to be. We were lost, miles from our rendezvous and we didn't have a radio – these things happen. So on that first night I just tried to be philosophical about it.'

Later, as Harry rested, he heard a noise at the cave entrance. Startled, he picked up his carbine and was ready to open fire when a man and a woman appeared. The man approached Harry with a gapped-tooth smile and offered him a cheroot, while the woman produced cooked rice wrapped in a banana leaf and a gourd containing fermented rice wine, both of which had an intoxicating effect, causing the pain to ebb away and allowing Harry to doze off. He awoke again a few hours later through thirst and hunger and once again found more Karens looking after him. Although they could only communicate with sign language, Harry felt very comfortable in their care and, despite his injuries, was delighted that he had volunteered for this particular mission and was looking forward to getting fit and ending the Japanese persecution of the Karens.

A few days later a doctor, Captain Harrison, arrived with the two other members of Harry's team, along with guides and elephants. Harry was passed fit to travel by the doctor, who had the respect of every member of the team in the Walrus area. Unlike many doctors operating in war zones, Captain Harrison, known as 'Doc', was armed. He later told Harry that he would rather fight his way out of a bad situation than be captured by the Japanese.

The stores were loaded on to the elephants, Harry was helped on to an elephant's back, where he sat in a cradle, and the small, somewhat unmilitary convoy moved off into the jungle, heading for a camp.

'I quickly realised that the heat and the humidity were far worse than I had appreciated. You were constantly wet from either sweat or downpours from the monsoon. The going was extremely tough and the elephants were allowed to rest every hour or so.'

Even though Harry wasn't actually walking, he found the journey to the camp exhausting. The constant swaying of the basket in which he sat on top of the elephant also left him feeling seasick.

The journey took three long days of trekking through thick jungle, skirting around tree-covered peaks which rose over 6,000 feet. The first two nights were spent in Karen villages, where the locals were only too happy to help the British soldiers and sell them what little food they could spare, such as vegetables and eggs. But the third night was spent in the bush and the soldiers slept on the jungle floor, wrapped tightly in their parachutes in which they resembled giant cocoons. The jungle floor came alive at night with beetles, ants, spiders and a whole host of other insects which liked nothing better than the taste of human flesh.

The convoy eventually arrived at their new camp the following day just in time for lunch, which was a welcome break from living off emergency rations. As they got there, Harry was amazed to see a Japanese soldier sitting beneath a makeshift shelter cleaning a US carbine.

'I was a bit shocked, to be honest, and my first instinct was to shoot him. I said, "What is he bloody well doing here?" And then the camp commander, Captain Campbell, appeared and said, "Don't worry about him. He's one of us now." I relaxed a bit, but I found it difficult being around a Japanese soldier.'

Harry later discovered that Captain Campbell had saved the life of the soldier, who had been injured and was about to be killed by the locals. The officer intervened and for some reason the Japanese soldier believed that his life now belonged to the British soldier.

The new team settled in to life in the camp, which was also home to a platoon of Burmese sappers and miners, who had been trained by the British and were now working alongside them. The Burmese irregulars were immensely brave soldiers and had a fervent hatred of the Japanese. They were also excellent guerrilla fighters who had become masters in setting ambushes.

Once settled in, Harry was given another examination by Doc Harrison, who told him that he was making good progress and with a bit of luck and rest he should be able to walk in a week or so.

The following morning Pop Tulloch arrived and explained how Walrus HQ operated. He gave Harry a breakdown of the names of the various officers involved in the mission. There were already two teams based in the Walrus area as well as a substantial headquarters. The third team, Harry's, was to be given a new area further east, close to the Siamese (now Thai) border. The total area of the Walrus operation was about 75 miles southwards from the town of Loi-Kaw and 50 miles westwards from the Siamese border. Maps which had been issued to the men earlier identified large areas as 'unsurveyed jungle'.

'I sat down with Pop,' Harry recalled, 'and he was keen to learn about my experience. I explained that I had initially been trained as an infantry soldier, then switched to the RAC and trained as a radio operator. I told him about my experience in France. He seemed very pleased and said he was delighted to have me on board.

'"Well, Harry," he said, "I have to tell you that your skills as a wireless operator may not be put to much use. The hills make radio communication very difficult and we don't have a spare radio transmitter, so we keep in touch using runners, which works remarkably well. You get yourself fit, and what I want you to do is to watch the back of your officers and to help train some levies who want to fight alongside us. All right with you?"'

While in Captain Campbell's camp in those first few weeks in the jungle, the members of Force 136 received some exciting news. 'I was listening to the radio, trying to pick up the BBC, and I heard someone announce that Germany had surrendered and that Hitler was dead. I turned to the others and I said, "'Ere, the war in Europe is over." There was a stunned silence, people stopped what they were doing for a few seconds and then the cheering began.

'We were all delighted because we were hoping that Japan would do the same and we would all be able to go home. We had a bit of a celebration, and a pig was slaughtered and a great deal of rice wine was consumed.'

That feast was one of the last wholesome meals Harry consumed during his time in the Burmese jungle. Rice, a foodstuff he had loathed since childhood, would become the staple, along with Australian or US pre-packed one-day rations (when they could get them).

Shortly after the meal finished the rain started – the monsoon season had begun – and there was a deluge like nothing Harry had ever witnessed before. Other soldiers in the camp began to strip off and wash their bodies with soap, and Harry joined in. It was the first time he had been able to have a proper wash since arriving in Burma. Then, as suddenly as it had started, the rain stopped.

Life continued in this way for the next few days, reasonably relaxed, if unexciting. While the other members of Harry's team were away ferrying supplies to other bases, Harry concentrated on getting fit and helping out with communications in the headquarters.

Around the end of the second week of May, when Harry's fitness had almost returned, he was invited to take part in an ambush being planned by Captain Campbell along a stretch of road in the Walrus area. Harry was delighted and jumped at the chance. He was getting bored sitting around the camp while others were involved in fighting the Japanese, and he was beginning to feel a little fed up.

Rangoon had been taken by the British on 4 May, as the Japanese were driven northwards. The British Army was also moving south along the coast, which limited the number of escape and resupply routes open to the Japanese, who it seemed had no intention of surrendering any time soon. One of the routes being used by the Japanese was through the Karen Hills, and Force 136 had orders to cause as much disruption as possible.

The plan was to ambush a Japanese convoy as it moved along one of the main supply roads running through their area. The ambush team consisted of two officers, Harry and a small group of Burmese sappers. They intended to mine the road in two areas, knocking out the first and last vehicles before opening fire and killing as many of the enemy as possible. Once the Japanese returned fire, the British party would make good their escape. Simple.

In the middle of May the ambush party left the base and hiked 12 miles or so to the road, where they also met up with a small party from another one of the bases. The ambush site was a straight stretch of road either side of which were deep irrigation ditches. The killing team located themselves on a steep hillside overlooking the road, which offered them the advantage of height and the best possible view.

Harry's team arrived at the ambush site tired but on schedule and with plenty of time to allow the sappers to lay the explosives. There was no real intelligence to suggest when the enemy might appear. It could be in an hour, a day or a week. So Captain Campbell organised a kind of shift rota system to allow some of the party to sleep, rest and eat while others kept watch.

That night Harry struggled to sleep, partly through the excitement of the impending attack but also because of the insects, which appeared intent on eating as much of him as possible. The following morning began as the previous evening ended with nothing but the noises of the jungle. Then shortly after breakfast they heard sounds of vehicles in the distance.

'There was a call to stand to. Everything was already packed away, so we watched and waited. The noise of the engines grew louder and we could eventually see the enemy convoy approaching.

There were three lorries which passed in a line then all of a sudden there was a massive explosion and the first vehicle burst into flames followed by another explosion. Those Japs who were still alive jumped from their vehicles and we began to open fire. We had a Bren gun firing burst after burst while the rest of us were opening fire with carbines. You could see some bodies falling who were either killed or injured. I knew we didn't have very long because pretty soon the Japs had jumped into the irrigation ditches and had started to return fire.

'I noticed that there was one soldier who may have been injured or wasn't being quick enough and his officer got his gun and bloody shot him. And I thought, What's he doing? He's shot one of his own men. Bloody hell. So I took a bead on him with my rifle and then the whistle went and I was told we had to go, and I said, 'No, no, I want to get him." I was so angry at what I had seen that I wanted to kill him. But one of the officers said, "That's it, we're leaving." I said to myself: You got away with it this time but it won't happen again. I really couldn't believe what I had seen, and that image plagued me right through the time I was there, but that was how it was in Burma.'

Harry was getting used to the privations of life in the jungle, but he missed some things a lot. 'The worst thing about being in Burma for me was no fags and no tea. So we used to make pipes out of bamboo and fill them with dog ends, tea leaves and a drop of rum or cognac or whatever we had to make our own tobacco. American K-rations – one-day rations – were quite good if you could get them, because they always had five cigarettes in them and we were always very short of ciggies. Then the locals had some cheroots, which were nice – they used to make you feel good and you always felt quite merry after one of them.

'Outside all the huts they had a gourd with rice and water which was brewing like beer. It would have a straw in it, and when you arrived in the village we would have a drink, and again that made you feel good – it was very refreshing. The villagers were very good to us; sometimes if things were OK they might give us a chicken. There was one time when we were on patrol and a couple of the

Burmese who were with us caught this thing which we used to call a flying fox. It had a sort of flap of skin between its legs and it would jump from tree to tree. The Burmese killed it, encased it in clay – they didn't bother to skin or gut it – and then threw it on the fire and cooked it. After a while, when it was cooked, they pulled it apart and handed it round to everyone. We were all so hungry and meat was such a rarity that we all tried some. To me it tasted like rabbit.

'I think I started to lose weight almost from the day I arrived. I was 10 stone 10 pounds when I went into the jungle and I weighed 9 stone when I came out. I lost a good stone in six months. Part of the problem was that we all suffered from chronic diarrhoea. You always had it; I think we picked it up from drinking dirty water. Nearly all of us were plagued with sores and ulcers. In the tropics even the tiniest scratch can quickly become infected, and because rations were so meagre the body never really had time to fully recover. Often the only way to get rid of dead skin and pus was to allow maggots to eat away at the wound. There were occasions when we were even barefooted, because our boots had rotted away before our supplies came in. The monsoon played havoc with the supply timetable and the RAF wouldn't risk a flight just to send us some extra kit.

'The insects were there all the time. When you were moving from one place to another at night and you stopped for a rest or some sleep, you would lie down on the ground and wrap a bit of parachute silk around your face, otherwise the insects would be in your mouth and ears – they would get everywhere. You would get covered by biting ants, so you would try and cover up as much of your body as possible.'

Every Karen villager Harry met told a terrifying story of Japanese brutality which most of the British soldiers found difficult to comprehend. After almost six years of war, tales of wanton violence and murder, especially in Eastern Europe, were nothing new, but this was the first time Harry had experienced such organised and calculated atrocities at first hand. Harry assumed that the Japanese high command realised that defeat was now just a matter of time and that those who committed war crimes would be made to atone for their actions, yet as they withdrew from Burma the Japanese exacted a terrible price from the local population, especially in the Karen Hills.

'You would come across a village that might have been there for hundreds of years until the Japs passed through, and everyone would be destroyed. All of the old people or those who couldn't flee would be shot or bayoneted. All the crops and grain stores would be destroyed, huts would be burnt down, and even the dogs were strung up and skinned. It was terrible, and you asked yourself why. Why did they do this? I couldn't understand it. I couldn't see what benefit the Japs thought they would get from such carnage. It was stupid apart from anything else, because there was nothing left for other Japanese troops passing through the same area. I never got used to seeing that. It did make you hate the Japanese, and you could understand why the local tribesmen always killed Japs whenever they caught one.'

Within the Walrus area lived a very belligerent, war-like tribe known as the Padaungs, who had developed a reputation for blood-curdling ferocity. Their weapon of choice was a long, razor-sharp machete which they would carry into battle and on ambushes, never hesitating to use it in hand-to-hand combat when the situation arose.

'The Padaungs were a very fearsome tribe and I was glad that they were on our side. They would track the Japanese to a village and wait for them to settle down for the night. Then they would sneak up to the huts, and one would wait by a door or a window, while others would make a noise outside or tap on the door. They would do this until a Jap soldier stuck his head out the window, and then they'd slice it off with one quick blow and disappear back into the jungle.

'We were also astonished by the behaviour of Japanese officers towards their men, which again is something I never really understood. The officers would beat the men and treat them appallingly. The soldiers were dressed in rags and were very underweight; they certainly weren't the supermen who had swarmed across the Far

East in 1942. We soon learnt that the best thing to do in an ambush was pick off the officers, because we found that as soon as that happened the men would run away as fast as they could, they didn't stop to fight. Strange, really, given all the stories you heard about how good the Japanese were and the battles they had. But we didn't meet any like that. They were very disillusioned.'

By the beginning of June 1945 Harry and his team had established their own base, from where they mounted reconnaissance patrols and ambushes. It had been hard work and supplies were running low, not just of food but also of clothes, ammunition and explosives. Then one day in June, when supplies were all but gone, the familiar drone of an aircraft could be heard circling in the distance. It appeared to be heading for an abandoned camp somewhere in the distance when Harry began signalling to the crew with a makeshift mirror. To the soldiers' amazement the aircraft, which by now had been identified as a Dakota, began heading towards them, eventually spotting the team's makeshift DZ and dropping sacks of rice and large boxes of ration packs.

'There was more food than we could have possibly imagined: eight-man ration packs of compo and large sacks of rice. I think it was more food than I had seen since my arrival in Burma. There were also explosives and ammunition, but no extra clothes or boots. No one seemed to worry and I think the whole camp was focused on getting stuck into some nourishing food for the first time in weeks. I had built an oven out of compo tins some weeks earlier, and that was put to good use as I prepared our evening meal of stew, vegetables and potatoes, and for pudding there were peaches in syrup. It was all tinned, of course, but tasted delicious.

'At the back of our minds were rumours we'd heard that the Japs were getting closer to our base. We assumed that they must have known we were in the area, because of the number of attacks which we had conducted. Pop had already suggested that we move back to his base before resettling elsewhere, and with this in mind we sent a significant quantity of the rations to him.'

Meanwhile a decision was taken to wire up the camp with explosives, even though Captain Coomber did not believe there was any truth in the rumours. Two days later he was proved wrong when the team were notified by a runner from a local village that there was an enemy fighting patrol composed of around 30 men heading their way.

'There was no choice but to make a run for it,' said Harry. 'We already had established an escape route and we were just about to pull out when Major Boal said that the fuses were too short. The problem was that the explosives would detonate before we were far enough away. Once the explosive had gone off the Japs would be drawn to the camp and would be able to pick up our trail, so there was no other option but to change the fuses. I gave my bergen pack, which weighed about 90 pounds, to two of the levies and they moved off first. Maung Tin, a Burmese I had become very friendly with, and two others went to a spot where the major and I would have to dash across open ground.

'While the major changed the length of the fuses, I set up a series of booby traps with grenades and instantaneous fuse wire. Job done, I got the all clear from Maung Tin and dashed across the open ground. I arrived on the other side and was just about to tell the major to run across when the Japs were spotted on the other side of the DZ. I signalled to the major to stand firm until the coast was clear, and once across we made good our escape. We were about a mile away when we heard the first explosion, and my heart sank at the thought of all that delicious food going to waste.

'Once we had put several miles between us and the Japs we began to relax a little but never dropped our guard. We came across a series of tracks and assumed that they were those of the levies, although we couldn't be sure. Then, when we came around one corner, slap bang in the middle of the track was my bergen. It didn't look right, because, rather than just being dropped, the rucksack appeared to have been carefully positioned.

'Maung Tin moved forward to take a closer look but I told him to be careful because it could be either booby-trapped or used as a marker. By now the rest of the team had closed in, and I quickly explained what we had discovered and told everyone to take cover in some boulders nearby. Then Maung Tin shouted "Japs!" and took aim with his carbine, while I raised my carbine and the major did the same – we had all spotted the Japs more or less at the same time. Then I noticed Maung Tin in a right old state, jumping up and down slapping his rifle – he clearly had a stoppage. Then Major Boal stood up – he had a stoppage too, and just as he stood up directly in front of me I pulled the trigger and in that split second I thought I had killed him, only then to discover that my carbine had also failed. The US carbine was a very good weapon but it had a simple design fault. The magazine release button and the safety catch were very close together and it was easy to press the wrong one. If you mistakenly pressed the magazine release catch, the magazine would drop and the rifle was unable to pick up a round and wouldn't fire, and exactly the same thing happened to all three of us at the same time.'

The opportunity missed, Harry told the rest of the party to make good their escape while he kept the enemies' heads down.

Harry pulled out a phosphorus grenade and waited for the enemy to appear while the rest of the team moved into the jungle. The Japs were still too far away, so Harry had to wait until they came closer. He quickly assessed the situation around him. The overhanging trees meant he would have to throw the grenade low and fast.

'So, as a practice shot, I threw a stone first. They must have thought it was a grenade because they all ducked down. Then, curiously, they all came out to have a look and I said to myself, "Yeah, you carry on, mate" – and that's when I threw the grenade. I didn't wait to see what happened. I jumped over a boulder, which was covered in green slime, and slid down as though I were on a horse's back. I gave out a loud scream and Major Boal came running over and saw me with my carbine in one hand and my manhood in the other, hobbling along with my face screwed up in agony. I just said, "Keep going, keep going."

'It wasn't long before the Japs were firing back at us, the bullets whizzing past us, but we escaped into the jungle and tried to reorientate ourselves and get on a bearing which would eventually take us back to Pop's camp.

'I had now lost all my kit. I was still irked by the food that had gone up with the camp, but now I had lost my bergen, too. The only equipment I had was that which I carried, and I wasn't looking forward to the inevitable miserable night sleeping in the bush.'

An uncomfortable night's sleep ended suddenly with a dawn downpour, and Harry and the others were only too happy to be on the move again. Their food had gone, and almost all of the group's water, and thirst soon became a serious problem as the temperature and humidity rose to almost unbearable levels. Even though it often rained in the jungle, water was often scarce. Streams and creeks would quickly run dry as water disappeared underground following a downpour.

'The going was very tough and we were all very thirsty – so thirsty that the desire for a drink of water begins to dominate your every thought. You hear the expression "driven mad by thirst", and after fighting in the jungle I can understand how a man could be driven mad. I took to sucking a pebble when thirst became a problem, just to keep the inside of my mouth moist.

'We were lucky to have Maung Tin with us and some of the Burmese levies, who were quite adept at finding water in the most unusual places. They showed us how to suck up water using a thin, hollow cane from the base of some plants where the water collected, which I think on the march probably saved our lives. They also managed to find some food, such as wild bananas and the stalks of some plants which were quite tasty and nutritious. The jungle is a very fertile place with lots of wildlife and you would have thought that food would be quite bountiful, but finding something edible and not poisonous was always a challenge.'

Two more nights sleeping on the jungle floor, the team pushed off once again deeper into the jungle, marching on a bearing which they hoped would take them to Pop's HQ. As well as keeping watch for the approaching enemy patrols and likely ambush points, the soldiers were also on the lookout for food and water.

Every clearing offered the hope that a small village, settlement or even a lone hut might be a source of food or water. But as soon as a hope was raised it was immediately dashed, and so the march through the early morning mist continued, the soldiers becoming increasingly desperate with every step.

Then Maung Tin spotted a path and told the rest of the team to follow him. They were barely able to contain their joy when it led to a small village.

The soldiers stopped and watched for a few minutes and waited to see if any locals were about. Major Boal, Maung Tin and Harry approached the village, carbines at the ready and with the distinct feeling that something was not quite right.

'It's too quiet,' Harry said out loud. 'There are no villagers, no animals – not even a chicken. Doesn't make sense.'

Harry handed his rifle to one of the others to hold. 'I'm going to shin up that tree and have a better look to see what's going on.'

As Harry watched, the door of one of the huts opened and a Japanese officer strolled out. 'He was spotless,' Harry recalled with a smile. 'His uniform was crisp and clean. He was wearing jodhpurs, a white shirt and a hat. He came outside on to a sort of veranda, and yawned. I said to Major Boal, "Quick, pass me my bloody rifle. There's a Jap officer. He's a sitting duck; I can't miss, it's a clean shot."

'"No, Harry," responded Major Boal. "We have no idea how many Japs are in the area and we are not well enough equipped to take on a large force."'

And very quietly Harry climbed down from the tree and the group withdrew into the jungle.

'Of course Major Boal was right, and I knew it. We were few in number, poorly armed and exhausted, and we might have been able to kill one or two of them but they would have got the better of us.'

Harry and the others marched for another three days, and were forced to cross one of the Japanese main supply routes which was picketed by sentries and climb a cliff, before they finally reached Pop's HQ. The men were in a sorry state by the time they arrived. Harry's clothes had been shredded by thorns and brambles and his jungle combat trousers were now shorts. Major Boal appeared to be suffering badly from dysentery or malaria or both, and even the

Burmese levies and Maung Tin were close to exhaustion. They were a sorry sight, all dehydrated, malnourished and covered with insect bites, but, despite their state, morale was high.

As they walked into the camp they were greeted first by Captain Coomber, who had safely arrived a few days earlier with a large amount of equipment and supplies from the air drop, along with some of the Burmese porters.

'We arrived exhausted but elated and the captain was especially delighted to see us because he thought we had either been killed or captured by the Japanese. We were fed and watered and given some new clothes, but we soon learnt that we would be on the move again very soon and that meant another hard march further north. The Japs had increased the number of patrols in the area of Pop's HQ and it was evident that they knew we were in the area and were trying to locate it. But that night we all slept like babies.'

Within a matter of days the headquarters had been abandoned and the teams had moved north, establishing a series of camps. Despite being forced to relocate to a new and much smaller area, Force 136 continued to hit the Japanese hard, and the enemy's morale was now beginning to suffer. They learnt that the enemy were unwilling to leave established tracks during the day or leave roads at night for fear of 'disappearing'. The poor fieldcraft of the Japanese made it much easier for the British to conduct successful ambushes.

The classic attack would take place along a track on which were rigged 'grenade necklaces', consisting of a dozen or so grenades on instantaneous fuses which could be detonated simultaneously by one or two soldiers. On one occasion a team of five, composed of two levies, an officer and Maung Tin, ambushed and killed a dozen Japanese soldiers without a shot being fired. Wounded enemy could not be taken prisoner, and searchers would move forward into the killing area, dispatching any who showed any form of life with one or two shots from a Colt .45 pistol.

★      ★      ★

On 15 August 1945 Harry and his team were conducting a recce patrol when, during a break, Harry began tuning in a small radio receiver. Harry knew the BBC would broadcast news reports every hour. Finding the right frequency, he listened intently and was amazed when he discovered that the Japanese had surrendered.

'I turned to Major Boal and Captain Coomber and told them the war had ended. They both looked at me and said nothing. So I said it again: "The war's ended. Emperor Hirohito has broadcast a message to the nation himself."'

Suddenly Harry's team was in a predicament. Under the rules of war it would be illegal to open fire on enemy troops unless it was a matter of self-defence. Major Boal decided that the only sensible action was to return to their base, try to make contact with their headquarters and await further orders.

Just as the team were about to leave, they saw a small enemy patrol moving through an area of cleared jungle along the edge of a paddy field.

'They were armed, the soldiers had rifles and the officer was carrying a sword. We had no idea whether they had been told the war was over and we had a discussion about what to do. I said we should ambush them, but Major Boal said that it was best just to let them past, given that the situation was still very confusing.

'So we moved off in the opposite direction through the jungle, making our way back to our camp. The country was very close and in situations like that I would sling my carbine over my shoulder and have my .45 in my hand ready for action. Then suddenly, as I came round a corner, a Jap came at me with a sword. He suddenly appeared in front of me, just feet away. I had my rifle in one hand so I quickly brought my .45 – it's strange but this sort of thing happens with me, it happened several times when everything seems to go into slow motion, and I could see him coming and I was firing at him. I did a double shot, twice in the chest, and killed him stone dead. The bullets hit him in one side of the chest, picked him up and spun him round and I could see all this in slow motion.

And then things came back to the normal speed and the two others came up and said, "You all right?" and I said yeah and they said, "You've got blood on you." And it was a scratch from the sword, about two inches long, on my sternum. It was where the sword had hit me, so I was very lucky. I don't know what happened to the rest of the Japs in the patrol, but they didn't show themselves after the officer was killed. I was never sure whether it was the same patrol we had seen some time earlier, but I was a hair's breadth away from being seriously injured or killed, and I have to say at the time there was part of me saying, "We should have bloody killed them."

'Later that night I thought about what had happened and recalled how the whole event seemed to take place in slow motion. I felt nothing, really. I had killed a man and I can honestly say that I felt nothing. But at that stage I had seen a lot of death, and things that would have been shocking a few years earlier were now commonplace.'

Later that night the team arrived tired, hungry and thirsty at a small village close to their base. News of Japan's unconditional surrender had clearly begun to spread across Burma. The soldiers were welcomed as honoured guests and a huge feast had been prepared. Even though the Karens had suffered from food shortages for many years, there was no holding back.

'There was lots of singing and a fun time was had by all and I think it was about that time that it began to dawn on us that the war was over and very soon we would be going home.'

Although the Japanese government had surrendered, there were still some isolated enemy units that had not been informed of the surrender, or else were either refusing to believe that their country had been defeated or simply ignoring requests to lay down their arms, and fighting on.

One morning in late August two young, immaculately dressed Japanese officers arrived at Harry's camp after being flown into their jungle location by the RAF. 'Neither of the officers could speak English, but we soon learnt with the help of an interpreter that they and other young officers had been sent into the jungle to try and convince the renegade forces that were still holding out to surrender.'

When they arrived at the camp and first set eyes on Harry and other members of the team, the Japanese must have wondered how they had lost the war. Most of the British soldiers had beards, and their hair was tied back in pony tails. Their uniforms were ripped and rotting, while some appeared to have adopted the dress of the locals and were sporting longyi skirts. Every member of the camp was malnourished, and most had legs covered with festering wounds. At first the British just stood and stared at the two officers, who bowed humbly to their victors.

'It was all very odd,' recalled Harry. 'We had two members of what were effectively the enemy in our camp putting us to shame because they were perfectly turned out, and frankly we didn't even look like soldiers, so God only knows what they made of us. I didn't really have a uniform any more, it had either been shredded by the jungle or had rotted away. Initially they were quite apprehensive, but I think when they saw us they sort of grew in confidence and actually started to behave in quite an arrogant manner.'

That morning after breakfast Harry went to one of the huts to await the arrival of the other members of the team. 'I walked into this room and saw these two Jap officers going through a series of exercises with their swords drawn. They were swiping and stabbing and shouted the occasional word. Then one of them turned and began moving towards me in a very aggressive manner, lifting the sword above his head as if he were about to strike. So I pulled out my .45, cocked it and pointed it at him very quickly and began shouting at him to put the sword down. I was creating merry hell, I really was, and I think that if he had taken another step forward I would have blown his head off. The Jap eventually lowered his sword and a look of fear crept across his face, but I wasn't satisfied. I kept saying, "Get down, get down!" until he was lying face down on the floor at my feet. I was absolutely furious and later demanded to know why they were allowed to carry swords. It was explained to me that the sword was part of the uniform and they would appear improperly dressed without them. "Fine," I said, "but that doesn't mean they should be entitled to wear them when they are in our camp." So it was decided that while they were with us they would not be allowed to carry swords.'

Later that morning Harry's team and the two Japanese officers, together with the Burmese sappers and miners, set off on a small expedition 15 miles down to the Loi Kaw road, where it was known that a small number of enemy soldiers were holding out. It was a tense journey, with Harry keeping a watchful and intimidating eye on his two former enemies. After about two hours the small convoy of vehicles arrived at the road, and the group dismounted and took up fire positions on one side of it.

Contact was eventually made with the Japanese soldiers through a temporary truce established by a white flag.

'These two Japanese officers moved forward and began speaking to their compatriots. There was lots of kowtowing. It wasn't looking good because the two young officers were getting a really hard time. They were being very submissive. I think they were terrified. The Japanese soldiers were really giving them a mouthful and the situation was getting pretty tense. Eventually the Jap officers got the wind up them and ran back to our side of the road and then all hell broke loose. The Japs opened fire and we fired back. During the firefight I saw a leg dangling from a tree so I opened fire. I couldn't actually see anything apart from this leg. I fired several rounds into where I thought the Jap might be and then a body fell down. I saw him lying on the ground bleeding from the side of his chest. He didn't move; he was dead. By that stage of the war I felt nothing. I just thought that by killing him there was one less to worry about.'

Virtually all attempts to encourage the Japanese to surrender failed, especially when the two Japanese officers were used by Force 136 teams. They seemed to have the effect of enraging the Japanese rather than pacifying them. Harry cannot recall what became of them, but believes they may have been shot dead while attempting to get their former comrades to surrender.

In November 1945, three months after the war ended, Harry's team were eventually withdrawn from Burma.

The team was flown out of a jungle airstrip by Lysander to Rangoon, where they were given a full medical examination before beginning the journey back home. The sores on Harry's legs had developed into abscesses and were to plague him for many years. A lack of toothpaste for almost the entire duration of the mission in Burma meant that Harry's teeth were also in a poor state.

'When I was in Rangoon, this female doctor looked into my mouth and said, "You haven't been cleaning your teeth recently, have you?" and I said, "No and we haven't been eating much either." I thought, What a silly thing to say.'

Much had happened while Harry was in Burma. The wars in Europe and the Far East had ended and Winston Churchill had lost an election and Britain was ruled by a Labour government. The various 'secret armies' which had sprung up during six years of war had also fallen out of favour, and the generals running the Army had ruled that they should be disbanded.

'As far as the generals were concerned we were not real soldiers. They said, "That's not how you fight a war, that's not cricket." Well, I say we weren't bloody playing cricket.'

Harry eventually returned to Britain, via a stint with the Gold Coast (now Ghana) Regiment in West Africa, and remained in the Army until May 1947. It was another year before Harry found work. His war service, working behind enemy lines with guerrilla forces, counted for little. The celebrations had been over for a long time. Harry eventually found employment with British Rail, where he remained until 1985, when he took early retirement aged 60. He lives in Beckenham in south-east London with his wife Elizabeth.

Harry Verlander has been a member of the Special Forces Club for most of his adult life. He became a member at the end of the war, when he was still only 19 years old. Today he is one of a diminishing number of former Special Operations Executive personnel still alive and, consequently, is treated as an honoured guest at the club when he attends functions there or gives talks about his life behind enemy lines.

# CHAPTER 10

# A Radio Operator at War

## John Sharp with the Jeds

'With advance information, costly mistakes can be avoided,
destruction averted and the way to lasting victory made clear.'
SUN TZU, The Art of War

In the evening of 7 June 1944, while hundreds of thousands of
Allied troops fought their way through the killing fields of
Normandy's *bocage*, Sergeant John Sharp nervously smoked one
last cigarette before climbing on board an ageing RAF Stirling*
bomber.

The aircraft was one of many that evening that lined the runway
of Fairford aerodrome in Gloucestershire. Every minute or so the
airfield would thunder into life as another consignment of British
troops or equipment headed east into the inky black night sky.

Despite the lateness of the hour, John, then 21, was wide awake.
His heart was racing and he was breathing heavily as he picked his
way through the semi-darkness of the aircraft's fuselage.

'All set?' At first John wasn't sure whether it was a question or a
statement from his commanding officer Lieutenant-Colonel James
Riley Holt Hutchison, who had fought in the First World War.

'Yes, sir,' John replied quickly.

'Good. Not long now. Sooner the better.'

---

* The Short Stirling was the first British four-engined heavy bomber of the
Second World War.

*John Sharp, second from left*

The two men were part of Jedburgh Team Verveine, and they were about to begin a journey into Nazi-occupied France from which the chances of returning were set at a generous 50 per cent.

John had never felt so lonely in his entire life. While he sat there wondering what fate the next few hours might hold, the aircraft began to fill with members of the Special Air Service undertaking a separate mission. All were young men, and all looked equally anxious.

There was no idle chat as they found room to sit and get comfortable. Everyone on board was fully aware that in the hours before D-Day a number of bombers, fighters and transports laden with US and British troops had been shot down by German anti-aircraft fire.

As John pondered his immediate future and whether he would live to see the light of dawn, the aircraft's four engines coughed and spluttered into life. John's stomach tightened and his throat became dry. But as the minutes passed the aircraft remained stationary. 'Get on with it, for Christ's sake,' John said to himself. Then ... nothing. The engines were cut and slowly muffled voices of complaint began to fill the silence.

'What now?' John thought when suddenly one of the aircraft's two rear doors opened. A young RAF airmen shone a torch into the darkness before shouting: 'Everybody out. You're not going anywhere.'

'What's the problem?' someone shouted, but there was no answer. 'Fucking RAF,' another muttered to grunts of agreement.

After all the waiting, the anti-climax was almost painful – only delaying an execution could be worse, thought John. It emerged some time later that there was a problem over in France, of which the detail was never quite explained, and so the mission was aborted.

As John waited at the airfield, over 160,000 Allied troops took part in the Normandy landings, otherwise known as D-Day, an operation involving the coming together of the largest invasion force in the history of the world.

The first troops to land in France were the men who took part in an airborne assault involving paratroopers and glider troops from the UK, America, Canada and France. The first troops parachuted shortly after midnight on 6 June 1944. Around 6.30am the same morning, armoured and infantry divisions conducted an amphibious assault on to the shores of Normandy across a 50-mile front, landing on beaches codenamed Omaha, Utah, Gold, Juno and Sword. The Supreme Allied Commander of the Allied force was US General Dwight Eisenhower, while the commander of the ground forces, 21st Army Group, was General Bernard Montgomery. The invasion force was composed of 73,000 US troops, 62,000 British troops and over 21,000 Canadian forces. Over 195,000 merchant and Royal Navy sailors in 5,000 ships were also involved in the operation.

The French Resistance's workload increased hugely in the buildup to D–Day, and in the hours that followed the first landings France's communication network came under relentless attack. The rail network was sabotaged, underground cables were cut, electricity stations were attacked and roads were blocked in a series of covert operations largely organised with the help of the SOE, who sent coded messages to the Resistance groups via the BBC.

Two days later, John and Colonel Hutchison, who at the age of 51 was old enough to be his father, readied themselves for a second time.

Once again the adrenaline pumped through John's veins and punched away the fatigue of two sleepless nights as he climbed aboard the now familiar aircraft.

'I remember seeing the pilot and he looked about 16, and I said to the colonel, "Is this young officer our pilot?" and he said, "Yes, that's him." I thought I hope he knows what he's doing because he looks as if he should still be in school.'

But the aircraft's four engines remained idle. There were storms over northern Europe and at one stage it looked as though the insertion of the Jedburgh Team and the SAS might be cancelled for a second time.

'I remember thinking, I hope this is it, because I can't take much more of this hanging around. You just wanted to get on with it.'

Then, as everyone assumed the operation was about to be aborted for a second time, the engines fired and minutes later the aircraft was airborne – the mission was on.

Mission Verveine's role was to parachute into the Massif du Morvan, a high-wooded region of central France, and coordinate the activities of the Maquis, a band of rural fighters who formed a large part of the Resistance. The Allies expected German reinforcements to flow eastwards towards Normandy when the Nazi high command appreciated that a full invasion was underway. The role of the Maquis in the Morvan region was to delay and disrupt German movement for as long as possible while the allies consolidated their bridgehead. Mission Verveine's secondary role was to report back to London on the strength of each Maquis unit, and to assess how their numbers could be increased and their training improved.

★    ★    ★

I'm chatting to John in the tidy kitchen of his spotless 1950s bungalow in Surrey. His wife Ivy makes a pot of tea and then leaves the room, explaining that she needs to work in the garden. 'I'll leave you two boys to chat about the war,' she says, closing the kitchen door.

I've only been in the 89-year-old John's company for a few minutes, but I immediately like him. He is a warm, chatty man with a gravelly voice and a wicked sense of humour, who is keen to hear about my travels in Afghanistan.

As John chats, he pulls photographs from an album and flicks them towards me. 'That's Colonel Hutchison,' he says, pointing at a figure in a black-and-white photograph. He is momentarily lost in thought and then adds: 'Hutchison was quite a card. He was the son of a wealthy Scottish ship owner, and had fought at Gallipoli with the 17th Cavalry of the Indian Army. A little bloke, only five foot six, but a waspish man and he didn't suffer fools at all. He was a good officer but very formal. You must remember that my background was lower middle class but he came from a shipbuilding family in Govan. He had an estate in Scotland and a town house in Chelsea; he was worth a few bob. He was a rather formal, regimental officer, and that was how things were in those days. Any officer automatically got our respect. He used to call me John, but I always called him Sir.'

★    ★    ★

For the next few hours John and the others jumping into France that night were buffeted by the appalling weather as the aircraft crossed the Channel and headed inland.

'I didn't find out till later, but the pilot's orders were that if he couldn't find our dropping zone we were to jump blind, and that is exactly what happened. We jumped blind. There was a great storm and it transpired that he dropped us at 3,000 feet rather than

600 feet. He couldn't do otherwise, because it was too dangerous for a single plane to hang about.'

At around 12.30am the RAF dispatcher began checking the soldiers' parachutes and their equipment containers. John too checked his own personal kit once again, in an attempt to settle his nerves.

'We wore battledress. I had a pistol, a Colt .45, a couple of magazines, a K-ration, a fighting knife, my codebook and most importantly my crystal, which is used to fix the radio wavelength. My radio set was in a container, along with my rifle and my pack.'

Then without any real warning the red light came on, a hatch in the floor of the fuselage was opened and the order 'Prepare for action' was given. John watched as the red light switched to green. Above the din of the engines, the command 'Go, go, go' could be heard. The 12 parachutists shuffled forward until they reached the hole where they took a single step into the black void.

'I was the last man out and the trouble was that we dropped so high that we were spread out all over the place. The sky was pitch black and full of thunder and lightning, the plane was being tossed about all over the place. The pilot just dropped us where he thought was the right place. At the time we didn't have any idea, of course – the dispatcher checked us and made sure we were ready and off we went, and I was just relieved to get out of the plane.

'It was a hell of a storm and I landed in a tree. It was like going into a cinema – I had total night blindness and I had no idea how high I was in this tree. I tensed myself up for a big fall, unclipped myself from my parachute harness and dropped. In fact I was only about 10 feet up, but when I hit the ground I shook every bone in my body. But I was safe and filled with a huge sense of relief.

'The 14 of us were all spread out over quite a large area. I was a field and a half away from the colonel, who had landed badly and broken a bone in his foot. The SAS blokes were all over the place too, and it was dawn before we all met up. After that we moved to a ridge that dominated the immediate area. We hid beneath some trees and used binoculars to scan the area, and we had the pleasure of watching Jerry pick up all of our gear. I lost everything – my radio, rifle, personal kit, rations. We waited for the Germans to leave and then we said goodbye to the SAS, who had also lost nearly all of their equipment. They were going on a separate mission, so we shook hands and wished them luck. I had a compass and there was nothing else to do but to walk on a bearing until we came to a village. We had no idea where we were. Obviously I knew we were in France, but that was about it, because we hadn't been dropped in the right area. We went in one direction and the SAS went in another.'

The Germans would have been aware that there were British parachutists around because of the equipment that had been found. Soon extra patrols started to flood the area and it became vital that the Jedburgh team quickly made contact with the Resistance.

'The following day, as we were moving across a field close to a hedge to give ourselves a bit of cover, we heard a battle erupt. The sound of the fighting came from the area where the SAS had been heading. We feared the worst but convinced ourselves that the SAS blokes would be able to handle themselves. We later learnt that they had run into the Germans and nine had been killed in the fight. Only their commander, Major Frost, managed to escape. They wouldn't have had much of a chance because all of their weapons and equipment had been lost – but they probably knew that if they were captured they would have been executed.

'Over the next few days the colonel and I managed to survive on my K-rations and by eating the berries we were picking. The colonel was hobbling along because he had this broken toe – he never complained but our progress was slow. We stopped one morning by a stone wall for a bit of a rest when I heard something; it was someone moving around. I whispered to the colonel, "There's somebody on the other side." We pulled out our persuaders – that's what we used to call our Colt .45s – useless really, only any good at close range, when they were a nasty weapon. We both ran round to the other side of the wall and said "Hands up!" in German. But rather than a German we found this little French bloke who was absolutely terrified. We questioned him and found out that he had been in the Spanish Civil War. The colonel said to me, "What shall we do with him, John? Shall we shoot him?" I was stunned. I thought to myself, You can't shoot him, he's French. But we knew that some of the French would give us away to the Germans. If the Germans came to his village and threatened him or some of the locals, he might point them in our direction. But I was only this middle-class ex-grammar school boy, so how was I meant to tell a colonel that he was wrong?

'But it was just a wind-up. Later, after the war, when I went to reunions at the Special Forces Club, the colonel used to pull my leg about that. He used to say to me, "You should have seen your face, John, when I said shall we shoot him!"

'The little bloke was shitting himself and the colonel told him that he was letting him go – and you could see the relief on his face. But before he was set free the colonel explained quite clearly that if he went to the Germans and told them where we were, our friends would, as he put it, find him and they would take him apart hair by hair – it was a hell of a risk to let him go, because we had no idea whether he was going to go to the Germans.'

John and the colonel pushed on for another few miles, when they came across a woman working in a field. The woman seemed to realise that they were British soldiers and took them to a house, where a few hours later two members of the Resistance arrived. It very soon became apparent that John and Colonel Hutchison had arrived at an outpost of the Maquis headquarters which had been their original goal.

'We had marched several days, without knowing where we were really going, and then just by chance we stumbled across our Maquis target. The farmer's wife was initially hostile and asked us what we were doing on her land. She then relaxed when she realised we were British and told us that there were no German soldiers in the area. For the first time in four days we could relax. The colonel told her that we wanted to meet up with the Resistance, and half an hour later she led us into another room where we were joined by two members of the local fighters. They looked serious and mistrustful. Both had bandoliers of bullets slung around their necks and they stared at us intently, their Sten guns pointing directly at us. Their uniform consisted of a beret and an armband with the letters FFI [Forces Françaises de l'Intérieur] imprinted on it. We knew immediately that they were Maquisards. But they seemed suspicious of us until the colonel showed them a letter signed by Général Marie-Pierre Koenig, the commander of the French Forces of the Interior.'

The letter read: 'The bearer of this document is a regular member of the Allied Forces under the command of General Eisenhower whose object is the liberation of your country from the enemy.

'It is required that you should give such members of the Allied Forces any assistance which they may require and which may lie within your power, including freedom of movement, provision of information, provision of transport where possible and provision of food and shelter.

'The Supreme Allied Commander counts upon your assistance in carrying out his wishes as expressed above, which are hereby endorsed by the French High Command.'

★    ★    ★

John Sharp was a 15-year old pupil at Clapham Central School in south-west London when war against Germany was declared in September 1939. When he was 18, working as a clerk in a factory in Battersea, he volunteered for active service.

Like many young men, John yearned to join the RAF, earn his wings and become a dashing pilot, but a minor sight deficiency ended those dreamy thoughts.

'I knew I wouldn't get into the RAF, and I'm jolly glad I didn't, because they suffered terrible casualties in Bomber Command – and I probably would have been one of those. Instead I joined the Royal Armoured Corps and trained at Bovington – it was a young soldiers' battalion. By the time I joined up quite a lot had happened in the war and I got posted to the 9th Battalion Green Howards, an infantry unit, which had just been converted to an armoured car unit. All we seemed to do was to paint these blinking armoured cars – no training or anything like that. A group of us who had been trained together, including Fred Bailey, decided that we had to get out.

'I knew, and the others thought the same, that if we stayed with the Green Howards we would get chewed up something rotten, because they were still thinking as infantrymen and knew nothing about fighting with armour.'

John's salvation came when he was told of the need for volunteers for special duties.

'A group of us put our names down as volunteers. We didn't know what we were volunteering for, we just wanted to get out of the battalion. I think all of us had volunteered for various different jobs within the Army, and so there was no expectation that we would automatically be accepted for this role. The one skill that counted in our favour was that the SOE needed radio operators. When I went along for the interview, I was given all sorts of tests; I was vetted and interviewed by psychiatrists.

'Those of us who were accepted were sent to Henley-on-Thames, where we did our signals training. It was very intense, with the focus on Morse, codes and cyphers. There was also a great deal of physical training. We were very young and we all thought it was great fun. We were typical arrogant English males who thought they could achieve anything, and only life could prove us wrong. The fun started at Milton Hall, in Cambridgeshire. That's where we were taught how to shoot, use a killing knife, and sabotage. The shooting was mainly with side-arms – the weapon we were issued with was the Colt .45 – but we also used American M1 carbines.

'Part of the way through the training we were sent up to Dunbar, East Lothian, where we began to take part in increasingly complex operations. There was a basic place where we were billeted, and the instructors used to come and collect us in lorries and dump us in the middle of nowhere for about a week. But we would make our way back to the headquarters, which was surrounded by a huge wall. The wall provided a bit of shelter. We would camp next to this wall and make radio contact with the HQ, and they would come back and say, "Your signal is strength five [very strong]" – what they didn't know, of course, was that that we were camped just 200 yards down the road.

'There was one occasion when we were camping in a barn and I had nipped out for some reason, and when I came back I found a farmer with a shotgun aimed at my friend. I went up to the farmer, pulled out my pistol, but I didn't put one up the spout – you never put one up the spout unless you are going to use it – and I said to him, "Put the gun down or I'll blow your head off." He looked terrified and dropped the shotgun. We hightailed out of there and when we returned to our HQ, the colonel said to us, "I've had a report that two British sergeants threatened a farmer and you two fit the description. Do you know anything?" We said, "No, sir," and he said, "Well, don't let it happen again."

'When we returned to Milton Hall I teamed up with an English major. We were going to form a team with another officer, but he hurt his leg during training and could not continue with the course – so I was all on my own while everyone else was in teams. I was called down to the SOE's London Headquarters in Baker Street, and that's where I was told that I would be teaming up with Colonel Hutchison. I was to be his radio operator. Even at that stage I wasn't sure exactly what our role would be. But when we were sent to Ringway airport for parachute training it became clear to most of us what we would be getting into.

'When you are in the services and you go over to what I used to call the "sticky side", proper combat, the main thing that keeps you going is fear. You don't want to be shown to be a coward in front of your comrades, and that was the main incentive, if not the biggest incentive, as far as I was concerned. When we started parachuting you couldn't back out even if you wanted to.

'When I discovered the full nature of what the Jeds were going to do – jump behind the lines and help organise the Resistance – it was a case of, well, we won't need any laxative for a bit. But we were too far in then – you couldn't back out.'

★　　★　　★

The two Maquisards hid John and the colonel in the back of a small van under a tarpaulin and drove for several miles along a rutted track deep into a wood.

The two men had been transported to their new headquarters, where they were met by a member of another Jed team, Major Duncan Guthrie. It was a welcome sight for the two tired soldiers, who were also given the extra and equally welcome news that most of their lost equipment, bar the radio, had been recovered after a skirmish with the enemy.

After the handshakes and warm greetings, Colonel Hutchison explained that his role was not to command the various Allied and Resistance units in central France but to let London know their strengths and locations, and to liaise between the Resistance and a unit from the SAS, who were now ensconced in the same wood.

While the colonel began informing the various groups of the current situation, John set about trying to acquire a new radio set. Finding his way to the SAS camp, he asked if they could arrange for another radio to be parachuted into the area as quickly as possible. The SAS signals officer duly obliged, and within a matter of days John was once again in communication with London – Mission Verveine was finally operational.

'I eventually got one of those proper agent radio sets, a B2 in a suitcase – it was brilliant, easy to carry and use. We spent a lot of time with SAS. They seemed to always be turning up. We had to constantly switch our HQ, so that the Germans could never target us. There was one occasion when we were staying in an SAS camp and I asked their commander if I could go out on patrol – he was delighted to have an extra pair of hands. But I never told the colonel because I knew he would say no. If anything happened to me the whole mission could be jeopardised. But I decided to risk it. I wanted to go out on patrol and earn my reputation as a soldier. It was all very exciting and different from what I had been doing before, but we didn't come into contact with any Germans. But the colonel found out and tore a strip off me. He was red in the face and shouted: "You realise, sergeant, I have the power to court-martial you, you know. You pull another trick like that again and I will bloody well reduce you to the ranks." And he was deadly serious.

'I was very crucial to the operation because I was the radio op and I couldn't be replaced without a lot of trouble; that's why the colonel got so cross when I went on patrol. If I had been killed he would not have been able to communicate with London. I was protected all the time, often with two people, who were always watching my back when I was transmitting.

'The colonel would often write messages which were on the long side and I would edit them and send them, as it was very unwise to stay on the air too long. Occasionally the Germans would send out detector vans to try and establish where we were. There was one occasion when I was on the radio in a building and I looked out of a window and saw a detector van and I thought I'd better get off the air quickly. We were only on the air for a maximum of 20 minutes. The messages were sent out from London twice a day, so if you missed it during the day you could pick it up again at night.

'A few days after that incident, a member of the Maquis came to me just after I had finished transmitting in the woods and said, "We've captured an SS colonel." He was a typical Nazi, very arrogant, very superior, and he wouldn't speak to me because I was an NCO. He also tried to claim that he didn't speak English. He was dressed in his riding boots and a very smart uniform. I went to the colonel and said: "The Maquis have captured a German colonel. He doesn't purport to speak English." The German officer was marched in front of the colonel, who asked him a few questions. He didn't answer any of them and just sneered at us. Then the colonel said: "He doesn't seem to speak English – he's no use to us. Take him outside and shoot him." And right at that moment this look of utter terror broke out across the officer's face and he started shouting in English, "You can't do that, you can't do that." And the colonel said, "Oh, I thought you couldn't speak English." After that he was taken away and I didn't see him again. We were 200 miles behind enemy lines so we couldn't take prisoners – I don't know what happened to him. Let's just say the Maquis had some problems with him and so he was dealt with.'

★   ★   ★

Life in France for John and the colonel was relatively comfortable, given the situation. The two men spent a lot of time living in farmhouses belonging to either members of the Resistance or those sympathetic to the cause. Food and wine was so plentiful that John actually put on weight. As time passed he began to acquire more and more equipment, so much so that transporting it became a bit of a problem. Then one day John saw the solution to his problems.

'We had stopped in a wood and I saw a donkey in a field and thought, "That is exactly what I need." We were in the area for a few days and I eventually found the owner and bought the donkey for 200 francs – or rather the Army bought it. Over the next few days I made a harness out of some old parachute straps that we acquired. The harness worked perfectly and I was able to load all of my equipment on to it. It was a blessed relief, and I was absolutely delighted, because by that stage I had also acquired an accumulator, which meant that I could run the set off mains electricity or the accumulator itself. Now the donkey was going to carry all of my communications equipment and my personal kit too.

'Then one day the Germans attacked us. Bullets were flying all over the place and we had to make a very quick exit. I quickly bundled all of my equipment on to the donkey, said "Come on, you," and walked him up to the gate. But when we got to the gate he wouldn't walk through, so I tried to pull him but he wouldn't budge – he refused to walk through the gate. I tried to walk him around the field to get to another gate, but he absolutely refused to move. We were tugging and pulling him and shouting, "Come on, you bastard!" but he wasn't going anywhere. He was so used to walking round that field that he didn't want to leave it. I had no other choice but to offload all my kit and carry it. The last I saw of him he was happily chomping on grass while this battle raged around us. The farmer did well out of the deal, he had 200 francs and managed to keep his donkey.'

Slowly the Maquis were shaped into an efficient fighting force, supplied with ammunition and weapons from air drops arranged by the Jed team.

'They were a good bunch and we formed strong relationships, but they had their limitations of course because they weren't trained soldiers. We had to make sure that they weren't overreaching themselves. But they were invaluable in gathering intelligence and going into areas where we couldn't.

'The intelligence was passed to the SAS and they would attack the German convoys passing through our area. The convoys were very well protected, and the ambushes needed to be carefully planned and you needed a lot of firepower if the attack was going to be successful. Those operations were left to the SAS. The SAS managed to arrange for jeeps and six-pounder anti-tank guns to be dropped. They were quite a force to be reckoned with. It was during that period that I met Colonel Paddy Maine, their CO. His jeep had hit a tree and was all cocked on one side, but he was still driving this bloody thing. He was a big, tall man, an Irish international rugby player, about six foot three, and he didn't suffer fools easily either. It was said to me that he should have got the VC, but the DSO and three bars isn't bad either.'

★     ★     ★

By the end of August the Jeds' role in France had almost come to an end. The French 1st Army troops landing in southern France had made rapid progress and had pushed well beyond Mission Verveine's operational area.

After eventually making their way to Paris, via a detour into the Nantes region of France, John and Colonel Hutchison finally parted company. There was little more the two could now achieve, and John was keen to get a little leave before volunteering again for another SOE mission.

'I said goodbye to Colonel Hutchison in Paris. We gave each other a firm handshake and said we would meet up again in London in the next few weeks. The war had become increasingly political; even as a sergeant I could see that. The US Army arrived on the outskirts two weeks before the Free French Army but was ordered to halt, so that de Gaulle could claim that he was the liberator of Paris – at least that what was what I was given to understand.

'While in Paris, I managed to get hold of a few really good bottles of wine, which I was going to give to friends and family. But when I flew into Northolt airport in London the customs officers searched my kit and confiscated them – I had a few choice words for them. Just after I arrived, the airborne operation "Market Garden" was launched, ending in the fiasco at Arnhem. I remember thinking what a balls-up – all those men killed and for what?

'The greatest mistake Hitler made was to fight on two fronts and not to trust his generals. If Hitler had left the fighting to men like Rommel, we'd have lost, no doubt about that.'

★   ★   ★

John returned to Milton Hall in Cambridgeshire for a thorough debriefing. 'Gradually all of the Jed teams who had been dropped into France began to return home. It was good to see all of my old mates, people who I had gone through training with. That was when we started to discover what had happened to all the various missions. Some had been very successful, while others complained that they did little, but most had been involved in some sort of action. We also learnt of colleagues who had been killed or injured.

'After the debriefing we had two choices: Burma, or return to our units, and the majority opted for the latter.' John was not one of those, preferring to volunteer for active duty.

Like all of the Jedburgh personnel posted to Burma, John had to make an arduous journey to India by boat, followed by a five-day train journey to the south of the subcontinent, before taking a ferry to Ceylon, now Sri Lanka, where he joined his new team.

'I think I was the first Jed to be posted to Burma, and when I got there I teamed up with my two new officers, who were part of Force 136, which was the Far Eastern element of SOE. The team was led by an Irishman called Major Tom Carew, who was 24 and later became a lieutenant-colonel. He wasn't like any officer I had ever met before. He seemed to be totally fearless. The other officer was Captain Tom Cox; he was 22, a year older than me. We spent a month doing jungle training and then received our orders, which were to jump into the Arakan and help organise the resistance. On paper it looked much the same as France, but I knew that the fighting and the conditions would be much tougher.'

Once training had been completed, the team moved north up to Calcutta, where they received their final orders and were joined by a Burmese interpreter before being parachuted deep behind enemy lines.

'We jumped in from a Dakota at night into a valley, an opening in the jungle. I was number one to jump, and my legs were shaking, but I exited the aircraft without a problem and watched as my parachute deployed and then I dropped gently down to earth. I landed without any problems at all and felt pretty pleased with myself. But there was no one else around and no reception committee. I looked up and despite the darkness could make out the silhouette of the plane as it flew away into the distance. I thought, Christ, what am I going to do now, and needless to say I didn't need a laxative. For a few minutes I felt completely lost. I thought that something had gone horribly wrong and the mission had been aborted after I had jumped out. I knew how difficult jungle navigation was, and that one man on his own surrounded by the enemy wouldn't last long. I was just beginning to curse my decision to volunteer when the aircraft returned, made another run over the DZ and the others jumped out.

'I later learnt that the Burmese interpreter, who was number two in the door, the next to jump, had frozen and the aircraft was forced to make a second run. When they came round a second time Carew just grabbed him and threw him out of the door.'

John's first mission into the Burmese jungle was something of a failure and, in circumstances similar to those experienced by Fred Bailey, little was achieved. The team contacted HQ and explained that they needed to be extracted because they had immediately been compromised by the Japanese. The team was ordered to move to a prearranged RV, a clearing in the jungle, and were extracted a few days later and flown back to India.

'The Japs must have seen us land because they were on our case immediately and we were pulled out after six weeks having achieved nothing. But after a few weeks we flew out again – and I think a lot better prepared.

'We parachuted into an area north of Rangoon, with effectively the same orders – to organise the resistance and to attack the Japanese as they attempted to retreat into Thailand.

'We quickly managed to set up our base and make contact with the Resistance fighters, the Karen tribesmen, and settled into a routine. The Karens were with us all the time. They would accompany us on patrol, act as guides and help us get food from the local villages when our rations ran short. They were excellent and completely loyal – and they also had a very deep hatred of the Japs.

'We helped in their organisation and training and managed to get them supplied with ammunition and explosives. The aim was to get them operating independently from us, so that they could plan and execute their own missions, which they soon did. We developed some very good friendships and they were very fond of Carew.

'I can distinctly remember one specific day when I thought Carew had lost it. I had just finished sending a radio message back to HQ when suddenly there was a hell of a lot of machine-gun fire and I thought we were under attack. I felt this huge surge of adrenaline and thought, 'We're for it now,' because the gunfire was so close. Then I realised it was Carew. There was a burst of machine-gun fire, then an explosion.

'I went over to where this racket was coming from and I saw Carew firing his machine-gun into the jungle. He had decided that he wanted to take down some trees and give us a bit more space in the camp. He had rigged up some explosive to the trees, which he detonated by firing at it. And it actually worked quite well, but Carew thought the whole thing was hilarious – he really was quite something else.'

While Carew and Coxie would often go out on patrol with the resistance fighters, John's main but not exclusive role was to remain back at the base monitoring the radio and preparing messages for transmission. One day Carew returned to the base location with one patrol member missing.

'A week or so after Carew was blowing up trees, Coxie managed to get himself captured by the Burmese National Army. I think they had run into an enemy patrol and Coxie had become separated. He was captured by a group of Indian soldiers, some former POWs who had been offered the chance of freedom if they fought for the Japs. At the time the Japs had a propaganda slogan, which was Asia for the Asiatics, and they were right of course because we had no right to be there. The Japs basically said fight with us and you fight against the imperialist. Of course it was all nonsense and, had the Japs won, India and the rest of Asia would have had an even worse time.

'Coxie was a schoolmaster, the epitome of Mr Chips, an intellectual, a really nice bloke, and Carew looked upon his capture as a personal affront. The resistance fighters were also angry and they set about trying to establish his whereabouts. Their intelligence network within the jungle was excellent, and they soon established the location of the BNA camp where we assumed Coxie was being held.

'Carew gave an outline of the plan and told me that I was coming too. I was delighted and it was a pretty straightforward operation.

'The BNA were probably intending to pass Coxie on to the Japs in the hope of some sort of reward. The Karens led us right into the camp and we got very close to them before we opened fire. I was armed with my carbine and fired off quite a few rounds, but I don't know if I killed anyone. The battle only lasted for what seemed like a few minutes before the BNA ran away. We quickly found Coxie and he was in pretty good shape, considering, and was obviously delighted to be free. He wasn't that badly treated, but we all knew that if he had been handed over to the Japs, in all likelihood he would have been killed.

'Life in the jungle was all right, but we all got malaria and dysentery, and everyone eventually got that, no matter how clean and careful you tried to be. Once you got ill, you sort of stayed ill. Even the Karens would suffer occasionally. We managed to get the occasional air drop, but when the weather changed and the monsoon came the drops stopped because the cloud was too low and the aircraft couldn't fly. The risk of crashing or being shot down was too great and so we became increasingly reliant on the Karen tribes-people for food.

'But the worst part on that mission was being shelled by our own 25-pounders, because we were between the 14th Army and the Japanese. It was terrifying, and by far the worst experience of the war for me, because you had no idea how long a barrage would last or where the shells would land.

'I think one of the things I found very difficult to get used to was the violence and brutality of the war in Burma. The Japs were very nasty pieces of work, and in every village they came across they would rape all the women and steal all of the food. The Karen resistance fighters absolutely hated the Japs because of the atrocities they had carried out during their occupation of Burma. If the Karens ever caught a Jap they killed them immediately. They never really took prisoners, they saw it as payback time.

'One day towards the end of the war the Karens captured a number of Japanese soldiers. We wondered what the Karens were going to do with them. Then one by one they marched them towards the edge of a cliff and shot them. I watched as they toppled over the cliff. You could see the look of sheer terror on the Japs' faces. Carew came up to me and said: "Now look here, John, don't you get involved in any of this."

I was a bit shocked by what I saw. There was no way we were going to try and stop the Karens killing the Japs – it was just tough luck. I think we all hated the Japs by that stage, but even so, watching a load of grown men knowing that they were about to die and then seeing them being killed one by one is not a nice experience. I have to say that I aged quite considerably between 1944 and 1945.'

By the early summer of 1945 the Japanese were attempting to escape from Burma. A force, estimated at around 10,000 soldiers, was heading for the Sittang River, a major obstacle which could only be crossed in boats. To reach the river the Japanese were forced to traverse thick jungle and paddy fields while being pursued by Allied forces attacking them at every opportunity.

'One of my lasting and strongest memories is watching the Japs being blown to pieces as they attempted to cross the Sittang River into Thailand, in dugout canoes. We had crossed the same river a few days earlier, and I was sitting on a hillside overlooking the river when the Japs arrived, thousands of them. As they tried to cross, waves of RAF Typhoons caught them. It was annihilation. There were dead bodies, bits of bodies floating everywhere. I didn't feel anything at the time – I had no pity for them. As far as I was concerned the Japs had brought all of this slaughter, death and destruction upon themselves. I think we all felt the same – there was no pity at all. The attack went on for several days. Some Japs made it across but a lot didn't.'

The slaughter of the Japanese at the Sittang River was the last real action John saw during the Second World War. The mission was at an end, and John, eager for some home leave, returned to India before travelling back to Britain.

'We all said goodbye and I was sorry to leave the team. But I was still a very young man and wanted to get home and see my family.'

John returned home to a changed Britain. London bore all the scars of five years of war but there was a sense of excitement and optimism in the air. His delight at seeing his family once again after so many months was followed by the surprise of discovering that he had been awarded the Military Medal.

'I got the Military Medal, Coxie got the Military Cross and Carew received the DSO. I had no idea that I was going to be awarded a medal – a letter came through the post with the citation saying that I had won the MM. I can't remember why now. There were so many people who were being awarded medals at the time and only a few could go to Buckingham Palace to receive them – I got mine through the post. I wasn't bothered, I was very proud.'

John later received a posting order and was ordered to return to a transit camp in India before being posted to the 25th Dragoons, an armoured car regiment stationed in the Indian state of Bihar.

The Second World War was over and the focus of the British forces in India had turned to partition and what part the British Army would play in its management.

'The violence which surrounded partition was getting worse and worse. I would lead patrols into the surrounding country which might last a week or so, and we would come across some terrible sights. Men, women and children all butchered. I actually saw more dead bodies during partition than I did during my involvement in the war. It was absolutely shocking.'

John was eventually demobbed in December 1946 and began a career in the oil industry. He became a member of the Special Forces Club.

'Every member of the Jedburgh Teams was made a member of the Special Forces Club. It was a wonderful place to meet up and reminisce. During the war we all had to sign the Official Secrets Act, and you weren't supposed to talk about your wartime activities. But the club was one of the places where you could meet up and chat with people you had served with.

'It was a very smart club and I suppose more geared towards officers than sergeants and non-commissioned officers, but the atmosphere was very friendly and I was always made to feel very welcome. As the years passed the number of Jeds and members of the SOE dwindled because those organisations no longer existed.

'Sadly many of my former comrades have passed away – but the stories have remained and I hope always will. Their tales of what they did live on through the club, which is a direct link to those dark days of the Second World War. It is an important part of this country's history.'

I switch off my tape recorder, and John and I agree to meet again in the coming weeks. He tells me, as others veterans have also done, that he greatly enjoyed our chat and he seems to be genuinely surprised that I want to include him in the book. As we shake hands and say goodbye, I tell him that his wartime experiences are remarkable.

'Seems like yesterday,' he says.

# Acknowledgements

Like all books, *Tales from the Special Forces Club* is a collaboration, involving the ideas and efforts of a wide group of people. But most thanks must go to a wonderful collection of Second World War veterans, the subjects of this book, without whose patience the book would not have been possible.

I am also much indebted to Roy Patterson of the Special Forces Association – a real expert on the role and history of Popski's Private Army, whose advice and opinions were invaluable.

Once again, I need to extend my deep thanks to my wife, Clodagh, and my two children, Luca and Rafe, who suffered my absences and frustrations over 18 months, with little complaint.

I would also like to thank Iain MacGregor, my editor at HarperCollins, and his team for their creativity and their seemingly endless patience.

Humfrey Hunter, my agent, also deserves credit for his inexhaustible advice on just about everything.

Lastly, I would also like thank Tom Smith, who witnessed a great deal of action with the Chindits during the Second World War. Sadly Tom died during the writing of this book, but his memories and descriptions of fighting in Burma were invaluable.